Human Rights on the Edge

This book grapples with the challenges inherent in an uncertain period for global human rights and explores the future of international human rights law and practice.

Many Western scholars are increasingly pessimistic about the future of international human rights law. However, the contributions to this volume demonstrate that far from collapsing in the face of duress, the concept of human rights has endured despite contractions and the spectre of co-option and manipulation by the powerful. In addition, law is a malleable tool that is deployed in novel ways to promote human rights. The book illustrates that the power of human rights lies not in their essentialized transcendence of time, culture, and context but in their enduring promise that a more just world can emerge from sustained and creative struggle through, against, and at the margins of states, law, and institutions. The key questions to emerge are not whether human rights law and practice will survive, but rather what are the forces that sustain, revitalize, and transform them? And what are human rights in the process of becoming?

This book will be of immense interest to those studying and researching across Politics, Human Rights, Gender and Law. It was originally published as a special issue of the *Journal of Human Rights.*

Heather Smith-Cannoy is a Political Scientist at Arizona State University, where she directs the Global Human Rights Hub and the undergraduate degree program on Social Justice and Human Rights. She has published three books, and 15 articles and book chapters on human rights, international law, sex trafficking and gender.

Tricia Redeker Hepner is a Political and Legal Anthropologist at Arizona State University. Her research focuses on migration and displacement, transnationalism, human rights, transitional justice, militarism, and conflict/peace. She has published four books and more than twenty peer-reviewed journal articles or chapters. She directs ASU's Master's Program in Social Justice and Human Rights.

Human Rights on the Edge

The Future of International Human Rights Law and Practice

Edited by
Heather Smith-Cannoy and Tricia Redeker Hepner

Routledge
Taylor & Francis Group
LONDON AND NEW YORK

First published 2023
by Routledge
4 Park Square, Milton Park, Abingdon, Oxon OX14 4RN

and by Routledge
605 Third Avenue, New York, NY 10158

Routledge is an imprint of the Taylor & Francis Group, an informa business

British Library Cataloguing in Publication Data
A catalogue record for this book is available from the British Library

ISBN13: 978-1-032-49570-5 (hbk)
ISBN13: 978-1-032-49571-2 (pbk)
ISBN13: 978-1-003-39446-4 (ebk)

DOI: 10.4324/9781003394464

Typeset in Minion Pro
by Newgen Publishing UK

Publisher's Note
The publisher accepts responsibility for any inconsistencies that may have arisen during the conversion of this book from journal articles to book chapters, namely the inclusion of journal terminology.

Disclaimer
Every effort has been made to contact copyright holders for their permission to reprint material in this book. The publishers would be grateful to hear from any copyright holder who is not here acknowledged and will undertake to rectify any errors or omissions in future editions of this book.

Contents

Citation Information

The chapters in this book were originally published in the *Journal of Human Rights*, volume 21, issue 2 (2022). When citing this material, please use the original page numbering for each article, as follows:

Foreword

The future of human rights: A research agenda
Alison Brysk
Journal of Human Rights, volume 21, issue 2 (2022), pp. 117

Introduction

Introduction to human rights on the edge: The future of international human rights law and practice
Tricia Redeker Hepner and Heather Smith-Cannoy
Journal of Human Rights, volume 21, issue 2 (2022), pp. 118–122

Chapter 1

NGO repression as a predictor of worsening human rights abuses
Suparna Chaudhry and Andrew Heiss
Journal of Human Rights, volume 21, issue 2 (2022), pp. 123–140

Chapter 2

New frontiers in international human rights: Actionable nonactionables and the (non)performance of perpetual becoming
Kamari Maxine Clarke
Journal of Human Rights, volume 21, issue 2 (2022), pp. 141–157

Chapter 3

Epistemes of human rights in Kashmir: Paradoxes of universality and particularity
Sarbani Sharma
Journal of Human Rights, volume 21, issue 2 (2022), pp. 158–173

Chapter 4

"Legal exhaustion" and the crisis of human rights: Tracing legal mobilization against sexual violence and torture of Kurdish women in state custody in Turkey since the 1990s
Nisa Göksel and Jaimie Morse
Journal of Human Rights, volume 21, issue 2 (2022), pp. 174–190

Chapter 5

The boundaries of religion in international human rights law
Shanna Corner
Journal of Human Rights, volume 21, issue 2 (2022), pp. 191–209

Chapter 6

Disentangling gendered peace: Observing gendered peace in policy
Anntiana Maral Sabeti
Journal of Human Rights, volume 21, issue 2 (2022), pp. 210–226

Chapter 7

The evolution of the global movement to end child marriage
Andrea Vilán
Journal of Human Rights, volume 21, issue 2 (2022), pp. 227–244

Notes on Contributors

Alison Brysk is Mellichamp Professor of Global Governance at the University of California, Santa Barbara, USA. She specialises in International human rights.

Suparna Chaudhry is Assistant Professor in the Department of International Affairs at Lewis & Clark College and an affiliated scholar with the International Justice Lab at College of William & Mary. Her research interests include human rights, international organizations and law, and political violence, with a specific focus on the causes and consequences of state persecution of NGOs and activists.

Kamari Maxine Clarke is Professor of Transnational Justice and Sociolegal Studies at the University of Toronto where she teaches in the Centre for Criminology and Sociolegal Studies and the Centre for Diaspora and Transnational Studies and holds a cross appointment at the Faculty of Law and the Department of Anthropology.

Shanna Corner is Visiting Assistant Professor of Sociology in the Department of Sociology and Social Work at Hope College. She is also a research affiliate at the Center for the Study of Religion and Society at the University of Notre Dame. Her research focuses on human rights, gender, religion, law, culture, and morality.

Nisa Göksel is Assistant Professor of Sociology in the School of Social and Behavioral Sciences in ASU's New College of Interdisciplinary Arts and Sciences. Her areas of research are gender and sexuality; feminist and women's movements in the Middle East; war, violence, and peace-making; human rights movements; and migration, displacement and diaspora studies.

Andrew Heiss is Assistant Professor in the Department of Public Management and Policy at the Andrew Young School of Policy Studies at Georgia State University. His research explores human rights and international nonprofit management and focuses on authoritarian regulation of civil society and international nongovernmental organization responses to administrative crackdown.

Tricia Redeker Hepner is a Political and Legal Anthropologist at Arizona State University. Her research focuses on migration and displacement, transnationalism, human rights, transitional justice, militarism, and conflict/peace. She has published four books and more than twenty peer-reviewed journal articles or chapters. She directs ASU's Master's Program in Social Justice and Human Rights.

Jaimie Morse, Ph.D., MPH, is Assistant Professor of Sociology at the University of California, Santa Cruz, and a Senior Visiting Fellow with the Global Health Justice Partnership at Yale University. Her research lies at the intersection of medicine, law, culture, and science and technology studies (STS). Broadly speaking, her work examines the politics of knowledge in biomedicine and global health, with a focus on the interplay between law, health, and human rights advocacy in processes of policy change.

Anntiana Maral Sabeti is a PhD candidate at School of Politics and Global Studies, Arizona State University. Her work lies in the intersection of women and peace.

Sarbani Sharma is Assistant Professor at the School of Development, Azim Premji University, Bengaluru, India. She works on itineraries of political aspirations and articulations of freedom and sovereignty in Kashmir.

Heather Smith-Cannoy is a Political Scientist at Arizona State University, where she directs the Global Human Rights Hub and the undergraduate degree program on Social Justice and Human Rights. She has published three books, and 15 articles and book chapters on human rights, international law, sex trafficking and gender.

Andrea Vilán is Associate Research Scholar at Princeton's School of International and Public Affairs and holds a PhD in Political Science from the University of California, Los Angeles. Her research focuses on transnational activism, children's rights, and international law.

Foreword—The future of human rights: A research agenda

Alison Brysk

In turbulent times, we stand at the leading edge of human rights. The previous generation of human rights scholarship debated the balance between a rising tide and an end times of human rights. From where we stand, we can discern both directions—and looking ahead, rising issues in the distance. Our research can only glimpse the social problems and power relations emerging at the horizon. These phenomena pose challenges to the continuing construction of human rights as a movement to expand norms and practices of *who is human*, *what is right*, and *who is responsible*.

The human rights agenda sits at the crossroads of historic progress and hard times. On the one hand, the arc of history bends through consequential advocacy campaigns—from antislavery to anti-apartheid, expanding rights frames, and a growing interactive regime of global, regional, national, local, and transnational institutions for monitoring, advocacy, socialization, capacity building, and accountability—that culminates in an unprecedented justice cascade. On the other hand, historic governance gaps threaten the lives, liberties, and well-being of people displaced from their homes, livelihoods, and identities by global forces beyond their control—from conflict to disaster to distorted development—while gender-based violence affects an estimated one of three women and girls worldwide. On every continent, illiberal ethnonationalists degrade democratic institutions, minorities and migrants, women's rights, sexual orientation and gender identity (SOGI) rights, and global governance, often posing counternorms to rights based in religious or populist claims: notably, in the United States, India, Turkey, Brazil, Hungary, Poland, the Philippines, and Israel.

Faced with these challenges, our research agenda can expand our analytic frameworks to meet the moment. This agenda must be situated within and beyond human rights law, as one expression and driver of a broader political process of human rights contestation. We can chronicle and theorize the growing modes and spaces to recognize a broader range of who is a human rights-bearing subject, the rising claims and bridging frames for what is right, and alternative regime mechanisms that increase the reach of who is responsible. At the same time, we must seek to understand the drivers and impacts of regime shortfalls, contractions, and backlash.

Engaged human rights scholarship can support the dynamic motion of human rights as practice. Our work can inform human rights struggles as we interrogate the dialectics and translation of normative appeals. Public-facing research can map leverage points and intersections, power relations of vulnerability and resources for resilience, the indivisibility of rights claims and the recognition of interdependence as a foundation for solidarity and coalitions. The research agenda of human rights can raise consciousness of the full range of the human rights repertoire, and help human rights campaigns to identify "the right tools for the job." Finally, as campaigns move from commitment to compliance, human rights research can provide guidance on pathways and barriers to access and fulfillment. Expanding our research agenda to the edge can help to construct as well as envision rights' future.

Introduction—Human rights on the edge: The future of international human rights law and practice

Tricia Redeker Hepner and Heather Smith-Cannoy

ABSTRACT

We convened a conference funded by the National Science Foundation at Arizona State University in April 2021. The 40 papers presented at the conference, a subset of which form this special issue, together demonstrated that, far from collapsing in the face of duress, law is a malleable tool that is deployed in novel ways to promote human rights. Collectively, the conference participants illustrated that the power of human rights lies not in their essentialized transcendence of time, culture, and context, but in their enduring promise that a more just world can emerge from sustained and creative struggle through, against, and at the margins of states, laws, and institutions. Ultimately, the key questions to emerge are not whether human rights law and practice will survive, but rather, what are the forces that continue to sustain, revitalize, and transform them? And what are human rights in the process of becoming?

The field of human rights constitutes a dynamic arena of struggle in law, politics, and practice. The resurgence of nationalist-populist governments in both the Global North and South has forced scholars to rethink the past, present, and future of this discursive and legal regime. Liberal democracies from the United States to India are clamping down on the rights of noncitizens and minorities, rolling back rights for women and girls, and instituting policies at odds with both the spirit and the letter of international human rights law. Escalating demands for economic justice and political reform pervade wealthy industrialized nations as well as developing ones, and authoritarian regimes and right-wing actors are as likely as liberal democracies and progressive social movements to invoke rights claims (Bob, 2019).

Many Western scholars are increasingly pessimistic about the future of international human rights law, suggesting that it is a poor mechanism for the promotion of rights (Moyn, 2010) or that it is simply ineffective in curtailing state excesses (Hopgood, 2013; Posner, 2014). Yet, despite pervasive cynicism about the role of governments and the United Nations, mass movements and civil society organizations that continue to stake demands in the language and law of international human rights proliferate globally.

Inevitably, critical questions abound: Will the body of law that has developed over the last 70 years collapse amid these new challenges? Will international rules and institutions persist but transform? How are local, national, and global dynamics intersecting in new ways to potentially reshape human rights law and practice? How do we make sense of the contemporary ferment of human rights pessimism and optimism and the curious blend of reactionary and progressive appropriations? Is it the case that, "Rather than a rise and fall, the better description of the place of human rights on the global agenda is one of continuous struggle … to remind shifting coalitions of states of the promises they have made to respect them" (Petrasek, 2019, p. 118)? Is it similarly true, as Bob (2019) argued from a legal realist perspective, that the normative and moral content of human rights claims may be "superfluous" to understanding their strategic deployment? Indeed, this is a critical moment for examining the future of international human rights law, politics, and practice.

We convened a conference funded by the National Science Foundation at Arizona State University in April 2021 to unpack some of these issues and questions. The 40 papers presented at the conference, a subset of which form this special issue, together demonstrated that, far from collapsing in the face of duress, law is a malleable tool that is deployed in novel ways to promote human rights. Collectively, the conference participants illustrated that the power of human rights lies not in their essentialized transcendence of time, culture, and context, but in their enduring promise that a more just world can emerge from sustained and creative struggle through, against, and at the margins of states, laws, and institutions. Ultimately, the key questions to emerge are not whether human rights law and practice will survive, but rather, what are the forces that continue to sustain, revitalize, and transform them? And what are human rights in the process of becoming?

Contradictions at the heart

At the heart of much human rights cynicism today lie at least two historical contradictions that accompanied the birth of the postwar human rights project. First, colonization and militarized imperialist expansion generated profound structural inequities within and across world regions, with material and ideological consequences that persist today. Second, the crystallization of statism and attendant ideals of sovereignty, autonomy, and nationalism occurred in tandem with the framework of international norms and institutions. The promise of human rights as accessible to all people and as a check on state power was deeply compromised from the beginning. Human rights have often looked more like a tool for advancing the interests of elites and powerful states than a vehicle for expanding the rights and freedoms of the most vulnerable and oppressed.

But this is far from the whole story. The evolution of human rights law and institutions during this era also helped to mobilize social forces around a common language of justice that ushered in important victories. Transnational forces invoked the language of human rights law to advance protections for women and girls, to better define torture and genocide, and to upend the brutal system of colonization. These institutions created new legal avenues for nonstate actors to monitor and report on human rights violations in ways that enhanced human rights protections. Enshrining civil, political, economic, social, and cultural rights into the cosmopolitan consciousness sent a powerful signal to those agitating for human rights in local struggles that the global community was moving toward a universal set of rights.

Still, much of this vision of human rights, articulated in the core UN human rights treaties, has yet to be realized: widespread poverty and inequality, corruption, democratic backsliding, and growing authoritarianism signal that the human rights project is far from complete. The legacy of the contradictions present at the birth of the human rights system have jeopardized meaningful progress on human rights both within states and between them. Within states, governments invoke the shield of sovereignty to repress local movements to advance rights. The language of human rights is routinely co-opted by powerful elites as a tool to further repress and disenfranchise citizens. At the international level, the powerful states that developed the early institutions of international human rights law created escape clauses, providing immunity for themselves while deploying law as a tool to pass judgment on weaker states.

The mixed legacy of the human rights system has led critics to call into question the current status and future of international human rights law. Yet, the work of the emerging human rights scholars that constitutes this special issue provides reason for guarded optimism. Their work illustrates the subtle and nuanced ways in which the ideas of human rights have created alternative sites of protest, struggle, institutional innovation, and reenvisioning of the project of human rights.

Warning signs and vital signs

The articles selected for this volume constitute clear vital signs for human rights, but they are not without warning. With the exception of distinguished senior scholar Kamari Maxine Clarke, the contributors are all emergent scholars whose research moves beyond normative and moral conceptualizations of human rights to engage with dynamic dimensions of power and practice. They show how informal mechanisms, situated knowledge, and attention to structural inequities are significant for the meaning and the making of law. And they highlight how—amid the failures, excesses, and corruption of states and institutions through which human rights have long been filtered—promising alternatives emerge at the margins.

Suparna Chaudhry and Andrew Heiss explore the recent growth and implementation of laws regulating nongovernmental organizations. Governments employ these nongovernmental organization (NGO) crackdowns, at first, employing milder forms of NGO repression to test the waters, before moving on to more severe forms. Chaudhry and Heiss show that the passage of these anti-NGO regulations alone does not predict future state repression, yet whether and how these laws are implemented predicts other forms of rights violations. Implementation of anti-NGO regulations contributes to moderate growth in political terror and an overall reduction in respect for human rights. Their work serves as a warning: When governments deploy and enforce the law to crack down on NGOs to shrink the space for civil society, the future deterioration of human rights may follow.

Kamari Maxine Clarke's analysis of postcolonial African states' withdrawal from the International Criminal Court (ICC) as a form of protest against structural and historical injustices points directly to the contradictions at the heart of the human rights project—and the enduring promise of it. Clarke argues that African states' efforts to establish the African Court via the Malabo Protocol, and their subsequent failure to ratify the latter, can be understood as both a form of "expressive law" and an "actionable nonactionable." The failure of the Malabo Protocol, Clarke argues, illustrates the potency of international human rights as an ongoing "space of becoming," in which aspirations for universal justice stand in tension with the persistent structural inequalities embedded in institutions like the ICC. For Clarke, the Malabo Protocol "symbolizes the possibility of ownership of international justice by Africans," and thus embodies the ongoing potential of what human rights could be.

Sarbani Sharma turns a critical and cautionary lens on contemporary India to illustrate how democratic countries ruled by majoritarian, nationalist ideology—in this case, *Hindutva*—can simultaneously appropriate the discourse of human rights to protect the powerful while claiming to do so as a "decolonizing" and culturally essentialist move against Western hegemony. Centering the Indian Army's repression and abuses of Muslim Kashmiris, including an incident in which soldiers used a Kashmiri civilian as a human shield, Sharma interrogates the complex intersections between "human rights discourse in India, neoliberal ethics of governmentality, and the *Hindutva* state," in which the "human" is redefined in ways that permit ongoing violations of Kashmiris. Her powerful analysis shows how postcolonial projects that purport to resist Western imperialism can, in fact, reiterate forms of racialized supremacy through the weaponization of redefined rights discourses.

Analyzing the "legal exhaustion" experienced by lawyers and Kurdish victims of state-sanctioned sexual violence in Turkey, Nisa Göksel and Jaimie Morse highlight how "international law has remained a key locus of local legal and human rights struggles," despite the impunity violators have enjoyed. Amid the legal exhaustion felt by lawyers and their Kurdish clients' search for justice both domestically and internationally, Göksel and Morse show how their daily struggles become generative forces revitalizing the commitment to human rights. In particular, lawyers' critiques of the European Court of Human Rights (i.e., as beholden to both state interests and global counterterrorism discourses) constitute a form of activism that calls on legal platforms to be more involved in national politics to implement change while linking women into advocacy networks. These developments highlight "two registers of law: the law as a tool of social control and violence and the law as a means of justice and human rights."

Building on critical feminist scholars' interrogation of the tenacious gendered dichotomies pervading human rights, including objective/subjective, legal/political, and binding/nonbinding, Shanna Corner argues that the unspoken reliance on the secular/religious dichotomy also limits our knowledge about people and dynamics present in intergovernmental institutions where human rights norms and laws are developed and shaped over time. Drawing on ethnographic work with members of the monitoring Committee on the Elimination of Discrimination Against Women (CEDAW), Corner shows how religious identities and personal knowledge inform committee members' interactions and the building of consensus that in turn shapes their evaluations, findings, and recommendations. Like Göksel and Morse, Corner finds that these informal engagements that occur within, against, and at the margins of the law are actually central to the conceptualization of human rights.

Much attention has been given to the human rights consequences of failed peace agreements. The violence, civilian death, and destruction that follows the collapse of an agreement makes understanding their duration all the more critical for scholars of human rights. Anntiana Maral Sabeti's article in this volume helps to close a critical gap in the literature on the duration of peace agreements, which has consistently shown that women's roles in the peace process matters for the sustainability of postwar peace.

Sabeti's work advances our knowledge by showing *how* women should be incorporated into these processes. Employing quantitative analysis, she demonstrates that agreements that focus on the social equality of women and those that invoke and apply international humanitarian law to women tend to last longer than those that do not. Sabeti also points to reforming constitutions so as to incorporate women into government as a vehicle for increasing the durability of peace agreements. Her work suggests that one of the core principles of the human rights project—gender equality and gender mainstreaming—may have a far broader and more significant impact than previously understood.

Assessing the factors that explain the success of the global movement to end child marriage, Andrea Vilán highlights the ways in which human rights advocates have invoked the language of human rights to broaden coalitions and mobilize a broad and diverse global network of actors to fight this practice. Vilán's work illustrates the power of human rights as a tool of mobilization for activists, who alternatively emphasize the role of child marriage in contributing to intimate partner violence, complications during childbirth, violence against women, and a reduction in access to healthcare and education. Yet her assessment, like Clarke's assessment of the ICC, reveals the dual nature of this success. Although new laws to reduce child marriage have been passed, Vilán warns that the success of the movement may be jeopardized by the potential for social backlash, conflicts over sexuality, and regional differences in the form of child marriage.

Conclusion

During his incarceration by the Fascist regime in the 1930s, Italian political philosopher Antonio Gramsci wrote, "The old world is dying, and the new world struggles to be born: now is the time of monsters." Gramsci was referring to the *interregnum*, in which liberalism had entered a period of crisis in the lead-up to World War II. It was out of the wreckage of that period, of course, that the modern human rights regime was born.

Many scholars have argued that the international (neo)liberal order is again in crisis today (Babic, 2020). As a key element of that order, and a register of its crisis, international human rights represent both a means and an end for contending forces in the struggle for ascendancy in an indeterminate present and future. And while human rights contain the vision and the possibility of a more just world, they also embody the historic and systemic injustices—from colonialism to Fascism—that necessitated them. Far from holding a fixed moral or principled essence, human rights may be strategically used as "instruments of conflict, tools of power" (Bob, 2019).

We do not yet know what will become of international human rights law and practice in the future, just as we do not know what new world order is emerging amid the current crisis—or if, perhaps, permanent crisis *is* the new world order. What we can do, however, is understand how human rights continue to unfold in our midst, and how contending forces deploy them in law and in practice, and for what ends.

The contributions to this special issue grapple with the challenges inherent in this uncertain period for global human rights. Far from collapsing, the concept of human rights has endured in spite of contradictions and the specter of co-option and manipulation by the powerful. The research in this volume provides hope. Both these emergent human rights scholars and senior scholar Clarke highlight together the novel and creative ways that advocates employ international human rights law and practice as a vehicle for social transformation and thereby help to reveal what they are in the process of becoming.

Funding

This work was supported by the National Science Foundation, Law and Social Science (2029490).

References

Babic, M. (2020). Let's talk about the interregnum: Gramsci and the crisis of the liberal world order. *International Affairs*, *96*(3), 767–786. doi:10.1093/ia/iiz254

Bob, C. (2019). *Rights as weapons: Instruments of conflict, tools of power*. Princeton University Press.

Hopgood, S. (2013). *The endtimes of human rights*. Cornell University Press.

Moyn, S. (2010). *The last Utopia: Human rights in history*. Belknap Press of Harvard.

Petrasek, D. (2019). Not dead yet: Human rights in an illiberal world order. *International Journal: Canada's Journal of Global Policy Analysis*, *74*(1), 103–118. doi:10.1177/0020702019827642

Posner, E. A. (2014). *The twilight of human rights*. Oxford University Press.

NGO repression as a predictor of worsening human rights abuses

Suparna Chaudhry and Andrew Heiss

ABSTRACT

An increasing number of countries have recently cracked down on nongovernmental organizations (NGOs). Much of this crackdown is sanctioned by law and represents a bureaucratic form of repression that could indicate more severe human rights abuses in the future. This is especially the case for democracies, which, unlike autocracies, may not aggressively attack civic space. We explore whether crackdowns on NGOs predict broader human rights repression. Anti-NGO laws are among the most subtle means of repression and attract lesser domestic and international condemnation compared to the use of violence. Using original data on NGO repression, we test whether NGO crackdown is a predictor of political terror and violations of physical integrity rights and civil liberties. We find that although *de jure* anti-NGO laws provide little information in predicting future repression, their patterns of implementation—or *de facto* civil society repression—predict worsening respect for physical integrity rights and civil liberties.

Over the last few decades, governments across the globe increasingly have been cracking down on civil society organizations (CSOs), particularly nongovernmental organizations (NGOs)—a phenomenon commonly known as closing or shrinking civic space (Carothers & Brechenmacher, 2014; Chaudhry, 2016; Dupuy et al., 2016; Dupuy & Prakash, 2018). More than 100 countries have proposed or enacted 244 different measures that have restricted, repressed, or shut down civil society since 2013 (International Center for Not-For-Profit Law, 2021). In Human Rights Watch's 2016 World Report, Executive Director Kenneth Roth argued that civil society was under more aggressive attack than at any time in recent memory. As seen in Figure 1, by the end of 2020, only 21 percent of countries had open and unrestricted civic space (Chaudhry & Heiss, 2021; CIVICUS., 2021).[1]

This hostility to civil society is not unique to autocratic governments or even illiberal democracies (Abramowitz & Schenkkan, 2018); long-established liberal democracies have also increased restrictions on civil society in their countries. Over the past decade, India has canceled the licenses of tens of thousands of NGOs; targeted major groups such as Greenpeace International, Amnesty International, and The Ford Foundation; and banned thousands of NGOs from receiving foreign funds (Press Trust of India, 2015, 2019). In 2013, Canada attempted to revoke the charitable status of NGOs for opposing the Northern Gateway pipeline and Canadian mining companies' initiatives abroad (CIVICUS, 2013). In 2019, activists from the US-based nonprofit No More Deaths were

Supplemental data for this article can be accessed on the publisher's website.
Data used in the study can be obtained for purposes of replication at: http://dataverse.harvard.edu/dataverse/jhr.

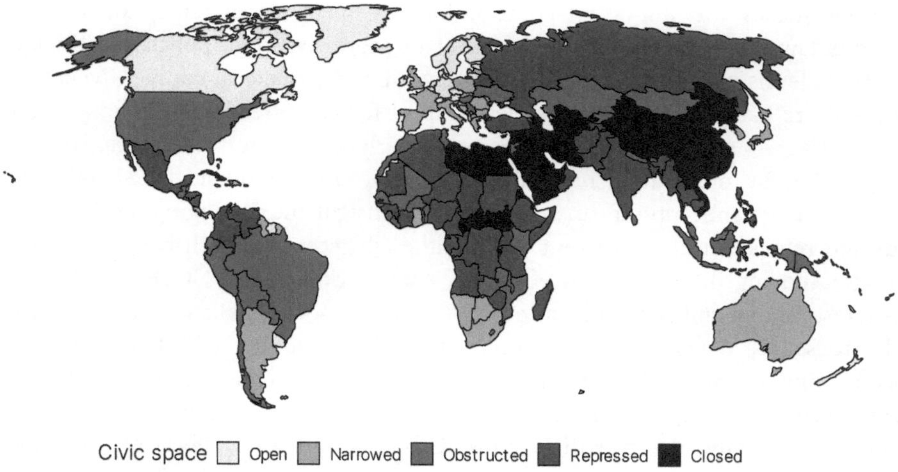

Figure 1. 2020 CIVICUS Monitor civic space ratings.

arrested for providing food and water to migrants at the US–Mexico border and faced a 20-year prison sentence before their convictions were overturned in 2020 (Cramer, 2020).

Much of this targeting of NGOs has been nonviolent. Rather than publicly arrest or beat activists, states implement "administrative crackdown," or the passage of anti-NGO laws to create barriers to NGO advocacy, entry, and funding (Chaudhry, 2022).[2] The use of legal tools instead of violent repression means that NGOs have to adapt their practices to stay within the bounds of permitted activities and operations (Heiss, 2017, 2019). Although this can lead to the depoliticization and avoidance of direct political activism by CSOs (Bloodgood & Tremblay-Boire, 2017), states cannot soften or neutralize all forms of political activity and advocacy in subtle, legal ways as they have with NGOs. Sooner or later, states may need to deal with threats to their stability in a more direct, violent, confrontational manner. Anti-NGO laws could be an important early warning sign—or a canary in the coal mine—of worsening human rights repression, signaling that a state will continue down the path of further repression. What does state targeting of NGOs tell us about the state's broader respect for civil society and the overall level of human rights repression? Can the crackdown on NGOs act as a predictor of subsequent increasing repression?

In this article, we explore the power of anti-NGO repression in predicting political terror and broader patterns of human rights abuses. We argue that information about NGO crackdown can be a valuable indicator of human rights trajectories. It can act as an early warning signal for worsening repression, suggesting which countries are testing the waters with comparatively "milder" methods of crackdown before enacting more violent forms of repression. To assess whether crackdowns on NGOs and activists can provide useful information about future repression, we use an original dataset on state crackdown on NGOs using anti-NGO laws across all countries from 1990 to 2013. We differentiate between two forms of NGO repression: *de jure* anti-NGO laws, and their *de facto* implementation. Whereas the former capture anti-NGO laws that seek to repress these organizations, the latter captures their effects when they are actually implemented or enforced. The distinction is important—laws may frequently be passed to create a chilling effect on civil society. They provide a legal threat that could compel NGOs to self-censor, without actually seeing any uniform or widespread implementation.

Using multilevel Bayesian modeling, we find that formal *de jure* laws provide a weak signal of future repression. Increasing *de facto* civil society repression, on the other hand, predicts both a moderate increase in the probability of moderate political terror and a deterioration in the overall respect for human rights in a typical country.

Our article makes two important contributions to the fields of repression and international human rights law. First, in predicting the onset of repressive state policies: Although structural factors such as levels of democracy, economic development, electoral competitiveness can identify countries that are likely to have more or less respect for civic freedoms, these factors are slow to change over time. As such, they may not be particularly suitable for forecasting short-term trajectories, especially for moderately repressive countries. On the other hand, state repression of NGOs is a more dynamic process that may provide insight into changing levels of human rights standards and repression in subsequent years. Although recent research has made important contributions to studying the extent and effects of state crackdown on NGOs, much of this focuses on *de jure* restrictions and their impact on NGOs and donors (Bakke et al., 2020; Bromley et al., 2020; Christensen & Weinstein, 2013; Dupuy et al., 2016; Dupuy & Prakash, 2018; Smidt et al., 2021). By looking at laws *and* their actual practices of implementation, we are able to assess the long-term effects of closing civic space on broader patterns of repression.

Second, by examining the growth in anti-NGO laws and their effects on patterns of human rights abuses, our results also have important implications for understanding the future of human rights legislation. Existing research on international human rights law shows that civil society groups play an important role in highlighting states' violations of their treaty commitments. By revealing the gap between treaty provisions and actual state behavior, these organizations play a vital role in reducing the "compliance gap" between legal commitments and state practices (Hafner-Burton & Tsutsui, 2005; Hathaway, 2002; Simmons, 2009). The dramatic rise in anti-NGO laws and their implementation through *de facto* civil society repression threatens to exacerbate this compliance gap. Indeed, recent research has found that when governments have committed to human rights treaties and continue to commit severe human rights abuses, they impose anti-NGO laws to escape monitoring (Bakke et al., 2020). Our findings support these arguments by showing that *de facto* levels of NGO repression are a possible predictor of broader patterns of human rights violations.

Below, we first look at existing literature on repression and political violence, outlining state motivations to repress NGOs. We then elaborate on why attacking NGOs may be an important predictor of subsequent repression. Using both original data and data from several existing datasets, we build an ensemble of predictive models and explore (1) the marginal effects of civil society repression on different forms of broader human rights repression, and (2) the out-of-sample predictive performance of each model. We then illustrate one of the mechanisms of our findings—the distinct impact of *de jure* and *de facto* anti-NGO repression—with a brief case illustration of Egypt's treatment of civil society since 2002. We conclude by discussing the implications of our findings on autocratic survival, and how states may manage NGOs as a strategy to remain in power.

Government repression and NGO restrictions

Repression is the use of coercive action against an individual or organization, for the purpose of imposing a cost on the target as well as deterring specific activities perceived to be challenging to government personnel, practices, or institutions (Conrad and Ritter, 2019, p. 15; Davenport, 2007a, p. 487; Goldstein, 1978, p. xxvii). Early literature on repression focused on the role of structural factors such as levels of democracy, economic development, and electoral competitiveness in predisposing a state to the increased use of repression. Most notably, democratic forms of government—and democratization in general—has a pacifying effect on state repression (Davenport & Armstrong, 2004; Krain, 1997; Richards, 1999). Democracies have a negative effect on repression largely because of the increased probability of sanctions against authorities for undesirable behavior (Davenport, 2007b, p. 47).

More recent research has focused on how the behavior of various actors shapes government response. One of the most consistent findings in the political violence literature is that authorities repress to counter ongoing challenges to the *status quo*. In other words, dissent increases repressive behavior (Davenport, 2007a). However, dissent and repression have an endogenous relationship: State authorities frequently engage in preventive repression to undermine or restrict groups' abilities to dissent (Conrad & Ritter, 2019; Ritter & Conrad, 2016). NGOs are one actor that can pose challenges to political authorities, and state repression of these actors—especially through anti-NGO laws—can be considered a form of preventive repression (Chaudhry, 2022).

This preventive repression of NGOs is a recent phenomenon. Although many saw the initial proliferation of NGOs in the 1980s and 1990s as leading to a "symbiotic relationship" between NGOs and states due to their mutual goals, this perception changed over time (Reimann, 2006, p. 63). With expanded powers and their perceived role in the color revolutions, NGOs began to be seen as having a real influence on both domestic and international politics (Carothers & Brechenmacher, 2014). State perception of NGOs as threatening became pervasive as these organizations demonstrated their ability to influence electoral politics (Dupuy et al., 2016; Weiss, 2009), mobilize aid (Bell et al., 2014; Boulding, 2014; Murdie & Bhasin, 2011), and threaten a state's economic interests (Dietrich & Murdie, 2017; Lebovic & Voeten, 2009; Nielsen, 2013).

Given this threat, a number of states decided to repress threatening NGOs. Although violence is often effective at curbing dissent, it can also backfire, leading to widespread protests, decreasing leaders' legitimacy and increasing their criminal liability (Kim & Sikkink, 2010; Sikkink, 2011). In contrast to violence, anti-NGO laws have fewer adverse consequences; citizens may see them as regulations rather than repression. Such laws may also circumvent concerns among state security or bureaucratic agents about illegitimate orders based on violent repression (Stephan & Chenoweth, 2008). There are also fewer international consequences, as laws—unlike violence—rarely invite condemnation or threats of aid withdrawal (Carothers & Brechenmacher, 2014).

These anti-NGO laws can provide convenient avenues for more violent repression and can foreshadow future government transgressions. Autocratic leaders want to avoid accountability, and NGOs often stand in conflict with that goal. Civil society organizations, including NGOs, can help shape the narrative of leaders' performance both domestically and internationally. Monitoring by NGOs and subsequent shaming can include significant external revenue loss to states in the form of loss of aid, trade, and foreign direct investments (Barry et al., 2013; Keck & Sikkink, 1998). Government attempts to repress NGOs through the use of law can signal the beginning of a deteriorating human rights situation. Such repression reflects a government's willingness and capability to use measures that can make it avoid accountability. Once a state targets NGOs, over time it may grow less hesitant to apply violent repression more widely and more severely, thus leading to broader contractions of civil and human rights throughout the country.

In exploring the impact of state crackdown on NGOs on subsequent human rights conditions, we look at both *de jure* measures—or formal legislation that seeks to repress NGOs—and the *de facto* implementation of these measures. This distinction is important; states may pass anti-NGO laws, but these laws can also lie dormant until governments feel the need to enforce them. For instance, Russia passed its 2015 Undesirable Organizations Law with the purpose of targeting and eliminating specific foreign-connected NGOs it deemed dangerous. One of the law's sponsors, Aleksandr Tarnavsky, described the law as a preventive measure that would not affect the majority of NGOs working in Russia. Rather, the law would be a "weapon hanging on the wall that never fires" and stand as a warning to potentially uncooperative NGOs (Kozenko, 2015).

Simply counting these laws may therefore miss the effect of their *de facto* implementation. Some governments may even pass laws to create a chilling effect on these organizations. By providing a legal threat, they could compel organizations to self-censor without even needing to implement the laws in any systematic or meaningful capacity. These laws, especially during moments of crises or contention, "highlight to the wider NGO community—and citizenry—that the government is willing and capable of using the law to repress dissent" (Brechenmacher, 2017, p. 94).

Moreover, the implementation of these laws may not be limited to their legal character. The government may also engage in harassment of NGOs and activists to dissuade NGOs from carrying out their operations. This may include measures such as detentions, short-term incarceration, and destruction of valuable property. Finally, counting official laws can also underestimate levels of NGO repression because governments can repress these organizations without relying on formal laws. As prior research in Egypt, Ethiopia, and Russia has pointed out, "rather than systematically enforcing all repressive legal measures-often impossible owing to capacity constraints," governments may choose to use extra-legal means to intimidate, harass, or prosecute a few NGOs or activists (Brechenmacher, 2017, p. 94) These measures can include arrests, trials, imprisonment, and other violent sanctions against NGO activists, such as beatings, threats to families, and attacks on property. As such, *de facto* crackdown in the form of not just legal harassment but also material and violent sanctions could lead to increases in both physical integrity and civil liberties violations.

Based on these various purposes of NGO restrictions and the different methods states use to implement them, we propose two empirical expectations about the relationship between civil society repression and general human rights:

Empirical expectation 1 (effect of *de jure* NGO repression): If a country imposes a formal anti-NGO law, it is likely to signal future deteriorating human rights conditions.

Empirical expectation 2 (effect of *de facto* NGO repression): If a country implements its formal anti-NGO laws and represses civil society, it is likely to signal future deteriorating human rights conditions.

Data and modeling approach

To test these empirical expectations, we used data on anti-NGO laws, as well as measures from several other larger datasets focused on human rights, political terror, and democratization. Table 1 provides a summary of our key variables.

Measuring *de jure* and *de facto* civil society repression

To measure *de jure* repression, we used data on anti-NGO laws from Chaudhry (2022), which includes official NGO laws for all countries (excluding micro-states) between 1990 and 2013. This measure of

Table 1. Outcomes and predictors.

Measure	Category	Description	Source
Outcomes			
Political Terror Scale (PTS)		Ordered category ranging from 1 (least terror) to 5 (most terror)	Gibney et al. (2019)
Latent human rights values		≈−3 to 5; higher values indicate greater respect for human rights	Fariss et al. (2020)
Predictors			
Total legal barriers	*De jure* laws	Count of all anti-NGO legal barriers	Chaudhry (2022)
Barriers to advocacy	*De jure* laws	Count of laws restricting NGO advocacy	Chaudhry (2022)
Barriers to entry	*De jure* laws	Count of laws restricting NGO entry, including registration	Chaudhry (2022)
Barriers to funding	*De jure* laws	Count of laws restricting NGO funding sources	Chaudhry (2022)
CSO repression	*De facto* repression	≈−3 to 3; higher values indicate less repression	Coppedge et al. (2020); v2csreprss

formal legal barriers does not necessarily represent individual laws. Instead, we count the presence or absence of specific types of anti-NGO legal barriers as a binary variable. If a country passes a law that implements several of these barriers simultaneously (e.g., making registration burdensome and restricting foreign funds), the values for each barrier will flip from 0 to 1. We created indices of the total number of legal barriers in each country based on three broad categories of laws: barriers to entry, funding, and advocacy. We also summed each of these indices to create an overall count of legal barriers.

- **Barriers to advocacy** (two possible barriers): (1) NGOs are restricted from engaging in political activities, and (2) advocacy restrictions differ if the NGO receives foreign funding.
- **Barriers to entry** (three possible barriers): (1) registration is burdensome, (2) NGOs are not allowed to appeal if denied registration, and (3) entry requirements differ if the NGO receives foreign funding.
- **Barriers to funding** (five possible barriers): (1) NGOs need prior approval to receive foreign funding, (2) NGOs are required to channel foreign funding to state-owned banks, (3) NGOs face additional restrictions if receiving foreign funding, and (4) NGOs are restricted or (5) prohibited from receiving foreign funding.

To measure *de facto* civil society repression in a country, we used the Varieties of Democracy's (V-Dem) CSO repression indicator (v2csreprss in Coppedge et al. (2020)), which captures the extent to which governments harass, deter, liquidate, and arrest members of civil society organizations. This variable captures repression using an ordinal scale, defining civil society repression as severe, substantial, moderate, weak, or absent. At the most severe levels, the government violently and actively pursues NGOs, seeking not only to deter their activities but also to liquidate them. On the least repressive end of the spectrum, NGOs are free to organize, associate, express themselves, and criticize the government without fear of government sanctions or harassment. This ordinal scale is then aggregated with a Bayesian item response theory measurement model and converted to a continuous scale that ranges from roughly −3 to 3, with higher values indicating less repression.

Figure 2 shows each of these types of legal barriers per country over time, as well as average levels of *de facto* civil society repression by regime type. Although anti-NGO laws have increased steadily since 1990, there has not necessarily been a corresponding rise in *de facto* civil society repression, which has remained fairly constant across different regime types. This divergence is likely indicative of the split between *de jure* laws and their *de facto* implementation: New legislation is not necessarily implemented immediately and does not always lead to broader NGO repression.

Measuring repression

To see how both *de jure* and *de facto* civil society restrictions influence general human rights repression, we used two different quantitative measures of repression, each of which captures different dimensions of political and civil violence. First, following Gohdes and Carey (2017), who used the killing of journalists to predict worsening human rights conditions, we used the Political Terror Scale (PTS), which assigns countries to one of five possible levels of repression each year (Gibney et al., 2019), with Level 5 representing widespread political violence—including arrests, imprisonment, political murders, disappearances, and torture. As seen in the top panel of Figure 3, the number of countries at Level 5 has decreased since the 1990s, and most countries are coded as Levels 2 and 3 (moderate levels of political terror).

The five levels of the PTS are helpful for conceptualizing broader trends in human rights abuses. However, these categories are not always granular enough to model or predict a country's

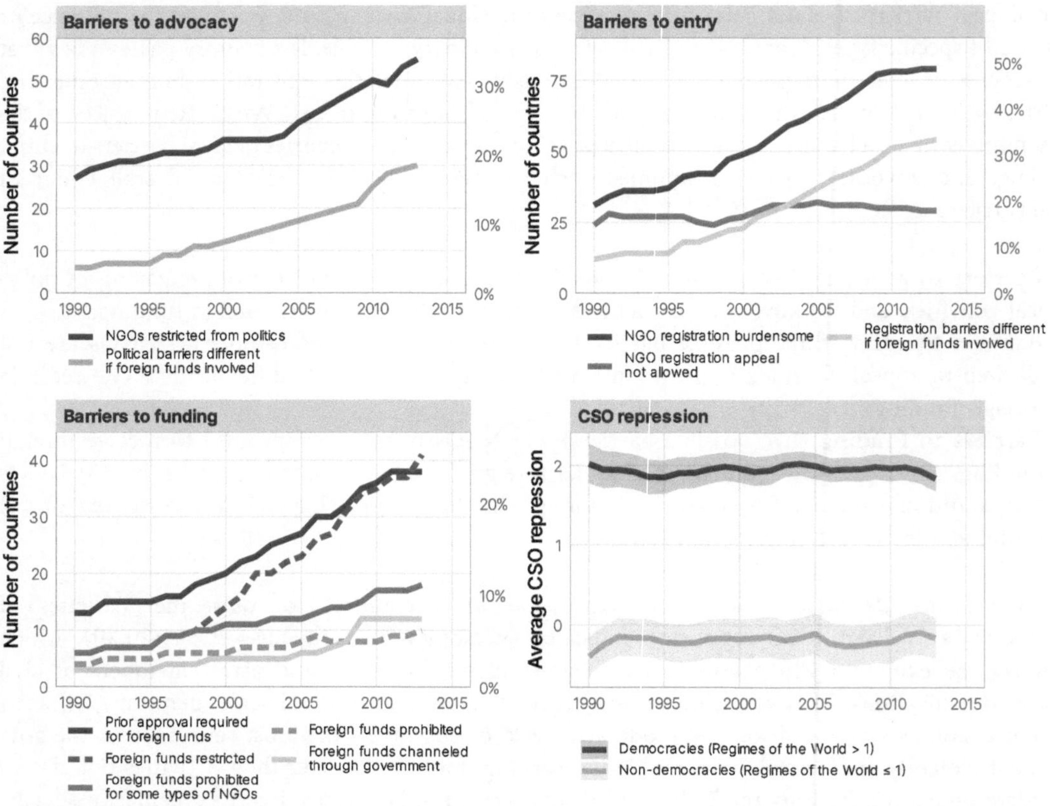

Figure 2. Number of legal barriers to NGO activity per country over time (*de jure* legislation) and average level of CSO repression across democracies and nondemocracies (*de facto* implementation).

level of political terror. Additionally, the PTS—along with most other measures of human rights abuses—does not account for the systematic changes in the way monitoring agencies have gathered information about human rights violations over time. Accordingly, we used latent human rights scores as an alternative measure of underlying repression (Fariss, 2014; Fariss et al., 2020). This variable is generated from a Bayesian measurement model that incorporates information about human rights abuses from a variety of published repression indices, including the PTS. Because the resulting measure is continuous, it picks up on more minute changes in national-level human rights. Moreover, this variable accounts for changing standards of accountability, which has led to the production of more stringent human rights reports as monitors look harder for abuse, look in more places for abuse, and classify more acts as abuse. When accounting for these changes, the bottom panel of Figure 3 demonstrates the global improvements in average latent human rights values over time.

Modeling approach

Because we looked at whether anti-NGO laws and their implementation can serve as an early warning signal for broader repression, we were primarily interested in *predicting* repression and not isolating the causal effect of civil society repression on general human rights abuses. We did not include a complete set of covariates to remove confounding relationships, but instead used a more parsimonious set of explanatory variables that strongly predict repression. Following Gohdes and Carey (2017), we controlled for a country's level of repression in the previous year

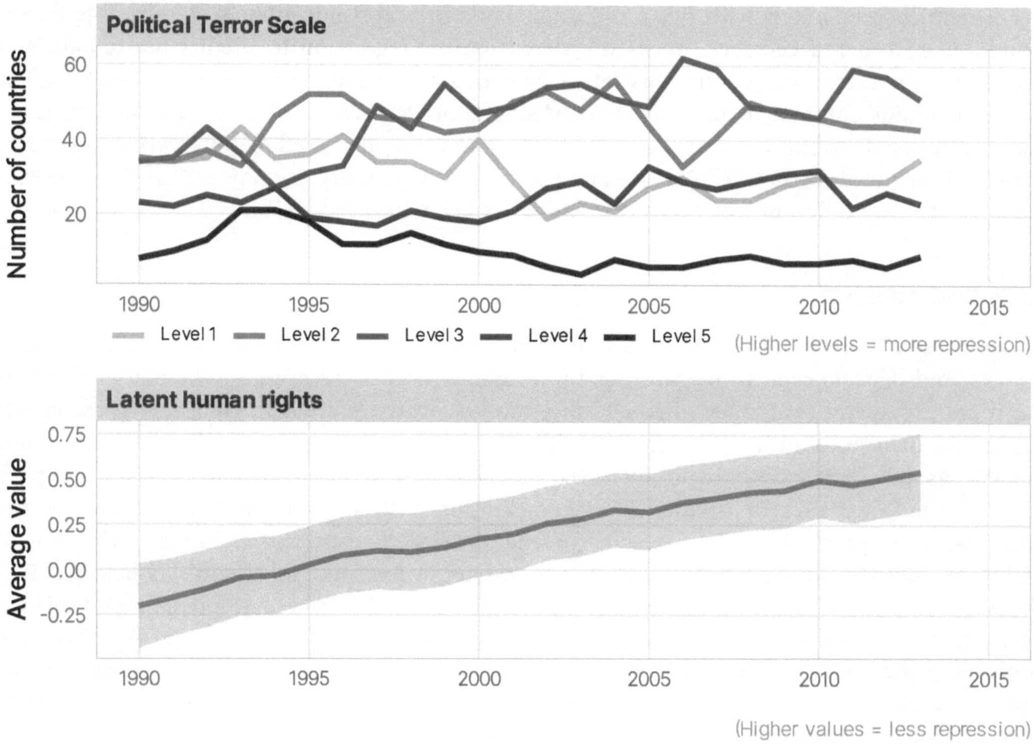

Figure 3. Key measures of repression over time.

(either PTS score or latent human rights value, depending on the model), its level of democracy as measured by V-Dem's polyarchy index, its logged GDP *per capita* (measured by the UN), the percentage of GDP attributed to trade (measured by the UN), and an indicator for whether the country witnessed more than 25 battle-related deaths (measured by Uppsala Conflict Data Program - Peace Research Institute Oslo (UCDP/PRIO) [2020] and Gleditsch et al. [2002]). Because changes in the human rights environment take time to be reflected by these larger indices, we modeled the effect of lagged explanatory variables on repression one year in the future. We also included the lag of civil society laws or repression to account for serial correlation.

We extended Gohdes and Carey (2017)'s previous modeling approach by accounting for country-level variation in repression with multilevel modeling and we included random effects for each country. Accounting for country differences this way resulted in intraclass correlation coefficients of around .7 for each of our three outcome variables, which means that the country-based structure of the data explains more than 70 percent of the variation in outcome, resulting in model estimates that are arguably more precisely measured. We ran multiple models for each of our empirical expectations, based on different combinations of our outcomes and key explanatory variables:

Expectation 1_a: Anti-NGO laws (total; advocacy, entry, funding separately) signal worsening political terror.
Expectation 1_b: Anti-NGO laws signal decreasing latent human rights respect.
Expectation 2_a: Civil society repression signals worsening political terror.
Expectation 2_b: Civil society repression signals decreasing latent human rights respect.

We generated predictions with two families of Bayesian regression models. Because the PTS is measured as an ordered category, we used ordered logistic regression to predict future values of the scale. We predicted the continuous latent human rights values with Gaussian models. The Appendix contains complete details of our modeling approach. We used median values from the models' posterior distributions as our point estimates and provided credible intervals using the 95 percent highest posterior density. We declared an effect statistically "significant" if the posterior probability of being different from zero (i.e., above or below) exceeds .95.

Results and analysis

Here, we present the results of our models in two stages. First, to see how minor shifts in anti-NGO laws and *de facto* repression influence future human rights, we examine the marginal effects of our main explanatory variables when all other model covariates are held constant. These effects are by no means causal; rather, they demonstrate how much variation in predicted human rights is possible as the legal environment for civil society improves or deteriorates within a typical country. Second, we present predictive diagnostics for each of our models to examine the improvements in predictions. The results of the ordered logistic regression models can be unwieldy to interpret with plain numbers due to varying intercepts and thresholds between PTS levels. Accordingly, we present graphical results for all our models wherever possible and include complete tables of model results in the Appendix (see supplemental Tables A2 and A3). For ease in comparing the count of NGO laws with civil society repression, we reverse the x-axis in the marginal effects plots for our second empirical expectation so that increasing the civil society repression represents *worse* repression rather than less.

Marginal results

How does repression change following increases in NGO laws?

In general, when holding all other covariates constant, the passage of an additional anti-NGO law is generally associated with a higher probability of more severe level of political terror in the following year. The probability of seeing different levels of political terror varies across different possible counts of NGO laws (see Figure 4). In the absence of formal laws, Level 2 of the PTS—an environment in which political imprisonment, torture, and beatings are rare—is the most likely category of political terror across all models, appearing a predicted 60 percent of the time. Level 1, in which a country is under secure rule of law, is the second most likely outcome, at slightly under 40 percent. The other categories of the PTS are extremely rare when there are no anti-NGO laws; as such, we collapse them into a single category.

As new laws are added, however, the distribution of probabilities for each of the PTS levels shifts. Adding new barriers to advocacy, entry, and funding decreases the likelihood of seeing Level 1 and increases the probability of a country turning to either Level 2 or Level 3 (with extensive political imprisonment and trial-free detention). The marginal effects of all forms of anti-NGO laws results in this turn from Level 1 to Levels 2 or 3+, but this switching effect is strongest following additional barriers to advocacy.

Anti-NGO laws do not predict more dramatic shifts in the PTS. Across all counts of anti-NGO laws, the overall probability of seeing Levels 4 and 5 is minuscule, and the passage of additional laws does little to shift that probability. This is not unexpected however: The PTS has a natural ceiling at Level 5. Specifically, in addition to measuring the scope and intensity of government violence, the PTS scale also looks at the proportion of population targeted for abuse. Countries that receive a 4 and 5 are rare, as 4 denotes that murders, disappearances, and torture are a common part of life, and 5 denotes that physical abuses are routinely perpetrated against citizens not involved in politics, and includes cases on which governments engage in "scorched

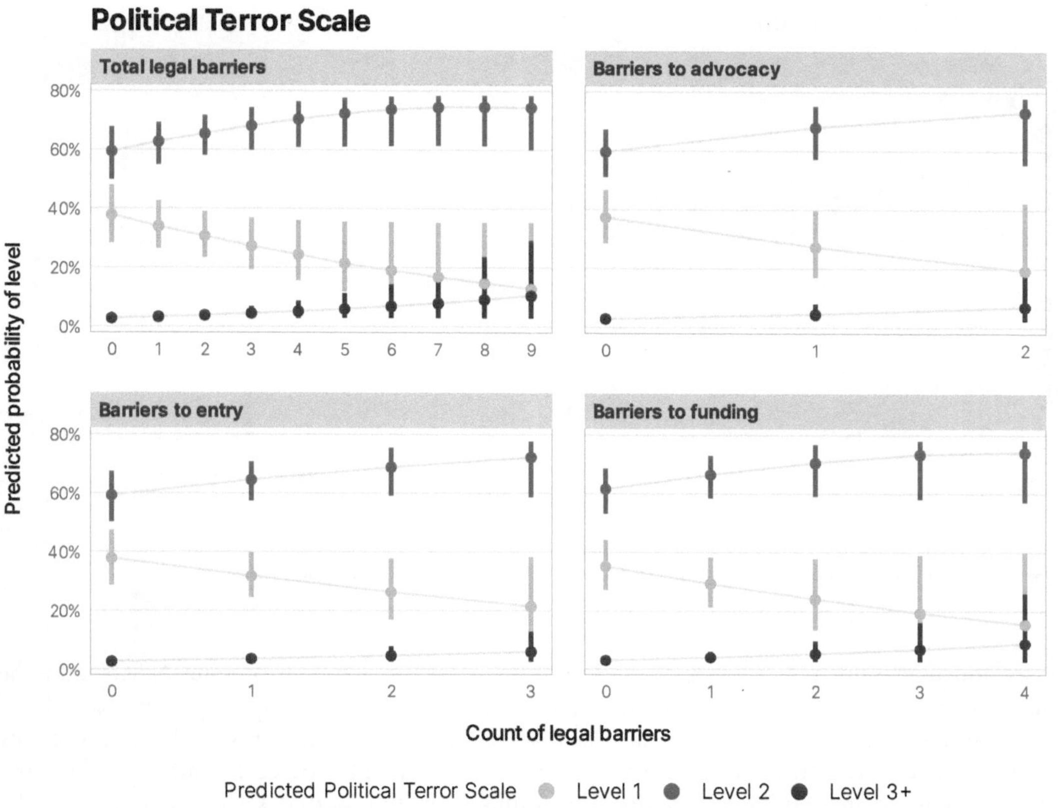

Figure 4. Marginal effects of increasing anti-NGO legal barriers on the probability of specific levels of political terror.

earth" counterinsurgency policies or summary executions based on class or ethnic affiliation (Gibney et al., 2019). The majority of movement across PTS categories should thus occur between Levels 1 and 3.

Figure 5 shows the marginal effects of additional anti-NGO laws on latent human rights scores. Across all four models for different categories of legal barriers, holding all other values constant, the predicted level of human rights respect decreases. Adding a new anti-NGO law is associated with a −.013-point decline in the level of respect for human rights in the following year, on average, representing a roughly 5 percent decline in predicted the predicted value. The marginal effect is larger (−.02, or a 9 percent decline) for additional barriers to advocacy and entry, which represent more burdensome registration requirements than barriers to funding.

At a marginal level, therefore, adding additional anti-NGO laws in countries with low levels of political terror could signal that higher levels of political repression are more likely in the future. Limited repression remains the most likely possible outcome, but the chance of seeing robust rule of law decreases rapidly as more laws are passed, all else equal. This pattern holds when looking at a more continuous measure of human rights protection: Countries with a low count of anti-NGO legal barriers tend to have higher predicted values of latent human rights scores, and average protection against abuses decreases as more laws are added.

How does general repression change following *de facto* civil society repression?

The weaker predictive power of formal NGO laws is likely attributable to the fact that *de jure* NGO legislation may take time to implement; many states need to first establish institutions that

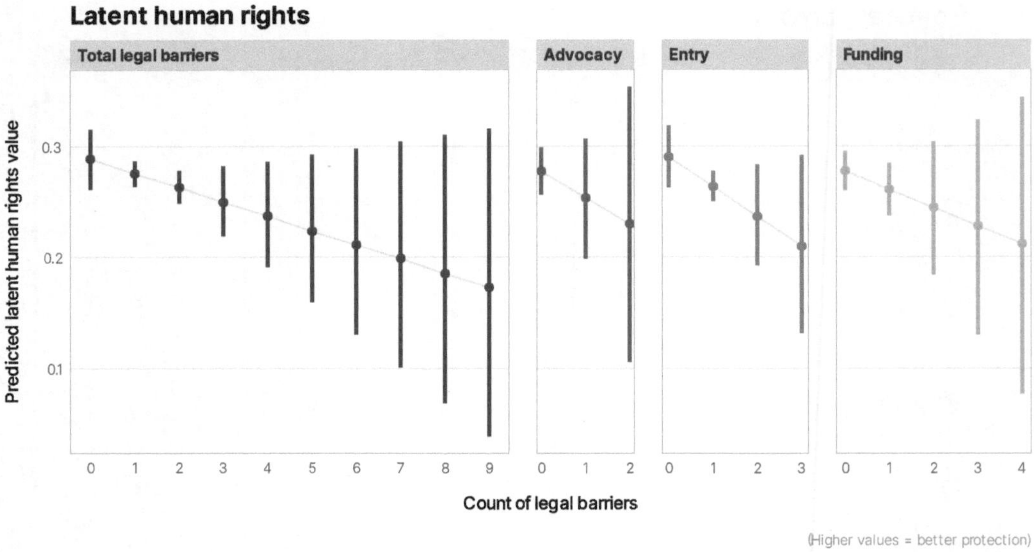

Figure 5. Marginal effects of increasing anti-NGO legal barriers on latent human rights values.

oversee the operation and funding of these groups or incorporate threatening NGOs into the regime apparatus (Naím, 2007). Furthermore, states that engage in political repression can do so with or without legal justification. *De facto* civil society repression, on the other hand, represents the actual implementation of anti-NGO strategies—both legal and extralegal—and might be more indicative of future human rights abuses. The results from our second set of models, using V-Dem's civil society repression index as the key predictor, confirm this.

The effect of *de facto* civil society repression on predicted values of the PTS mirrors what we found previously with our first empirical expectation. As seen in left panel of Figure 6, at the lowest levels of repression, Levels 1 and 2 are the most common predicted outcomes and are each equiprobable at roughly 50 percent. As *de facto* CSO repression increases, however, the probability of seeing Level 1 decreases and is replaced with either Level 2 or Level 3. More severe levels of political terror remain exceptionally improbable at any level of preceding civil society repression; we again collapse these into a single category.

De facto civil society repression has a noticeable effect on latent human rights values (see the right panel of Figure 6). When holding all other model parameters at their typical values, increased civil society repression predicts a strong decrease in respect for broader human rights: A one-unit change in civil society repression is associated with a .05-unit change in overall latent human rights. To illustrate the magnitude of this effect, a typical simulated country with a civil society repression index of 0 is predicted to have a latent human rights score of .22. This predicted outcome drops to .17 with a one-unit decrease in civil society repression, representing a 24 percent decline in respect for human rights in the following year.

When holding all other factors equal, the *de facto* implementation of anti-NGO laws thus appears to be a stronger marginal indicator of future repression than simply the passage of these laws. Although these laws may be intended to have a chilling effect on civil society (and certainly have a chilling effect on levels of aid and NGO operations, as shown by recent literature), *de jure* laws by themselves do not have similar adverse consequences on respect for physical integrity rights and civil liberties. In countries with low levels of political terror, it can potentially serve as a weak signal of a more general increase in political violence in the future, but predict more substantial changes in general respect for human rights. The difference in the effects of laws vs. their *de facto* implementation could also potentially be explained by the time frame of these strategies.

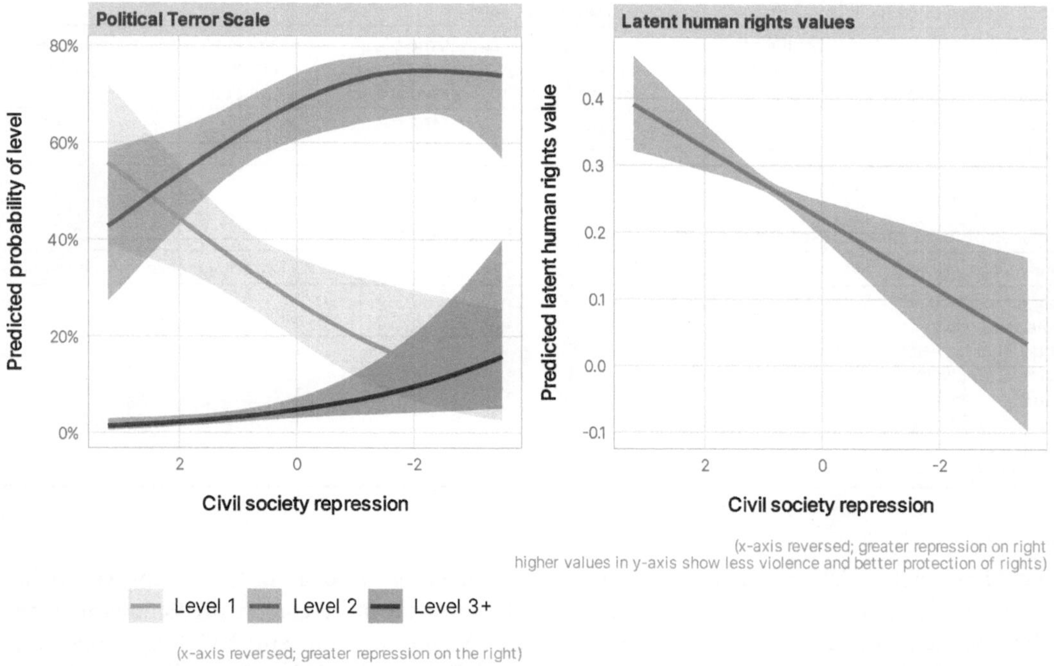

Figure 6. Marginal effects of changing levels of civil society repression on the probability of specific levels of political terror and predicted latent human rights values.

As we explore in the next section, *de jure* civil society laws constitute a long-term strategy to prevent threats to the regime from coalescing in the first place. As such, the effects of these laws in terms of their predictive power may require a much longer time period under study. In contrast, *de facto* crackdown on NGOs may signal that a state needs to react sooner due to the immediacy of the threat.

Predictions

These predicted probabilities and outcomes are conditional on all other model parameters being held at their average values and show the effect of hypothetically changing a single predictor to different values. They do not show how well these models work with actual data. Following Ward and Beger (2017) and Gohdes and Carey (2017), we tested the predictive power of both sets of our models using out-of-sample prediction. We divided our complete data into a training set and a test set—the training set includes data from all countries from 1990–2010, and the test set includes the last three years of data (2011–2013). We reran each of our models using our training data and then used the estimated parameters to predict political terror, physical violence, and private civil liberties for the test data. Additionally, we estimated a model for each outcome without predictor variables for civil society laws or repression as a baseline measure of model performance.

We assessed predictive power in a few different ways, depending on the model used to predict the outcome. For the ordinal PTS, Table 2 shows a count of correct and incorrect predictions from each model. We measured the predicted accuracy of our latent human rights models with the root mean squared error (RMSE), provided in Table 3. In the Appendix we include lists of country-year cases that see improved predictions when taking civil society laws and repression into account.

Table 2. Counts of correctly and incorrectly predicted cases across different PTS models.

Prediction	Baseline	Total legal barriers included	Barriers to advocacy included	Barriers to entry included	Barriers to funding included	Civil society repression included
Wrong	109	107	110	108	108	111
Correct	376	378	375	377	376	374

Table 3. Root mean squared error across models predicting latent human rights.

Latent human rights values	RMSE	Percentage change from baseline
Baseline model	.1862	–
De jure repression		
Total legal barriers	.1872	.54
Barriers to advocacy	.1872	.53
Barriers to entry	.1863	.03
Barriers to funding	.1880	.95
De facto repression		
Civil society repression	.1857	−.27

Including civil society restrictions—both *de jure* and *de facto*—does little to improve predictions of political terror. As seen in Table 2, no model provides more correct predictions than the baseline model, and some models perform worse. Accounting for anti-NGO activities does improve predictions in eight cases (see supplemental Table A1 in the Appendix), but it also results in an equal number of incorrect predictions.

When looking at the overall latent human rights values in a country, including *de jure* and *de facto* repression does little to improve predictive accuracy. As Table 3 shows, accounting for *de facto* civil society repression only reduces the Root Mean Square Error (RMSE) by .27% compared to the baseline, and accounting for *de jure* laws worsens the models' predictive power slightly. Although these gains in predictive power appear negligible, they are somewhat comparable with the findings of previous work. For instance, in their work on the effect of the murder of journalists on predicting future political terror, Gohdes and Carey (2017) found that accounting for violence against the media adds five correctly predicted cases of PTS scores and improves predictions in seven cases.

We thus again find that *de facto* civil society repression is a stronger predictor of worsening human rights in the future than formal laws on their own. Actual government interference in civil society acts as a possible signal of future abuses of civil and human rights better than simply the presence of a law that could potentially be used at some point in the future.

Discretionary disconnect between *de jure* and *de facto* NGO repression: The case of Egypt

When looking at both marginal effects and improvements in predictive power, we found that the *de facto* implementation of anti-civil society measures is a stronger indicator of future repression than *de jure* anti-NGO laws. One reason for this disconnect between law and implementation is that laws targeted at NGOs are often not designed to be used immediately, but instead serve to protect regimes against potential threats in the future. Egypt provides a prime example of this mechanism.

In the wake of domestic terrorist attacks in the late 1990s, the Egyptian Parliament passed Law 84 of 2002, or the Law on Associations and Foundations (Agati, 2007, p. 60). The new law imposed specific limits on international and foreign-connected NGOs and required that all NGOs register with the Ministry of Social Solidarity. Any revenue from foreign associations to nonprofit organizations working in Egypt required both recipients and donors to submit multiple

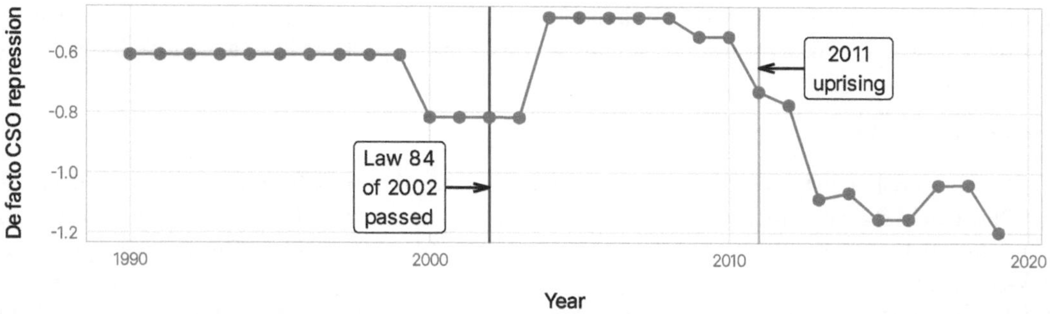

Figure 7. The disconnect between Egypt's *de jure* 2002 law and the widespread *de facto* repression of civil society a decade later.

applications to the Ministry of Foreign Affairs and state security, and the latter maintained ultimate veto power over the approval process (Thabet, 2004, p. 162).

Although it granted the government substantial oversight power over NGOs, Law 84 also allowed for enormous discretion in enforcement. In spite of the strict legal framework, the Egyptian NGO sector nearly doubled in size between 1993 and 2011 (Brechenmacher, 2017), largely because of the government's selective and targeted enforcement of the law. When NGOs became too contentious or posed a threat to the regime, officials could use minor infractions in more obscure parts of the law to fine or shut down the organization, but these attacks on NGOs were limited to specific NGOs. As seen in Figure 7, Egypt saw its highest, most stable, and most open level of broader civil society repression in the decade following the passage of Law 84.

The calculus of enforcement changed as the state faced increased threats to its stability. Following Hosni Mubarak's removal as president in February 2011, the Supreme Council of the Armed Forces (SCAF) took temporary control over governing the country. SCAF worked throughout the year to curtail protests and often resorted to violence to break up demonstrations, which led to larger and more violent protests in response. The tension culminated on December 16, when troops filled Tahrir Square to put down an anti-SCAF demonstration, killing 10 and wounding more than 400. Two weeks later, Egyptian security forces raided the offices of 17 local and international NGOs—including Freedom House, the National Democratic Institute, and the International Republican Institute—and arrested dozens of domestic and international NGO staff (Fadel & Warrick, 2011). The stated legal pretext for this raid was that the organizations were not officially registered and thus in violation of Law 84. The *de jure* law—constantly looming in the background, but enforced selectively—was finally implemented and enforced more expansively. In the years after the 2011 uprising, postrevolutionary regimes have enforced the law more consistently, further constricting the space for civil society (Ruffner, 2015), as seen in the rapid drop in broader civil society repression in Figure 7.

Law 84 (and its replacement, Law 70 of 2017) is thus a useful lever for selectively controlling the allowable space for dissidence and leaving open the possibility of future human rights abuses. The law's built-in discretionary authority permits the government to give the appearance of concessions and openness to civil society while simultaneously providing it with the ability to target individual NGOs and the right to engage in broader crackdowns of associational rights.

This trend holds across many other countries as well. For instance, even though India passed an anti-NGO law (containing multiple barriers to funding and advocacy) in 1976, it has not always been uniformly implemented. Rather, having an anti-NGO law on the books serves the state's long-term strategic interests, enabling it to crack down on NGOs when they start posing electoral or economic threats to the state (Chaudhry, 2022). Anti-NGO laws can therefore serve as a useful avenue for future human rights abuses, sometimes with years separating the official passage of a law and the large-scale implementation of the law, explaining why *de facto* levels of NGO repression serve as a stronger predictor of worsening respect for human rights abuses.

Conclusion and implications

Strengthening civil society is an important precondition for democratic transition and consolidation. This article shows dramatic growth in *de jure* regulations constraining NGOs—laws that can lay the foundation for subsequent *de facto* repression of civil society. Given these potential knock-on effects, in this article we have posited that the ongoing global crackdown on NGOs could predict worsening human rights abuses. Using original data on *de jure* and *de facto* NGO repression from 1990 to 2013, we found weak support for the predictive power of *de jure* restriction on political terror and overall latent human rights values. Marginal predictions showed that—all else held equal—adding new anti-NGO laws increases the probability of seeing moderate levels of political terror and is associated with worsening human rights conditions more generally. However, in contrast to *de jure* laws, *de facto* levels of NGO repression—including both legal and extra-legal means of crackdown—tend to increase the probability of more moderate political terror. Additionally, this repression is associated with worsening respect for broader human rights in the future.

Importantly, the weak predictive power of anti-NGO laws by themselves reflects the purpose of NGO restrictions. Encroachments on private civil liberties such as restricting freedom of association and funding are not nearly as violent as events like physical integrity rights violations and political terror. Anti-NGO laws could possibly be a side effect of authoritarian stability-seeking behavior, similar to election tampering, media censorship, cronyism, and rent seeking, rather than an overt signal of impending serious human rights abuses. The global shrinking of civic space or increasing passage of anti-NGO laws is thus not likely an early warning sign for future violent repression: States typically signal their future repressive intentions with more violent methods, such as the persecution or murder of civil society activists and the media. Instead, civil society is a possible canary in the coal mine for impending violations of other civil rights, such as the freedom of religion, labor rights, property rights, and the freedom of movement.

However, it is also important to state that although anti-NGO laws do not seem to be predictors of broader human rights repression over the period under study, this does not imply they are not having a chilling effect on NGO operations. The broader literature on state repression of NGOs has shown that *de jure* laws can have numerous adverse consequences. Foreign funding laws have led to a 32 percent decline in bilateral aid flows (Dupuy & Prakash, 2018). NGOs that are underfunded and understaffed tend to shut down when faced with increasing restrictions (Heiss, 2019). In sum, although *de jure* laws do not affect levels of physical integrity and civil liberties violations in particular, research has found that they do have other adverse consequences. Moreover, because the actual implementation of these laws through *de facto* civil society repression can have negative effects on broader patterns of human rights abuses, the passage of these laws may still be a concerning first step that paves the path for future implementation.

The dramatic growth in these laws has important implications for the power of the human rights regime and international human rights law. The UN Special Rapporteur on the Right to Freedom of Peaceful Assembly and Association has pointed out that the right of NGOs to seek, receive, and use resources is an essential component of the right to association (Kiai, 2013). Anti-NGO laws, including barriers to funding, violate core human rights treaties such as the International Covenant on Civil and Political Rights. In contrast to the influential work on the impact of transnational advocacy networks and international law—which places immense value on the ability of civil society groups to monitor, shame, and reform state behavior—the results in this article show that reforms resulting from international legal pressure and mobilization may be short-lived. Rather, states may be learning to counter these dynamics by ramping up repression.

Notes

1. Following CIVICUS, open civic space in a country indicates that the state enables and safeguards citizens' freedom to form associations, authorities are tolerant of criticism from CSOs, and laws governing freedom of peaceful assembly adhere to international laws and standards.
2. In this article, we use the terms *anti-NGO laws* and *de jure NGO laws* and *NGO restrictions* interchangeably.

Acknowledgments

We would like to thank participants of the 2021 International Studies Association (ISA) convention, and the "Human Rights on the Edge: The Future of International Human Rights Law and Practice" workshop hosted by the Global Human Rights Hub at Arizona State University for their comments and feedback.

Disclosure statement

The authors report there are no competing interests to declare.

ORCID

Suparna Chaudhry http://orcid.org/0000-0003-3506-7590
Andrew Heiss http://orcid.org/0000-0002-3948-3914

References

Abramowitz, M., & Schenkkan, N. (2018, April 6). How illiberal leaders attack civil society. *Foreign Affairs*. Retrieved December 10, 2021, from https://www.foreignaffairs.com/articles/central-europe/2018-04-06/how-illiberal-leaders-attack-civil-society

Agati, M. (2007). Undermining standards of good governance: Egypt's NGO law and its impact on the transparency and accountability of CSOs. *International Journal of Not-for-Profit Law*, *9*(2), 56–75.

Bakke, K. M., Mitchell, N. J., & Smidt, H. M. (2020). When states crack down on human rights defenders. *International Studies Quarterly*, *64*(1), 85–96. doi:10.1093/isq/sqz088

Barry, C. M., Clay, K. C., & Flynn, M. E. (2013). Avoiding the spotlight: Human rights shaming and foreign direct investment. *International Studies Quarterly*, *57*(3), 532–544. doi:10.1111/isqu.12039

Bell, S. R., Bhasin, T., Clay, K. C., & Murdie, A. (2014). Taking the fight to them: Neighborhood human rights organizations and domestic protest. *British Journal of Political Science*, *44*(4), 853–875. doi:10.1017/S0007123413000100

Bloodgood, E., & Tremblay-Boire, J. (2017). Does government funding depoliticize non-governmental organizations? Examining evidence from Europe. *European Political Science Review*, *9*(3), 401–424. doi:10.1017/S1755773915000430

Boulding, C. (2014). *NGOs, political protest, and civil society*. Cambridge University Press.

Brechenmacher, S. (2017). *Civil society under assault: Repression and response in Russia, Egypt, and Ethiopia*. Carnegie Endowment for International Peace. Retrieved December 10, 2021, from http://carnegieendowment.org/2017/05/18/civil-society-under-assault-repression-and-responses-in-russia-egypt-and-ethiopia-pub-69953

Bromley, P., Schofer, E., & Longhofer, W. (2020). Contentions over world culture: The rise of legal restrictions on foreign funding to NGOs, 1994–2015. *Social Forces*, *99*(1), 281–304. doi:10.1093/sf/soz138

Carothers, T., & Brechenmacher, S. (2014). *Closing space: Democracy and human rights support under fire*. Carnegie Endowment for International Peace.

Chaudhry, S. (2016). *The assault on democracy assistance: Explaining state repression of NGOs* [PhD thesis]. Yale University.

Chaudhry, S. (2022). The assault on civil society: Explaining state crackdown on NGOs. *International Organization*, 1–42. doi:10.1017/S0020818321000473

Chaudhry, S., & Heiss, A. (2021). Closing space and the restructuring of global activism: Causes and consequences of the global crackdown on NGOs. In C. L. Pallas & E. Bloodgood (Eds.), *Beyond the boomerang: New patterns in transcalar advocacy*. University of Alabama Press.

Christensen, D., & Weinstein, J. M. (2013). Defunding dissent: Restrictions on aid to NGOs. *Journal of Democracy*, *24*(2), 77–91. doi:10.1353/jod.2013.0026

CIVICUS. (2013). *Global trends on civil society restrictions: Mounting restrictions on civil society: The gap between rhetoric and reality*. CIVICUS.

CIVICUS. (2021). *CIVICUS monitor*. Retrieved December 10, 2021, from https://monitor.civicus.org/

Conrad, C. R., & Ritter, E. H. (2019). *Contentious compliance: Dissent and repression under international human rights law*. Oxford University Press. 10.1093/oso/9780190910976.001.0001

Coppedge, M., Gerring, J., Knutsen, C. H., Lindberg, S. I., Teorell, J., Altman, D., & Ziblatt, D. (2020). *V-Dem [country-year/country-date] dataset v10*. Varieties of Democracy (V-Dem) Project. 10.23696/vdemds20

Cramer, M. (2020, February 5). Judge reverses convictions of activists who left water for migrants. *The New York Times*. Retrieved December 10, 2021, from https://www.nytimes.com/2020/02/05/us/tucson-border-activists-conviction-reversed.html

Davenport, C. (2007a). State repression and political order. *Annual Review of Political Science*, *10*(1), 1–23. doi:10.1146/annurev.polisci.10.101405.143216

Davenport, C. (2007b). *State repression and the domestic democratic peace*. Cambridge University Press. 10.1017/cbo9780511510021

Davenport, C., & Armstrong, D. A. (2004). Democracy and the violation of human rights: A statistical analysis from 1976–1996. *American Journal of Political Science*, *48*(3), 538–554. doi:10.1111/j.0092-5853.2004.00086.x

Dietrich, S., & Murdie, A. (2017). Human rights shaming through INGOs and foreign aid delivery. *The Review of International Organizations*, *12*(1), 95–120. doi:10.1007/s11558-015-9242-8

Dupuy, K., & Prakash, A. (2018). Do donors reduce bilateral aid to countries with restrictive NGO laws? A panel study, 1993–2012. *Nonprofit and Voluntary Sector Quarterly*, *47*(1), 89–106. doi:10.1177/0899764017737384

Dupuy, K., Ron, J., & Prakash, A. (2016). Hands off my regime! Governments' restrictions on foreign aid to non-governmental organizations in poor and middle-income countries. *World Development*, *84*, 299–311. doi:10.1016/j.worlddev.2016.02.001

Fadel, L., Warrick, J. (2011, December 29). Egyptian security forces raid offices of U.S., Other democracy groups. *The Washington Post*. Retrieved December 10, 2021, from https://www.washingtonpost.com/world/middle_east/egyptian-security-forces-raid-offices-of-us-other-democracy-groups/2011/12/29/gIQA2jlbOP_story.html

Fariss, C. J. (2014). Respect for human rights has improved over time: Modeling the changing standard of accountability in human rights documents. *American Political Science Review*, *108*(2), 297–318. doi:10.1017/S0003055414000070

Fariss, C. J., Kenwick, M. R., & Reuning, K. (2020). Estimating one-sided killings from a robust measurement model of human rights. *Journal of Peace Research*, *57*(6), 801–814. doi:10.1177/0022343320965670

Gibney, M., Cornett, L., Wood, R., Haschke, P., Arnon, D., Pisanò, A., Barrett, G. (2019). *The Political Terror Scale 1976–2018*. http://politicalterrorscale.org/

Gleditsch, N. P., Wallensteen, P., Eriksson, M., Sollenberg, M., & Strand, H. (2002). Armed conflict 1946–2001: A new dataset. *Journal of Peace Research*, *39*(5), 615–637. doi:10.1177/0022343302039005007

Gohdes, A. R., & Carey, S. C. (2017). Canaries in a coal-mine? What the killings of journalists tell us about future repression. *Journal of Peace Research*, *54*(2), 157–174. doi:10.1177/0022343316680859

Goldstein, R. J. (1978). *Political repression in modern America: From 1870 to the present*. G. K. Hall.

Hafner-Burton, E. M., & Tsutsui, K. (2005). Human rights in a globalizing world: The paradox of empty promises. *American Journal of Sociology*, *110*(5), 1373–1411. doi:10.1086/428442

Hathaway, O. A. (2002). Do human rights treaties make a difference? *The Yale Law Journal, 111*(8), 1935–2043. doi:10.2307/797642
Heiss, A. (2017). Amicable contempt: The strategic balance between dictators and international NGOs (PhD thesis). Duke University.
Heiss, A. (2019). Taking control of regulations: How international advocacy NGOs shape the regulatory environments of their target countries. *Interest Groups & Advocacy, 8*(3), 356–375. doi:10.1057/s41309-019-00061-0
International Center for Not-For-Profit Law. (2021). *The civic space initiative*. Retrieved December 10, 2021, from https://www.icnl.org/our-work/global-programs/the-civic-space-initiative
Keck, M. E., & Sikkink, K. (1998). *Activists beyond borders: Advocacy networks in international politics*. Cornell University Press.
Kiai, M. (2013). *Report of the Special Rapporteur on the rights to freedom of peaceful assembly and of association*. Retrieved December 10, 2021, from https://www.ohchr.org/Documents/HRBodies/HRCouncil/RegularSession/Session23/A.HRC.23.39_EN.pdf
Kim, H., & Sikkink, K. (2010). Explaining the deterrence effect of human rights prosecutions for transitional countries. *International Studies Quarterly, 54*(4), 939–963. doi:10.1111/j.1468-2478.2010.00621.x
Kozenko, A. (2015, May 21). Pure pragmatism—nothing personal. *Meduza*. Retrieved December 10, 2021, from https://meduza.io/en/feature/2015/05/21/pure-pragmatism-nothing-personal
Krain, M. (1997). State-sponsored mass murder: A study of the onset and severity of genocides and politicides. *Journal of Conflict Resolution, 41*(3), 331–360. doi:10.1177/0022002797041003001
Lebovic, J. H., & Voeten, E. (2009). The cost of shame: International organizations and foreign aid in the punishing of human rights violators. *Journal of Peace Research, 46*(1), 79–97. doi:10.1177/0022343308098405
Murdie, A., & Bhasin, T. (2011). Aiding and abetting: Human rights INGOs and domestic protest. *Journal of Conflict Resolution, 55*(2), 163–191. doi:10.1177/0022002710374715
Naím, M. (2007). Rogue aid. *Foreign Policy, 159*, 95–96.
Nielsen, R. A. (2013). Rewarding human rights? Selective aid sanctions against repressive states. *International Studies Quarterly, 57*(4), 791–803. doi:10.1111/isqu.12049
Press Trust of India (2015, April 28). Foreign funding: Government cancels licences of nearly 9,000 NGOs. *The Indian Express*. Retrieved December 10, 2021, from http://indianexpress.com/article/india/govt-cancels-licences-of-nearly-9000-ngos/
Press Trust of India (2019, December 4). 14,500 NGOs banned by government from receiving foreign funds. *The Times of India*. Retrieved December 10, 2021, from https://timesofindia.indiatimes.com/india/14500-ngos-banned-by-govt-from-receiving-foreign-funds/articleshow/72366997.cms
Reimann, K. D. (2006). A view from the top: International politics, norms and the worldwide growth of NGOs. *International Studies Quarterly, 50*(1), 45–67. doi:10.1111/j.1468-2478.2006.00392.x
Richards, D. L. (1999). Perilous proxy: Human rights and the presence of national elections. *Social Science Quarterly, 80*(4), 648–665.
Ritter, E. H., & Conrad, C. R. (2016). Preventing and responding to dissent: The observational challenges of explaining strategic repression. *American Political Science Review, 110*(1), 85–99. doi:10.1017/S0003055415000623
Ruffner, T. (2015). *Under threat: Egypt's systematic campaign against NGOs* (Report). Project on Middle East Democracy (POMED). Retrieved December 10, 2021, from https://pomed.org/under-threat-egypts-systematic-campaign-against-ngos/
Sikkink, K. (2011). *The justice cascade: How human rights prosecutions are changing world politics*. W. W. Norton & Company.
Simmons, B. A. (2009). *Mobilizing for human rights: International law in domestic politics*. Cambridge University Press. 10.1017/cbo9780511811340
Smidt, H. M., Perera, D., Mitchell, N. J., & Bakke, K. M. (2021). Silencing their critics: How government restrictions against civil society affect international 'naming and shaming. *British Journal of Political Science, 51*(3), 1270–1291. doi:10.1017/S0007123419000693
Stephan, M. J., & Chenoweth, E. (2008). Why civil resistance works: The strategic logic of nonviolent conflict. *International Security, 33*(1), 7–44. doi:10.1162/isec.2008.33.1.7
Thabet, A. (2004). The human rights situation in Egypt. In P. T. Zeleza & P. J. McConnaughay (Eds.), *Human rights, the rule of law, and development in Africa* (pp. 157–172). University of Pennsylvania Press.
Uppsala Conflict Data Program - Peace Research Institute Oslo (UCDP/PRIO) (2020). *UCDP/PRIO* armed conflict dataset codebook. https://ucdp.uu.se/
Ward, M. D., & Beger, A. (2017). Lessons from near real-time forecasting of irregular leadership changes. *Journal of Peace Research, 54*(2), 141–156. doi:10.1177/0022343316680858
Weiss, M. L. (2009). Edging toward a new politics in Malaysia: Civil society at the gate? *Asian Survey, 49*(5), 741–758. doi:10.1525/as.2009.49.5.741

New frontiers in international human rights: Actionable nonactionables and the (non)performance of perpetual becoming

Kamari Maxine Clarke

ABSTRACT

This article explores the emergence of various international justice narratives that operate as legal nonperformatives, making the law and law making seem liberatory. It shows that the ratification of a treaty may not qualify as a form of state expression or a speech act advocating human rights. Instead, it can be interpreted through semiotics as sending a signal about a stance. By examining this proleptic space, we can begin to make sense of what we cannot yet see, and perhaps begin to forecast whether the core tenets of international human rights will soon be reinvented or merely perpetuated.

Introduction

The theoretical concept of "expressive law" has been developed at the intersection of political science, sociolegal studies, and legal studies. Scholarship in this area begins with the premise that a central function of state behaviors, governance, and action is to take stances on social and political thought that might otherwise be outside of the state's control. This work shows that expressive functions of a legal action, including the way those modalities handle and impose social meaning, can explain how legal action manifests on the ground. As a concept, expressive law has been employed by scholars to illuminate how "norm regulation" translates into dominant social reality.

Legal scholars trace the genealogy of expressive law to Murray Edelman, who, in *The Symbolic Use of Politics* (1964), explored how state behaviors, acts, and documents can have direct "instrumental" as well as expressive "symbolic" purposes. Evoking John Searle, scholars of expressive law (e.g., Anderson & Pildes, 2000) have used the concept of "intentions" to explain why states engage in acts of expressive law, considering to what extent they *mean* to do so. This approach perpetuates a way of viewing the state as a consistent and rational actor, and in so doing conflates expressive practices with performative acts that state actors use to signal or communicate something to a particular audience (Hamlin & Jennings, 2011). In fact, expression is distinct from communication, a distinction that is critical to understanding human engagement with the legal state (Anderson & Pildes, 2000). Expressive approaches to analyzing law making involves the way that legal acts are animated through intentional action. However, performative approaches project state behavior through the situational enactment of social action.

John Austin's influential *How to Do Things with Words* (1975) introduced the idea that a speech "act" is performative when it does what it says: "the issuing of the utterance is the performing of an action" (p. 6). For Austin, failed performatives are unhappy; the condition required for the action to succeed goes unmet (Ahmed, 2021, p. 2). Complicating Austin's framework, Judith Butler later argued that "performativity must be understood not as a singular or deliberate 'act,' but, rather, as the reiterative and citational practice by which discourse produces the effects that it names" (Butler, 1993, p. 2; see also Ahmed, 2021). More recently, various theorists have argued that this notion of performativity, as producing consequences within the world, has limits: It assumes that consequences that emerge from actions are always tangible and visible. Sara Ahmed's helpful conceptualization of the "nonperformative" advances our understanding of what is accomplished in social reality when an act of "saying" that claims performativity produces no real-world transformation of social reality and, in fact, serves paradoxically to reify hegemonic norms (Ahmed, 2006a).

This article builds on the work of Austin, Butler, and Ahmed to develop the concept of the *actionable nonactionable*. This notion occupies a space between the performative and the nonperformative, a space of perpetual becoming. It names the kind of act that, although (like the nonperformative) it fails to produce the real-world consequences it purports to bring about, nevertheless contains the possibility of bringing about a different set of future consequences. As such, the term's value lies in its ability to make visible the potentiality that inheres in speech acts—especially acts of refusal and protest—that appear to have failed at bringing about their intended effects. It also, therefore, helps scholars to attend to that which has not yet been actualized—to becoming rather than to being—countering the tendency within hegemonic frameworks to focus on the present and the legible at the expense of the speculative or the proleptic. I use the term *actionable* rather than *performative* to highlight this relation of speech in action, speech that does not simply actualize but is part of an ongoing negotiation of a future that is always in the process of becoming.

I develop this notion in dialogue with and as an explanation for a series of African state protests against structural inequality. The body of the article consists of an analysis of announcements of the withdrawal of African states from the International Criminal Court (ICC), these states' subsequent creation of an African court with criminal jurisdiction, and the protracted delays that followed in signing and ratifying the Malabo Protocol—the treaty that sought to establish the African Court as a judicial body whose jurisdiction would cover a greater range of international crimes even than the ICC. The African states' rejection of the ICC functioned to produce the conditions it purported to resist. Yet as a form of performative protest against the long and continuing history of structural inequality between Africa and the Global North, this rejection pointed to new potentialities, even while maintaining the *status quo*. The concept of the actionable nonactionable indexes this logic.

Africa and the ICC: Inequality in case selection

Many arguments have been launched about the systemic imbalance and perceived inequalities of international decision-making processes in relation to the ICC. From its inception in 2002 until June 2020, the ICC pursued 28 cases in 13 situations, 10 of them in African states: the Central African Republic (CAR), the Democratic Republic of the Congo (DRC), the Ivory Coast, Sudan, Uganda, Kenya, the Republic of Mali, Libya, and Burundi ("Cases," 2021; "Situations under investigation," 2021; also see Clarke, 2019; Muleefu, 2019). It issued indictments for 36 individuals, including 27 warrants of arrest and four summonses to appear before the court ("Cases," 2021). As of November 2021, six individuals had been put on trial, and proceedings were concluded in nine cases: four individuals were convicted, four acquitted, two had charges dismissed, one had charges withdrawn, three had charges vacated, one was held inadmissible, and four individuals had their cases terminated following evidence of death—all African cases ("Cases," 2021; "Situations under investigation," 2021). Throughout this period, the ICC's focus on African cases led to accusations of selectivity, resulting in strained relations between the ICC and African states.

A key tipping point was the March 2009 arrest warrants issued against Sudanese President Omar Al Bashir and other members of the Khartoum regime for international crimes allegedly committed in Darfur ("ICC: Bashir Warrant Is Warning to Abusive Leaders," 2010; *The Prosecutor v. Omar Hassan Ahmad Al Bashir*, 2009). As a result of the perceived undue focus on African cases, at subsequent Heads of States Government (HOSG) summits the African Union (AU) called for solidarity among AU member states in their opposition to the proceedings launched against Al Bashir. The matter was further complicated in December 2010, when Uhuru Kenyatta and William Ruto were named with four others by the prosecutor of the ICC as suspects in crimes against humanity (International Criminal Court, n.d.-a, 2016; "Kenyatta & Ruto," 2012). In response, Kenya formally requested that the ICC defer investigations and prosecutions to allow for a domestic mechanism to address the cases (Situation in the Republic of Kenya, 2011). Despite this request, Kenyatta and Ruto were indicted in March 2011 and charges were confirmed against them (and Joshua Arap Sang) in September 2011 ("Why Is There a War?" 2020). In March 2013, presidential elections in Kenya resulted in victory for a Kenyatta–Ruto alliance. Kenyatta became the first serving head of state to appear before the ICC.[1]

AU leaders were further angered by the June 2011 issuance of arrest warrants for Muammar Gaddafi (then president of Libya); his son, Saif al-Islam Gaddafi; and his brother-in-law, Abdullah al-Sanussi, for the commission of crimes against humanity (Abraham, 2015; Assembly of the African Union, 2011). At its July 2011 Summit, the AU Assembly held that the arrest warrants seriously complicated efforts aimed at finding a negotiated political solution to the crisis in Libya and decided "that Member States shall not cooperate in the execution of the arrest warrant" against Gaddafi (Abraham, 2015; Assembly of the African Union, 2011).

At subsequent HOSG summits, Assembly decisions continued to call for solidarity among AU member states in their opposition to the proceedings launched against Al Bashir, and to call on the UNSC to defer the ICC's prosecutions against Al Bashir, Kenyatta, and Ruto under Article 16 of the Rome Statute (Assembly of the African Union, 2011, 2012). In the January 2012 Summit, the Assembly affirmed that countries that had received President Bashir "were implementing various AU Assembly Decisions on non-cooperation with the ICC on the arrest and surrender of President Omar Hassan Al Bashir of The Sudan" (Assembly of the African Union, 2011, 2012).[2]

The matter escalated at the October 2013 Summit in Addis Ababa, when some AU member states called on all signatory African states to withdraw their membership of the Rome Statute (Assembly of the African Union, 2011). The Assembly also formally decided that "no charges shall be commenced or continued before any International Court or Tribunal against any serving AU Head of State or Government or anybody acting or entitled to act in such capacity during their term of office." These various speech acts reflected attempts to realign power and establish stances that were publicly oppositional to the work of the ICC.

The UN Security Council and the *de facto* immunity of politically powerful states

The involvement of the UN Security Council (UNSC) has raised questions about which states are under the ICC's jurisdiction, the process of selecting cases, and the role of the UNSC's referral and deferral mechanism. In relation to Africa's peripheral role, some have argued that the referral and deferral powers vested in the UNSC through articles 13(b) and 16 of the Rome Statute create a *de facto* immunity for its five permanent members and their allies (Schuerch, 2017). Under the UN Charter, the Security Council's primary responsibility is to uphold international security and peace (U.N. Charter art. 24, para. 1). Composed of 15 members, 10 rotating and five permanent (the United Kingdom, China, France, the Russian Federation, and the United States), the Security Council is responsible for determining the existence of a threat to peace and taking the appropriate action, diplomatic or military, to control the conflict (United Nations Security Council, n.d.-a). No African countries are permanent members of the UNSC.

Of the five permanent members, France and the United Kingdom are the only states that have ratified the Rome Statute (United Nations Security Council, n.d.-b). South Africa's initial withdrawal from the Rome Statute pointed to this unfairness; the state's Minister of International Relations and Cooperation wrote in a declaratory statement: "Questions of the credibility of the ICC will persist so long as three of the five permanent members of the Security Council are not State Parties to the Statute" (Nkoana-Mashbane, 2016).

South Africa's notification of withdrawal from the Rome Statute was submitted with the argument that perceptions of inequality at the ICC "do not only emanate from the Court's relationship with the Security Council, but also by the perceived focus of the ICC on African states, notwithstanding clear evidence of violations by others" (Nkoana-Mashbane, 2016). This has raised a range of questions about equity and the way law exists in practice (*de jure*) and in fact (*de facto*). The *de facto* dimension, meaning in all practicality or fact although without legitimacy (Black, 1991, pp. 325–326), has been exemplified by China and Russia's use of veto power to block referral of the situation in Syria to the ICC (Schuerch, 2017). Criticism of such forms of immunity has been raised in the context of inconsistent applications of *de facto* immunity: immunity granted and affirmed at law through the brokering power of the UNSC. This is also illustrated by the fact that Sudan fell under ICC jurisdiction despite not being a party to the Rome Statute, whereas nationals from other nonparty states are actively excluded from its jurisdiction (Schuerch, 2017).

The United Kingdom (as a state party to the treaty) and the United States (not a party to the treaty) have both played active roles in assisting the court in pursuing various African perpetrators but have blocked attempts to pursue investigations involving their own states. President Kagame of Rwanda, for one, has publicly accused the ICC of bias on multiple occasions. In May of 2013, he declared that his state "cannot support an ICC that condemns crimes committed by some and not others or imposes itself on democratic processes or the will of sovereign people" (Lamony, 2013), and again in 2018 he criticized the fact that the "ICC was supposed to address the whole world, but it ended up covering only Africa" ("Rwanda's Paul Kagame," 2018).

Both the United States and the United Kingdom have been understood as benefiting from *de jure* immunity, both regarding their role in the US invasion of Afghanistan that began in 2001. Requests for investigations into the war and its significant civilian casualties have been denied on multiple occasions, although on March 5, 2020, the Appeals Chamber of the International Criminal Court unanimously authorized the investigation (International Criminal Court, n.d.-a), prompting backlash from US representatives including then-Secretary of State Mike Pompeo. It remains to be seen whether this development marks an enduring shift in the ICC's selectivity track record, and what the outcome will be.

For prosecutions against African leaders to be considered legitimate, international institutions are expected to follow the state equality principle. The issues described above—related to selectivity of cases, determining which states are under the ICC's jurisdiction, and the UNSC—have all raised questions about the fairness of the international system. But as we will see, the potential solution proposed in response has turned out to be equally controversial.

The contours of AU international justice negotiations

African states that participated in the Rome Statute for the ICC did so with the expectation that if it did not serve them appropriately, amendments would be possible. When it was felt that the Rome Statute was failing to align with the expectations of a fair international judicial system, reforms were deemed necessary. The pressure for change was by two African members of the Assembly of State Parties (ASP)—South Africa and Kenya—endorsed by the African Union, and reviewed by the ASP. Through the introduction of amendments to the Rome Statute through the ASP in November 2014, African states underscored the importance of undertaking reforms, especially relating to Articles 16 and 27 (African Union, 2016). Amendments were seen as a viable strategy for preserving African state participation in the ICC (African Union, 2018). In particular, proposed reforms included (1) Article 27—Irrelevance of official capacity; (2) Preambular part of Rome Statute to allow for complementarity of regional judicial institutions; (3) Article 16 on the deferral of cases; (4) Article 70—offences against administration of justice; and (5) Reduction of the powers of the Prosecutor (African Union, 2018).

By the January 2016 Summit (Assembly/AU/Dec.590 (XXVI)), African states had become frustrated at the lack of progress with the amendments and launched a media campaign that highlighted an African state withdrawal strategy (Clarke, 2019). The decision articulated in this campaign stated:

> The Open-ended Ministerial Committee's mandate will include the urgent development of a comprehensive strategy including collective withdrawal from the ICC to inform the next action of AU Member States that are also parties to the Rome Statute, and to submit such strategy to an extraordinary session of the Executive Council which is mandated to take such decision (Clarke, 2019; AU, n.d., para. 10 (iv))

Once this committee was established, it identified the relevant issues and set up a two-phase strategy that involved the option of a collective withdrawal from the Rome Statute if particular reforms did not take place, as well as the potential withdrawal of individual states. Key to the AU strategy laid out by the Open-Ended Ministerial Committee was the delivery of justice in a fair and equitable manner, to allow for the regionalization of international criminal law to flourish in the continent (AU, n.d., para. 18). Echoing the mantra, "African solutions for African problems," it advanced the objectives of the Union and the African members of the Rome Statute by proposing three steps: the reform of the Rome Statute, the reform of the UNSC referral system, and the ratification of both the Protocol on the Statute of the African Court of Justice and Human Rights and the Protocol on the Amendments on the Statute of the African Court of Justice and Human Rights by Member States of the African Union (the Malabo Protocol).

It is here that we begin to see, first, how states with less political power in the international system use the treaty as a form of political protest to communicate disagreement with the institutions of power that contribute to such disparity. Furthermore, we see that they use these strategies to exert pressure through the use of the symbolic capital of the international system. In the case of the management of violence in African states, it is international law that becomes a domain for the symbolic production of political refusals to engage or comply with international spheres of inequality. Burundi's, South Africa's, and Gambia's declarations of withdrawal from the Rome Statute—their communications of nonparticipation—open up a space for understanding the performativity of refusal in African postcolonies.

In October 2016, Burundi became the first country to commence the withdrawal process from the Rome Statute for the ICC, an international treaty signed and ratified by two-thirds of the world's states (International Criminal Court, n.d.-b). The context for the withdrawal was the ICC's investigation of the deaths of 430 people in Burundi's capital in April 2015 and the subsequent displacement of 230,000 Burundians following related political violence. Anti-impunity groups supported by the ICC investigative team alleged that the government's security forces had perpetrated acts of violence (International Criminal Court, n.d.-b). When the ICC's Office of the Prosecutor began to speak of launching a preliminary examination into the violence, Burundian President Nkurunziza accused the ICC of acting as an "instrument" to destabilize "poor [African] countries" (Gouvernement du Burundi, 2016). Following claims that the ICC's actions were tantamount to supporting a Western regime-change strategy, Burundian leaders insisted that the ICC's preliminary examination could contribute to "potentially negative forces and their cronies" committing acts of violence (Gouvernement du Burundi, 2016). They asserted later that the "government considers that maintaining Burundi as a party to the Rome Statute of the International Criminal Court cannot be justified" (Gouvernement du Burundi, 2016).

On October 11, 2016, President Nkurunziza signed the withdrawal legislation with overwhelming support from Burundi's lawmakers. Later that week they submitted a letter of notification to the UN Secretary General and initiated the required one-year waiting period for formal separation from ICC jurisdiction; Burundi has now accomplished full withdrawal from the ICC.

This was not a singular development on the continent. The South African parliament followed suit. Prior to a ruling by the North Gauteng High Court (Masuthao, 2017; United Nations, 2017; *Democratic Alliance v. Minister of International Relations & Cooperation & Others*, 2017) that its withdrawal was unconstitutional (*Democratic Alliance v. Minister of International Relations & Cooperation & Others*, 2017), South Africa's leadership released a declaratory statement: "Under these circumstances South Africa is of the view that to continue to be a State Party to the Rome Statute will compromise its efforts to promote peace and security on the African Continent" (Democratic Alliance v Minister of International Relations & Cooperation & Others, 2017).

Burundi and South Africa's withdrawal actions were followed by the announcement of The Gambia's intentions to withdraw (later reversed by a new president).[3] As noted by its spokesperson at the time, "Despite being called International Criminal Court, [it] is in fact an International Caucasian Court for the persecution and humiliation of people of color, especially Africans" ("Gambia Withdraws," 2016).

Burundi, South Africa, and The Gambia each displayed acts of theatrical utterance in their attempts to extract themselves from what they saw as structural inequality in the exercise of international justice.[4] The 34 African states that signed the Rome Statute in 1998 initially embraced the rule-of-law movement as an extension of their commitments to Africa's emancipatory future. The violence that had unfolded in Africa in the 1980s and 1990s helped compel states to try to prevent a repetition of the international community's inaction during the Rwandan genocide and South African apartheid, and the indifference or interference of Western "democracies" *vis-à-vis* decades of anticolonial struggles against European imperialism. With these realities in mind, the various leaders in these states initially accepted the ICC as a beacon of emancipation—a potential solution for their continent's injustices.

By 2016, this hope had faded. Prior to the individual withdrawal announcements, African states had been considering a collective withdrawal[5] from the Rome Statute to signal their dissatisfaction with the targeting of African leaders. This strategy shifted in recognition that the treaty required unilateral action, and states instead staged separate withdrawal announcements meant to articulate coordinated stances of rejection of what was described as structural patterns of racialized targeting, including the application of the ICC to achieve externally driven regime change in African states (a form of political interference with deep colonial roots). This coordinated resistance entailed a particular form of international engagement in which less politically influential states mobilized allied states to participate in a spectacle of rebellion, even if protest action was not legally viable. Alongside the positions being taken by states, anti-impunity civil society counter-mobilizations in courts and in the media worked to discredit the withdrawing governments and to prevent them from succeeding through legal action. This civil society action led to reversals of the notification of withdrawal in South Africa and The Gambia.

Despite these reversals, the progressively worsening public relationship between African and European states nevertheless nurtured the political will to pursue in Africa a means to adjudicate the alleged crimes of European states. This manifested in an effort to expand the jurisdiction of the African Court.

A (non)performance of perpetual becoming: African-led justice and the Malabo Protocol as actionable nonactionable

In 1980, the UN General Assembly labeled apartheid in South Africa a crime against humanity (United Nations Security Council, 1984) and then explored the establishment a special international criminal court to try persons for this crime. This did not result in judicial action, and states were left to enact their own legislation to prosecute apartheid (Dugard, 2008). The lack of criminal action resulted in feelings of injustice on the part of stakeholders working on behalf of African states through the predecessor to the African Union Commission: the Organization of African Unity (OAU; Clarke, 2019). African stakeholders continued to develop a human rights infrastructure, leading to the African Charter on Human and Peoples' Rights (Abass, 2013; Clarke, 2019) and the 1987 establishment of the African Commission on Human and People's Rights, the quasi-judicial oversight body tasked with interpreting the charter and hearing complaints (United Nations Security Council, 1984; Dugard, 2008). In 1998, a protocol to the charter was adopted that created the African Court of Human and Peoples' Rights (ACHPR). That protocol came into force on January 25, 2005; currently, 52 of 54 possible states are signatories and 30 states have ratified it (Assembly of the African Union, 2017). As of 2019, the ACHPR has received 248 applications in contentious matters and 13 requests for advisory opinion since its establishment in 2006 (African Union, 2020).

The ACHPR sits in Arusha, Tanzania, and hears applications relating to human rights violations brought before it by the AU Commission, as well as African intergovernmental organizations and member states (Abraham, 2015). In 2001, a second interstate court structure was included in the AU's Constitutive Act and was further developed in the 2003 Protocol of the Court of Justice of the AU, becoming known as the African Court of Justice (ACJ; African Union, 2003). The push to establish the ACJ was motivated, in part, by the need to strengthen the African human rights system by enhancing its capacity to engender positive responses from states through binding decisions, given that the decisions of the African Commission are mere recommendations. Its sources of law were based on the African Charter on Human and Peoples Rights, the Protocol Establishing the Court, and any other relevant (human rights) instrument ratified by the states concerned (African Union, 1998). The ACJ was intended to be the principal judicial organ of the AU, with authority to rule on disputes over the interpretation of AU treaties. The ACJ has entered into force; however, the court has not been established, because its protocol was superseded by the push to establish a judicial mechanism in Africa with international criminal jurisdiction.

A range of developments have led to attempts to establish international justice alternatives in Africa with greater significance and reach. Within months of the adoption of the Merger Protocol, however, the AU's Assembly of Heads of State and Government asked the AU Commission, in consultation with the African Commission on Human and Peoples' Rights and the African Court on Human and Peoples' Rights, to examine the implications of empowering the court with jurisdiction to adjudicate international crimes (African Union, 2009a). During its Twelfth Ordinary Session held February 1–3, 2009, in Addis Ababa, only months after having adopted the Protocol Establishing the Merged Court, the Assembly of Heads of State and Government requested that the AU Commission (Secretariat) consult with the African Commission on Human and Peoples' Rights, and the African Court on Human and Peoples' Rights, to examine the implications of empowering the court to adjudicate international crimes. And at the close of its Thirteenth Ordinary African Union Commission Session in Sirte, Libya, in July 2009, the AU Commission urged the AU Assembly to renew its desire to have the process sped up, and urged the Commission to aim for "early implementation" of its February decision. This was the decision to adjudicate international crimes in Africa, leading to the establishment of the African Court of Justice and Human Rights (African Union, 2009b).

A range of factors contributed to this move to establish an African court with the ability to adjudicate both human rights abuses and criminal legal matters. The principal concerns were related to (1) arrest warrants and/or extradition requests for nonstate parties to the Rome Statute and for states that were still willing to pursue investigations prior to ICC interference, and (2) the ICC's selective focus on African cases and the reality that most of the politically powerful countries, including those in the Security Council, were not under the jurisdiction of the ICC. What unfolded as a result of these factors was a particular push to establish a regional mechanism to adjudicate criminal cases in Africa.

Known as the Protocol on Amendments to the Protocol on the Statute of the African Court of Justice and Human Rights (the Malabo Protocol for the African Court), this treaty was set up to go into force 30 days after the ratification of 15 of the AU member states (African Union, 2014, art. 11). In a move that clearly signaled a desire among African states to assert their own sovereign authority to bring neocolonial state and corporate powers to justice, the authors of the Malabo Protocol sought to substantially expand the four core political crimes that were within the ICC's jurisdiction: (1) genocide, (2) crimes against humanity, (3) war crimes, and (4) the crime of aggression. The expanded list of 14 included (5) the crime of unconstitutional change of government, (6) piracy, (7) terrorism, (8) mercenaryism, (9) corruption, (10) money laundering, (11) trafficking in persons, (12) trafficking in drugs, (13) trafficking in hazardous wastes, and (14) the illicit exploitation of natural resources.

This range of issues is addressed across three distinct branches within the single court: the Human and Peoples' Rights Section, the General Affairs Section, and the International Criminal Law Section. Legal scholars have pointed to this expanded scope as a significant innovation in international law (African Union, 2014). However, despite the expansion of AU criminal jurisdiction through the Malabo Protocol and the publicly stated positions *vis-à-vis* the ICC, African states have fallen short of actually ratifying the protocol.

The remainder of this article addresses the question of why this is, and what this limitation can tell us about the African states' rejection of the ICC. Indeed, the pace of ratification of the Malabo Protocol has been unusually slow, even as compared with other AU treaties. In the five years since the protocol's adoption in 2014, only 15 states have signed it. None of those states has progressed to ratification. The median time for entry into force of all OAU/AU treaties is just over three years, while human rights and juridical treaties generally require five years and five years seven months, respectively, to enter into force. At that pace, the Malabo Protocol should have entered into force by January 2020. To date, there has been no progress.

It may be especially instructive to consider ratification trends of AU/OAU treaties with similar subject matter. In light of the unique nature of the Malabo Protocol—a treaty establishing a court with jurisdiction over both human rights and international crimes—I examined OAU/AU treaties in three different areas: (1) human rights, (2) international and transnational crimes, and (3) court establishment. To date, six key OAU/AU human rights treaties have entered into force:

1. Protocol to the African Charter on Human and Peoples' Rights on the Rights of Women in Africa
2. African Union Convention for the Protection and Assistance of Internally Displaced Persons in Africa
3. OAU Convention Governing the Specific Aspects of the Refugee Problem
4. African Charter on Human and Peoples' Rights
5. Protocol to the African Charter on Human and Peoples' Rights on the Establishment of an African Court on Human and Peoples' Rights[6]
6. African Charter on the Rights and Welfare of the Child

Of these, the Protocol on the Rights of Women entered into force the fastest, after a mere two years and four months, whereas the African Charter on the Rights and Welfare of the Child took the longest at over nine years. On average, these six treaties entered into force five years after their adoption, while the median was just under five years. Figure 1 shows the length of time from adoption to entry into force of the major OAU/AU human rights treaties.

Of note, ratifications do not happen all at once. Rather, they occur over a period of time, with some states taking less time and others more depending on their priorities, the length of their domestic ratification processes, and other events occurring in the country (e.g., elections, economic or political crises, conflict). In the case of the African Court, for example, two states (Burkina Faso and Senegal)

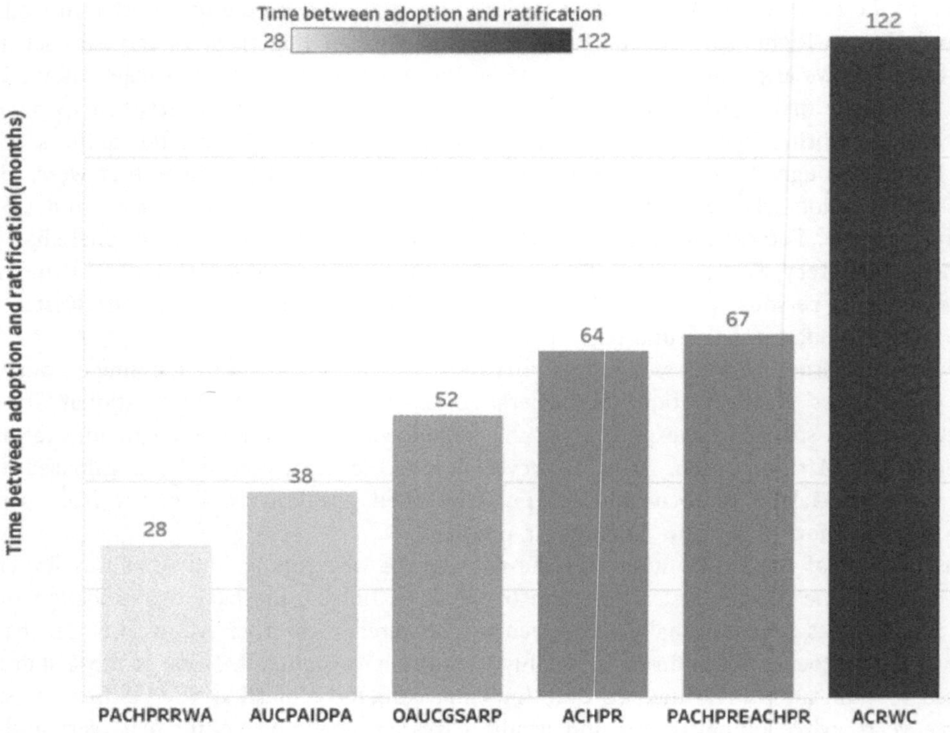

Figure 1. Length of time in months from Adoption to Ratification of African Human Rights Treaties. Source: https://au.int/en/treaties.

ratified the protocol the same year it was adopted; three (Gabon, The Gambia, and Mali) ratified the protocol in 1999 and 2000, and the remaining ratifications necessary for entry into force occurred between 2001 and 2003. The year after the ACJ protocol was adopted, seven states ratified it.[7] By contrast, no country had ratified the Malabo Protocol more than five years after it was adopted.[8]

It is also illuminating to compare the countries that quickly ratified the protocols of the African Court and ACJ with those that have signed the Malabo Protocol. Only three of the 15 early adopters of the African Court protocol (Comoros, Togo, and Uganda) and two of the 15 early adopters of the ACJ protocol (Comoros, Mozambique) have signed the Malabo Protocol. The lack of signatures by many states that previously showed strong support for regional judicial institutions indicates that the delay is not simply a technical issue of moving from signature to ratification. Instead, if states that support regional judicial mechanisms are not signing the Malabo Protocol, it is an indication that they, and possibly others, have serious reservations.

Further support for the conclusion that concerns about the protocol—rather than domestic ratification procedures and other technical issues—constitute at least part of the reason for the delay can be drawn from an analysis of trends in the ratification of human rights and juridical treaties by African states. Human rights treaties have a relatively high rate of ratification among African countries. The African Charter on Human and Peoples' Rights, for example, has been ratified by 54 countries, second only to the 55 ratifications of the AU's Constitutive Act (African Union, 2017). Ratifications of the protocol establishing the African Court, although somewhat fewer, still stand at a respectable 30 (African Union, 2016).[9] Yet many of the states that have ratified the African Court Protocol—Algeria, Burkina Faso, Cameroon, Côte d'Ivoire, Gabon, Lesotho, Mali, Malawi, Mauritius, Nigeria, Niger, Rwanda, South Africa, Senegal, Tanzania, and Tunisia, and others—have not even signed the Malabo Protocol.

The data presented here, based on a two-year investigation,[10] provide strong evidence that concerns with the Malabo Protocol have likely constituted a key, although not necessarily exclusive, impediment to ratification. To identify those particular concerns, my research assistants and I conducted, along with the AU's Office of Legal Counsel, a survey of African states and numerous informal interviews with state officials involved in treaty ratification. A variety of issues were identified in that process, from technical questions about how the Malabo Protocol works, to substantive concerns with the content of the protocol, to rational considerations about how ratification might impact relationships with donors. Notably, despite ongoing reminders by AU bodies, only four of 55 states completed the survey.

One of the most controversial aspects of the Malabo Protocol is contained in Article 46 A *bis*, the impunity clause, which grants serving heads of state or government and other senior state officials protection from prosecution. During interviews collected over the course of the study that informs this article, the 46a *bis* provision was identified by African states as being the single most important impediment to ratification of the protocol. The article reads as follows: "No charges shall be commenced or continued before the Court against any serving African Union Head of State of Government, or anybody acting or entitled to act in such capacity, or other senior state officials based on their functions, during their tenure of office."[11]

The exact scope of the provision has been one of the many issues under debate since the Amended Protocol was released in June 2014. In the absence of precise definitions for terms such as "African Union Head of State or Government," "anybody acting or entitled to act in such capacity," and "senior state officials," concerns have raised over the ambiguity regarding who exactly benefits from immunity (Van Schaack, 2014; Tladi, 2015; Du Plessis, 2014). Immunity is a procedural rule (International Court of Justice, 2002; Van Alebeek, 2008),[12] which concerns whether and when a court has jurisdiction over a particular individual. For example, a head of state with immunity *ratione personae* cannot be brought before a criminal court during his or her term in office, but this does not exonerate him or her from criminal responsibility: He or she may still be prosecuted, and thus held criminally responsible, after leaving office (International Court of Justice, 2002; Van Alebeek, 2008)[13]. This is different from the issue of criminal responsibility, a substantive rule of law that concerns whether a government official can be held responsible, at all, for his or her acts (International Court of Justice, 2002; Van Alebeek, 2008). The immunities recognized in Article 46 A *bis* are a form of immunity *ratione personae*, meaning that the immunity attaches to the office and is possessed by the officeholder only so long as he or she remains in office (Akande, 2004). This form of immunity dates back hundreds of years and was developed to ensure that certain high-ranking officials, including but not limited to heads of state, can discharge their functions unhindered by potentially politically motivated charges (Akande, 2004; Du Plessis, 2014).

Some have argued that the immunity clause is at odds with the African Union's foundational principles and therefore undermines the African Court's legitimacy. Although under customary international law serving heads of state and senior state officials are safeguarded from criminal jurisdiction of a third state, such officials do not enjoy immunity before international criminal courts (Amnesty International, 2017). Critics have condemned the clause as (1) a highly politicized and blatant attempt to shield African leaders, (2) an affront to the twentieth-century core principle that no one—not even heads of state—should be immune from prosecution for international crimes, and (3) a direct conflict with international law as well as a breach of obligations to the Rome Statute for the ICC.

In May 2014, more than 30 civil society and international NGOs appealed to a meeting of African ministers of justice and attorneys general not to include Article 46 A *bis* in its draft of the Malabo Protocol (ACADHOSHA, et al., 2012). In addition, organizations including Human Rights Watch, the International Bar Association, the International Federation for Human Rights, Amnesty International, the South African Litigation Center, the New York City Bar Association, and many others have released statements sharply criticizing the provision as retrogressive and inconsistent with ensuring that perpetrators are held to account (Human Rights Watch, 2014; Lahidji, K., et al., 2014). Malawi's Center for Human Rights and Rehabilitation, in an open letter joined by 140 civil society organizations, maintained that "immunity indirectly legitimizes the chronic disease of impunity," "goes against the very essence of promoting human rights, peace and stability, and is a setback to advances made towards democracy and the rule of law in Africa."[14] Meanwhile, Kenyans for Peace with Truth and Justice said that the immunity provision "undermine[s] the raison d'être of the Court" and speculated that African leaders had added it to the Malabo Protocol "simply out of self-interest and a desire to avoid being held accountable for their actions."[15]

Some African states have also aligned themselves with these critiques of the immunity provision, publicly asserting that rejection of immunity is a moral imperative that cannot be compromised without compromising the pursuit of justice itself. As Botswana proclaimed in a different context related to the African Court, opposition to prosecution for sitting heads of state is:

> a serious setback in the battle against impunity in Africa and undermines efforts to confront war crimes and crimes against humanity which are committed by some leaders on the continent. Such a move also places Africa on the wrong side of history. It is a betrayal of the innocent and helpless victims of such crimes. … We need to have the political will and the moral courage to hold accountable, without fear or favor, anyone in authority—including a sitting Head of State—when he or she is suspected of having committed crimes against innocent people.[16]

Collectively, civil society and state critiques have created a political discourse that positions the court as an institution for the maintenance of impunity. The AU as a political bloc has responded by repeatedly stressing its commitment to combating impunity—including with respect to abuses by leaders—while objecting to prosecutions of *sitting* heads of state and other senior state officials because under "international customary law … sitting Heads of State and other senior state officials are granted immunities during their tenure in office." (African Union, 2013) These immunities "apply not only to proceedings in foreign domestic courts but also to international tribunals."

Despite the assertion that such immunities exist, African states have been unwilling to ratify the Malabo Protocol for the African court for a number of reasons. The most significant have to do with external pressures from economic donors and other states threatening to withdraw aid. The challenge for a geopolitical analysis is to account for different forms of pressure—financial, social, and political—that often remain unarticulated. As such, the AU held that the immunity clause, far from undermining the pursuit of universal justice, was in accordance with international conventions: Hence, the inclusion of this provision functioned in part as a rejection of what the AU perceived as the ICC's inequitable application of international law.

The debate over the African court and its related controversies over the immunity of African heads of state is not necessarily a disagreement with the principle that "no one should be beyond the law," even if the dispute has been publicly framed as such. Rather, it is really about the perception held by (most) African states that there is an unequal application of justice and the conditions for justice through the apparatus of international law, which is itself a vestige of colonial law. Yet this framing of the debate is rarely permitted space to assert itself, let alone to enact change. The vision of an African Court with the jurisdiction to try a range of criminal cases in Africa has emerged in the historical context of several generations of (neo)colonial plunder and domination in Africa (Clarke, 2009; Sirleaf, 2017). Pan-African efforts to counter those forces through legal means date back to the establishment of institutional criminal legal strategies in the 1960s, the 1981 establishment of an African human rights court, and later the Malabo Protocol (Clarke et al., 2019). The last of these is the latest in a series of ongoing, often toothless shows of resistance in relation to a profoundly uneven international legal system. Symbolic and overt protests against African inequality in international politics deploy communicative strategies that threaten withdrawal from that system and construction of a new form of practice with the authority to push back. It is not expressivism that explains the seeming contradiction of the non-ratification of the African court. Rather, it is the role of a particular communicative practice in which protest is used to referentially index refusal and nonagreement with the production of inequality of Africa and Africans in international law.

There is thus a curious paradox between the aspirational aspects of the Malabo Protocol and the threat that it is seen as protecting or even promoting. On one side is the extraordinary expansion of accountability through the African Court with three jurisdictions that would seek to generally reduce impunity on the African continent as well as the aspiration to influence international frameworks of power, particularly as they relate to international justice and the underlying economic, environmental, and political drivers of conflict. On the other side is a vehement debate over the integrity of judicial innovations that appear to undermine the (neo)liberal anti-impunity framework. The paradoxical nature of the provision exemplifies the concept of the *actionable nonactionable.*

Various international justice narratives operate as legal nonperformatives that make the law and law making appear liberatory even as they shore up the *status quo.* The 46 A *bis* provision functions as a claim to performativity but produces no direct real-world consequences in the effort to promote human rights. This is because the speech act fails in its commitment—that is, it fails to commit a person, organization, or state to enact what they say (Ahmed, 2006, p. 1). Yet crucially, the act is not necessarily entirely inconsequential: It also holds within itself the proleptic possibility of becoming something else—a force of protest. As such, the provision exemplifies the logic of the actionable nonactionable. Such acts contain a force of protest that can become actionable, a refusal that can make a real impact in the world. These acts exist in a perpetual state of future possibility that is never quite realized, even as the *status quo* is able to further entrench itself through a productive tension with the stance of resistance.

In Article 46 A *bis*, what we see is an attempt to defend the need for the immunity provision from a doctrinal perspective on the grounds that immunities provided for by international law apply not only to proceedings in foreign domestic courts but also to international tribunals, and that states cannot circumvent such obligations by establishing an international tribunal (Akande, 2014). Consistent with these principles, the AU has repeatedly stressed its commitment to combating impunity[17]—including with respect to abuses by leaders—but has objected to prosecutions of sitting heads of state and other senior state officials because, under "international customary law … sitting Heads of State and other senior state officials are granted immunities during their tenure in office." These immunities "apply not only to proceedings in foreign domestic courts but also to international tribunals." However, despite the AU state declarations, African states have been unwilling to ratify the Malabo Protocol for the African Court, suggesting that there is something else at play. This seeming contradiction is not about a widespread attempt on the part of African states to evade justice or to put in place an institutional mechanism that will ultimately fail.

By reducing the Malabo Protocol to its immunity provision, these depictions of the proposed African court create a stark dichotomy: Support for the protocol is glossed as an embrace of impunity and a betrayal of victims, and only rejection of the protocol can confirm a state's position in favor of human rights, peace, and stability. One must either be a hero or a villain; there is no other option (Tladi, 2019). This polarization is evident in remarks by organizations within Africa as well outside the continent. Yet, despite the pressure of international criticism, various African states have defended the Malabo Protocol as a mechanism that at least symbolizes the possibility of ownership of international justice by Africans. For example, Burundi's foreign minister has insisted that Burundi wants to "put on the record [its] unwavering support to the AU call for the respect of immunities in favor of acting Heads of State and Government, as is accepted in the International Law (Nahimana, 2015)." The failure to ratify the Malabo Protocol can be explained *via* the dialectical tension between aspirations for universal justice and the protest of structural and historic inequality as reflected in the forms of justice being meted by international law.

What is accomplished (or not accomplished) when a strong signaling of a stance of resistance and the investment of political capital in the creation of an alternative legal institutions fails to translate into the operationalization of such an alternative? The project of the African Court is shaped by several important currents of historic and contemporary struggle for African state autonomy and Pan-African solidarity. It is also a response to the generational and persistent lack of judicial activity in African jurisdictions for crimes of slavery, imperialism, colonialism, apartheid, and subsequent forms of economic plunder—crimes that remain willfully invisibilized as open secrets while contemporary anti-impunity campaigns exclusively target Africans for criminal responsibility regarding crimes that take place within spheres of structural inequality. Analyzing stance taking in relation to intentions and affects can be useful for making sense of these contradictions.

African state protest speech and the associated actions that led to the conceptualization yet ultimately failed adoption of the treaty to establish an African Court with expanded crimes exemplifies the actionable nonactionable. If a performative speech act holds the ability to transform and engender the social reality it describes (Ahmed, 2006, p. 4), then a nonperformative does the opposite. Rather than initiating action, the speech is itself the action, with inaction emerging in its wake (Ahmed, 2006, p. 4). An actionable nonactionable occupies a space between the performative and the nonperformative, a space of perpetual becoming. The notion of becoming is among the most underengaged domains in human rights, where hegemonic legal frameworks traced to Western logics persist in privileging phenomena that are either legible to present states or government control over visions of alternative logics as illuminated through protest. Becoming is about future possibility and the potential to transform our world—not what is. It is not actualization, and it is not (yet) legible to the law. Actionable nonactionables gesture quite precisely and even forcefully to alternative worlds, while continually falling short of actually authorizing them.

Conclusion

Despite promising to be a functioning institution grounded in the rule of law and pursuit of justice, the renewed African Court appears to exist purely to court public approval—by agreeing to conditions that purposely pander to justice rhetoric while seeking to undermine the pursuit of justice entirely. In this sense, it is a legal nonperformative. Yet ratifying a treaty such as the Malabo Protocol is better understood not as a speech act but as sending a signal about stance.

The Malabo Protocol is part of a long history of attempts by African states to create counternarratives in opposition to imperial forces. However, this protest remains aspirational and discursive, as actual state participation in treaty ratification faces several complex barriers. In the absence of the actual ratification of the treaty, we see instead the actionable nonactionable: a space that reflects remaining tensions between aspirations of progress and attempts to counter subordination through negation.

The Malabo Protocol reflects a Pan-Africanist vision in which African stakeholders insist on their technocratic authorship of African social formations while also undermining equality by undermining the vision of justice for all. By examining the African court project as a proleptic space for the dual maintenance of the *status quo* and of possibility, we can begin to make sense of what we cannot yet see, and perhaps begin to forecast whether the core tenets of international human rights are on the edge of reinvention or merely perpetrated.

Notes

1. For a detailed discussion of the Sudan and Kenya cases, refer to the memo on peace and justice sequencing dated August 4, 2015.
2. Doc. EX.CL/710(XX).
3. Just one week after that, on October 25, 2016, The Gambia announced its intent to withdraw as well.
4. Burundi's withdrawal will not affect the past obligations the country may have in relation to ongoing proceedings or investigations, and it will not come into effect until after a one-year waiting period has elapsed and the subsequent notification of withdrawal is registered with UN treaty office.
5. At the time of these deliberations, I served as a technical advisor to the African Union Legal Office and we conducted the research being requested of us at the time: to assess whether there were precedents for a collective withdrawal from the Rome Statute and under what conditions a collective withdrawal was possible.
6. The protocol establishing the current African Court is included in both the human rights and juridical treaty groups.
7. ACJ Protocol Status List (the protocol was adopted in July 2003 and entered into force in February 2009).
8. Malabo Protocol Status List.
9. African Court Status List.
10. Regarding methods, between 2017 and 2018, I and ACRI researchers and staff from the AU's Office of Legal Counsel (OLC) conducted interviews with state officials about the Malabo Protocol at three AU summits. I also created a survey questionnaire regarding treaty ratification and the Malabo Protocol, which was distributed to all African States by the OLC. In addition to these primary sources, ACRI collected and analyzed data on AU treaty ratification trends; assessed public statements by African State officials on the Malabo Protocol and other supra-national courts; examined relevant provisions in state constitutions and laws; and reviewed academic articles, policy reports, and media commentary on the Malabo Protocol. This research confirmed the validity of the concerns that prompted this study: namely, that the pace of ratification of the Malabo Protocol has been unusually slow, even by AU standards. A comparison of signature and ratification trends of the Malabo Protocol with other AU treaties plainly demonstrates that ratification of the Malabo Protocol is well behind schedule.
11. AU, Protocol on Amendments to the Protocol on the Statute of the African Court of Justice and Human Rights, Article 46A *bis*.
12. The phrase "African Union Head of State or Government" refers to people occupying such an office in a state which is party to the AU Constitutive Act; D. Tladi, at 6., that a broad interpretation could result in the inclusion of all ministers and even all members of parliament in some states, whereas a narrow one could confine the definition to a deputy head of state or government and Beth Van Schaack and M. du Plessis, who noted that the term "senior officials" is not defined and suggests that it has been left to the new court to determine the reach of the term (du Plessis, at 8; Van Schaak). There is also a lack of clarity on what exact "functions" are likely to result in the granting of immunity (ibid.).
13. Confirming that immunity from criminal jurisdiction is "procedural in nature."
14. Human Rights Watch.
15. Africa Centre for Open Governance, *supra* note 101, at 15.
16. Botswana Keynote Address at the 2011 ASP, at para. 35.
17. E.g., AU Decision on the Application by the International Criminal Court (ICC) Prosecutor for the Indictment of the President of the Republic of Sudan, *supra* note 156, at para. 6; AU Decision on the Meeting of African States Parties to the Rome Statute of the International Criminal Court, *supra* note 156, at 4; AU Decision on the Report of the Second Meeting of States Parties to the Rome Statute on the International Criminal Court (ICC), *supra* note 260, at para. 3.

Acknowledgments

The author wishes to thank the following individuals for their critically important contributions to the research and conceptualizations that informed this article: Alysson Ford Ouoba, Ermias Kassaye, Wumi Asubiara Dada and Fela Dada. A special thank you to the OSIWA for their funding of the research for this project and NSF for their support in the final write up.

References

Abass, A. (2013). Prosecuting international crimes in Africa: Rationale, prospects and challenges. *European Journal of International Law*, *24*(3), 933–946. doi:10.1093/ejil/cht042

Abraham, G. (2015). *Occasional paper. Africa's evolving continental court structures: At the Crossroads?* South African Institute of International Affairs (SAIIA). https://saiia.org.za/research/africas-evolving-continental-court-structures-at-the-crossroads/.

Acadhosha, Ahrao. (2012, May 3). *Joint letter to the justice ministers and attorneys general of the African states parties to the International Criminal Court regarding the proposed expansion of the jurisdiction of the African Court of Justice and Human Rights*. Human Rights Watch. https://www.hrw.org/news/2012/05/03/joint-letter-justice-ministers-and-attorneys-general-african-states-parties

African Union. (1998). *Protocol to the African Charter on Human and Peoples' Rights on the Establishment of an African Court on Human and Peoples' Rights*.

African Union. (2003). *Protocol of the Court of Justice of the African Union, Adopted by the 2nd Ordinary Session of the Assembly of the Union on 11 July 2003*. https://au.int/sites/default/files/treaties/36395-treaty-0026_-_protocol_of_the_court_of_justice_of_the_african_union_e.pdf

African Union. (2009a). *Decision on the Implementation of the Assembly Decision on the Abuse of the Principle of Universal Jurisdiction*. Doc. Assembly/AU/Dec.213.

African Union. (2009b). *Decision on the meeting of African States Parties to the Statute of the Rome Statute of the International Criminal Court on 3 July 2009*. Assembly/AU/13(XIII).

African Union. (2013). *Decision on Africa's relationship with the International Criminal Court (ICC)*. http://www.iccnow.org/documents/Ext_Assembly_AU_Dec_Decl_12Oct2013.pdf.

African Union (2014). *Protocol on Amendments to the Protocol on the Statute of the African Court of Justice and Human Rights*.

African Union (2016). *Decision on the International Criminal Court, 26th Ordinary Session, AU Assembly Doc. EX.CL/952(XXVIII)*, (para. 52). https://au.int/sites/default/files/decisions/29514-assembly_au_dec_588_-_604_xxvi_e.pdf

African Union (2017). *List of Countries which have signed, ratified/acceded to the Constitutive Act of the African Union*. https://au.int/sites/default/files/treaties/7758-sl-constitutive_act_of_the_african_union_2.pdf.

African Union (2018, September 24). *The AU Open-ended Committee of Ministers of Foreign Affairs on the International Criminal Court Convene 7th Meeting on the Sidelines of the UN General Assembly* [Press release]. https://au.int/en/pressreleases/20180924/au-open-ended-committee-ministers-foreign-affairs-international-criminal

African Union (2020). *Activity Report of the African Court on Human and Peoples' Rights*. EX.CL/1204(XXXVI). https://archives.au.int/handle/123456789/8522?locale-attribute=ar

Ahmed, S. (2006). *Queer phenomenology: Orientations, objects and others*. Duke University Press.

Ahmed, S. (2006a). The nonperformativity of antiracism. *Meridians*, *7*(1), 104–126. doi:10.2979/MER.2006.7.1.104

Ahmed, S. (2021). *Complaint!*. Duke University Press.

Akande, D. (2004). International law immunities and the International Criminal Court. *American Journal of International Law*, *98*(3), 407–433. doi:10.2307/3181639

Akande, D. (2014, October 7). *The African Union's response to the ICC's decisions on Bashir's immunity: Will the ICJ get another immunity case?* EJIL Talk! http://www.ejiltalk.org/the-african-unions-responseto-the-iccsdecisions-bashirs-immunity-will-the-icj-get-another-immunity-case/

Amnesty International (2017). *Malabo protocol: Legal and institutional implications of the merged and expanded African Court*. Amnesty International.

Anderson, E. S., & Pildes, R. H. (2000). Expressive theories of law: A general restatement. *University of Pennsylvania Law Review*, *148*(5), 1503–1575. doi:10.2307/3312748

Assembly of the African Union. (2011). *Decision on the Implementation of the Assembly Decisions on the International Criminal Court, Decisions, Declarations and Resolution, Doc.* EX.CL/670(XIX). https://au.int/sites/default/files/decisions/9647-assembly_au_dec_363-390_xvii_e.pdf.

Assembly of the African Union. (2012). *Decision on the Progress Report of the Commission on the Implementation of the Assembly Decisions on the International Criminal Court, Decisions, Resolution and Declarations, Doc.* EX.CL/710(XX). https://au.int/sites/default/files/decisions/9649-assembly_au_dec_391_-_415_xviii_e.pdf.

Assembly of the African Union (2017). *List of Countries which have Signed, Ratified/Acceded to the Protocol to the African Charter on Human and Peoples' Rights on the Establishment of an African Court on Human and Peoples' Rights.* https://au.int/sites/default/files/treaties/36393-sl-protocol_to_the_african_charter_on_human_and_peoplesrights_on_the_estab.pdf

Austin, J. L. (1975). *How to do things with words.* Oxford University Press.

Black, H. C. (1991). *A dictionary of law: Containing definitions of the terms and phrases of American and English jurisprudence, ancient and modern; including the principal terms of international, constitutional, and commercial law; with a collection of legal maxims and numerous select titles from the civil law and other foreign systems.* West Publishing Company.

Butler, J. (1993). Critically queer. *GLQ: A Journal of Lesbian and Gay Studies, 1*(1), 17–32. doi:10.1215/10642684-1-1-17

Cases (2021). *ICC.* Retrieved June 17, 2020, from https://www.icc-cpi.int/Pages/cases.aspx.

Clarke, K. M. (2009). *Fictions of justice: The international criminal court and the challenge of legal pluralism in sub-Saharan Africa.* Cambridge University Press.

Clarke, K. M. (2019). *Affective justice: The international criminal court and the pan-Africanist pushback* (p. 384). Duke University Press.

Clarke, K., Jalloh, C., & Nmehielle, V. (2019). Introduction. In K. Clarke, C. Jalloh, & V. Nmehielle (Eds.), *The African court of justice and human and peoples' rights in context* (pp. 2–4). Cambridge University Press.

Democratic Alliance v Minister of International Relations and Cooperation and Others (Council for the Advancement of the South African Constitution Intervening) (2017). 83145/2016. ZAGPPHC 53; 2017 (3) SA 212 (GP); [2017] 2 All SA 123 (GP); 2017 (1) SACR 623 (GP) (22 February 2017). http://www.saflii.org/za/cases/ZAGPPHC/2017/53.pdf.

Dugard, J. (2008). *Convention on the suppression and punishment of the crime of apartheid.* United Nations Audiovisual Library of International Law. https://legal.un.org/avl/ha/cspca/cspca.html

Du Plessis, M. (2014). Shambolic, shameful and symbolic-implications of the African Union's immunity for African leaders. *Institute for Security Studies Papers, 2014*(278), 16. https://issafrica.s3.amazonaws.com/site/uploads/Paper278.pdf

Gambia Withdraws from International Criminal Court (2016, October 25). Al Jazeera. https://www.aljazeera.com/news/2016/10/gambia-withdraws-international-criminal-court-161026041436188.html

Gouvernement du Burundi (2016, October 7). *Communique de Presse de la Réunion du Conseil des Ministres du Jeudi 06 Octobre* [Press release]. http://www.burundi.gov.bi/spip.php?article1534.

Hamlin, A., & Jennings, C. (2011). Expressive political behaviour: Foundations, scope and implications. *British Journal of Political Science, 41*(3), 645–670. doi:10.1017/S0007123411000020

Human Rights Watch. (2014, Nov 12). *Statement regarding immunity for sitting officials before the expanded African Court of Justice and Human Rights.* https://www.hrw.org/news/2014/11/13/statement-regarding-immunity-sitting-officials-expanded-african-court-justice-and

ICC: Bashir Warrant Is Warning to Abusive Leaders (2010). *Human Rights Watch.* [Blog]. Retrieved 19 February 2020, from https://www.hrw.org/news/2010/02/03/icc-bashir-warrant-warning-abusive-leaders.

International Court of Justice. (2002). *Case concerning the arrest warrant of 11 April 2000 (Democratic Republic of the Congo v. Belgium).*

International Criminal Court (2016). *Case information sheet—Ruto and Sang.* https://www.icc-cpi.int/CaseInformationSheets/RutoSangEng.pdf

International Criminal Court (n.d.-a). *Afghanistan.* https://www.icc-cpi.int/afghanistan.

International Criminal Court (n.d.-b). *Burundi.* https://www.icc-cpi.int/burundi

International Law Commission. (2013). *Report of the International Law Commission, 65th session.* https://legal.un.org/docs/?symbol=A/68/10

Kenyatta and Ruto to face ICC trial over Kenya violence (2012, January 23). *BBC News.* https://www.bbc.com/news/world-africa-16675268.

Lahidji, K., Belhassen, S., Nabachwa, S. M., Senga, D. K., Traore, D., Nsapu, P., Mogwe, A., & Fall, M. (2014, June 10). *Immunity of heads of state and government for international crimes? The African Union must act with coherence and political courage.* International Federation for Human Rights. https://www.fidh.org/en/15601-immunity-of-heads-of-state-and-government-for-international-crimes-the

Lamony, S. (2013). *Rwanda and the ICC: Playing Politics with Justice.* African Arguments. https://africanarguments.org/2013/10/rwanda-and-the-icc-playing-politics-with-justice-by-stephen-a-lamony/

Masuthao, T. M. (2017, December 4). *Opening Statement, ASP 16 General Debate, Sixteenth Session of the Assembly of State Parties of the International Criminal Court.* https://asp.icc-cpi.int/iccdocs/asp_docs/ASP16/ASP-16-ZA.pdf

Muleefu, A. (2019). *The independence of the international criminal court: Between a rock and a hard place.* Intersentia.

Nahimana, H. E. V. (2015). *Statement of H.E Vestine Nahimana Ambassador of Burundi during the 15th session of the assembly of states parties.* https://asp.icc-cpi.int/iccdocs/asp_docs/ASP15/GenDeba/ICC-ASP15-GenDeba-Burundi-ENG.pdf

Nkoana-Mashbane, M. (2016). *Declaratory statement by the Republic of South Africa on the decision to withdraw from the Rome Statute of the International Criminal Court.* https://www.parliament.gov.za/storage/app/media/CommitteeNotices/2017/february/16-02-2017/docs/Withdrawal_from_the_Rome_Statute_of_the_International_Criminal_Court_tabled_Friday_4th_November_2016.pdf.

Rwanda's Paul Kagame accuses ICC of bias against Africa (2018, April 29). *Al Jazeera News.* https://www.aljazeera.com/news/2018/04/rwanda-kagame-accuses-icc-bias-africa-180429050656022.html.

Schuerch, R. (2017). *The international criminal court at the mercy of powerful states.* Springer.

Sirleaf, M. (2017). The African justice cascade and the Malabo Protocol. *International Journal of Transitional Justice, 11*(1), 71–91.v. doi:10.1093/ijtj/ijx002

Situation in the Republic of Kenya, Application on Behalf of the Government of the Republic of Kenya Pursuant to Article 19 of the ICC Statute, ICC-01/09-01/11 and ICC—01/09-02/11. https://www.icc-cpi.int/CourtRecords/CR2011_03107.PDF.

Situations under investigation (2021). ICC. Retrieved June 17, 2020, from https://www.icc-cpi.int/pages/situation.aspx

The Prosecutor v. Omar Hassan Ahmad Al Bashir, Warrant of Arrest for Omar Hassan Ahmad Al Bashir, ICC-02/05-01/09-1 (2009). https://www.icc-cpi.int/Pages/record.aspx?docNo=ICC-02/05-01/09-1.

Tladi, D. (2015). The immunity provision in the AU amendment protocol: separating the (doctrinal) wheat from the (normative) chaff. *Journal of International Criminal Justice, 13*(1), 3–17. doi:10.1093/jicj/mqu081

Tladi, D. (2019). *Article 46A Bis: Beyond the rhetoric. The African Court of Justice and Human and Peoples' Rights in context: Development and challenges.* Cambridge University Press, p. 850.

U.N. Charter art. 24, para. 1.

United Nations (2017). *South Africa: Withdrawal of Notification of Withdrawal, C.N.* 121.2017.TREATIES-XVIII.10. https://treaties.un.org/doc/Publication/CN/2017/CN.121.2017-Eng.pdf

United Nations Security Council. (1984). *Resolution adopted by the Security Council on 23 October 1984.* 2560th meeting. S/RES/556. https://digitallibrary.un.org/record/71588?ln=en

United Nations Security Council (n.d.-a). *Current members.* https://www.un.org/securitycouncil/content/current-members.

United Nations Security Council (n.d.-b). *Frequently asked questions.* https://www.un.org/securitycouncil/content/faq

Van Alebeek, R. (2008). *The immunity of states and their officials in international criminal law and international human rights law.* Oxford University Press.

Van Schaack, B. (2014). *Immunity before the African Court of Justice & Human & Peoples Rights—The potential outlier.* Just Security. https://www.justsecurity.org/12732/immunity-african-court-justice-human-peoples-rights-the-potential-outlier/

Why is there a war in Afghanistan? The short, medium and long story. (2020, February 29). *BBC News.* https://www.bbc.com/news/world-asia-49192495

Epistemes of human rights in Kashmir: Paradoxes of universality and particularity

Sarbani Sharma

ABSTRACT

Human rights violations through militarized control have been the cornerstone of Indian statecraft in Indian-administered Kashmir. This article offers a close reading of the April 2017 episode of using a civilian Kashmiri Muslim man as a human shield by the Indian Army in Indian-administered Kashmir. Whereas the existing scholarship on the relationship between militarization, human rights violations, and *Hindutva* politics have employed political or feminist analytical frameworks, this article focuses on rereading the episode of human shield usage to analyze how "universality" of human rights in India is being redefined. It reflects on how the ruling right-wing government in India appropriates the language of violations and afflictions to embolden its strategies to alter the grammar of human rights in India. Drawing on a discourse analysis of the human shield event, the article deliberates on how anthropology of *Hindutva* and right-wing extremism research could pay greater attention to the conversation between *Hindutva* theology of rights and neoliberal ethics when approaching questions of recurrent human rights violations in Kashmir.

Introduction

On April 9, 2017, a photograph of a human shield used by the Indian armed forces in the Indian-administered Kashmir Valley went viral on various social media platforms. The photograph showed a middle-aged man, later identified as Farooq Ahmad Dar, tied with a rope to the bonnet of an army vehicle while holding up a placard (message illegible). Farooq Ahmad Dar used to work as a Kashmiri shawl weaver. Media reportage about his narrative showed his trepidation and humiliation of being dragged around by Indian Army personnel in front of his entire village. He was strapped onto the bonnet of an armored SUV and paraded on the village streets to instill a sense of fear among protesting locals.

There was widespread shock and condemnation of the use of a human shield by the armed forces of a nation signatory to the Universal Declaration of Human Rights and Geneva Conventions of War. Shockingly, yet not unexpectedly, the Indian Army officer responsible for this action was congratulated by the ruling right-wing government committed to a *Hindutva*[1] state with appreciative recommendations and cash rewards. The felicitations for the officer cited appreciation for the "innovative" work of using a human shield to manage a protest by residents in a conflict zone. This article focuses on the specificity of this episode of human rights violation and how the brazen validation of the violation illuminates the epistemic consequences of redefining the particularities of "human" in the human rights discourse of the Indian state. The article highlights the consequences of the tactical transactions that are occurring between human rights discourse in India, neoliberal ethics of governmentality, and the *Hindutva* state.

The questions around who could be defined as a human and who deserves human rights have been the center of various academic debates for decades. Biological and philosophical anthropologists have long debated with theologians and advocates of various rights and equality projects to compare the entitlement and treatment of "contested" and "uncontested" human beings (Evans, 2016). In a similar spirit and much like the international law, human rights and its regimes have also encountered critics who have addressed the stakes involved in rethinking the reason and discourse of "universality" of human rights. Given the historical overlap of colonial conquest, capitalist aggression, and statist consolidation with the articulation of universal dignity, modernity, freedom, democracy, rule of law, and development, this skepticism has been articulated, and at times tangentially amounted to, a dismissal of "human rights" (Rudy, 2020, p. 21–23).

In continuation of this critique, the rise of contemporary right-wing populist and authoritarian governments across the globe has witnessed a renewed interest in overturning the discourse of "universal humanity" embedded in human rights. The fact that human rights asserts universal equality and ascribes to all humans an equally abstract feature that papers overs the undeniable cracks of inequality of distinct humans has been used by statist and right-wing movements as a justification to unravel "colonialist logic inherent in the discursive logic of proclaiming 'universal humanity'" (Rudy, 2020, p. 24). The negation of this transcendental feature of universal humanity within the human rights discourse of "equal rights for all" has been at the core of neocolonial, occupational forces, and reactionary right-wing responses (Perugini & Gordon, 2015). Therefore, the humanitarian and egalitarian logic of human rights discourse gets co-opted and mimicked by the right-wing *Hindutva* ideological state to argue for "new" human rights projects that "do not necessarily find a riposte emerging from the 'universal' human right discourse" (Rudy, 2020, p. 26).

This paradox has developed a new dimension in contemporary times. On one hand, almost no right-wing populist authoritarian government outrightly denounces the international human rights directives, but on the other, instances of human rights violations against certain communities and identities have grown under the pretext of national security, preservation of sovereignty, and imagined threats to the majoritarian sensibilities.

Within the context of postcolonial India, the combination of neoliberal ethics of development and persistent structural inequalities and discrimination have given rise to a virulent form of Hindu identity politics. "*Hindutva*" is commonly defined as a politicized use of the Hindu religion to transform the Indian state into a united Hindu nation (*Hindu Rashtra*), one that follows a militant "Hindu First" position (Kapila, 2022).

According to *Hindutva* ideology, India as a nation is identified with the worldview of Hindus, the dominant group in Indian society, and only those narratives that value the role of this group are seen as patriotic (Sundar 2005). Much like other majoritarian populist projects in global contexts, patriotism, according to proponents of *Hindutva*, means glorifying an ancient Hindu past, extolling the virtues of one's own country over others, glossing over events of violence and injustice, and minimizing discussion on "internal problems" such as caste oppression, gender-based violence, and discrimination against *Adivasis*[2] as well as sexual and religious minorities (Sundar 2005).

Historically, many human rights violations in Kashmir have been justified in the name of protecting Indian democracy and sovereignty. An assumed economic rationality and a moral superiority of the democratic principles of the Indian nation-state drives the political, economic, and social attitudes toward Kashmir. The rhetoric of "postcolonial economic rising power" in dialogue with the "resurgent Hindu cultural masculinity" produces varying dynamics of violence in Kashmir (Kaul, 2018, p. 137). The logic of strong, muscular, resurgent Hindus who need to discipline and enlighten the only Muslim-dominated region of India bases itself on the amalgamation of anxieties that both perceives a tangible threat to the Hindu-majority nation from the untrustworthy Kashmiri Muslim "other" and seeks to reclaim complete territorial control of a fictitious ancient Hindu land (Kaul, 2018).

Since the beginning of Prime Minister Narendra Modi's first five-year term in 2014, backed by right-wing Hindu nationalist ideology, human rights violations in Kashmir have crossed all previous thresholds in the political history of post-1947 independent India (Kanjwal, 2019). Banning of newspapers; internet and telecommunication blackouts lasting months; use of often lethal pellet guns to blind unarmed protestors, including children; occupying of school and college buildings for military use; arrests and surveillance of human rights defenders; abuse of draconian laws like the Public Safety Act[3] and the Unlawful Activities (Prevention) Act (UAPA)[4] to criminalize dissent; imprisonment of proresistance leadership; and the complete invisibilization of aspirations for self-determination and freedom from the Indian state are a few instances in the long track record of human rights violations in Kashmir.

Kashmir's modern history does not lack previous instances of human rights violations. Alterations in the grammar of the language used to talk about these violations are recent, however. The singularity of the human shield episode highlighted in this article lies in its brazen validation and the clear change in the definition of "human" in human rights. I relate the change in this definition of human in the Indian polity to the state's appropriation of so-called "decolonization" and "indigenization" of the universal ideas of human rights that have often been critiqued as "Western," in a bid to claim an oppressive reimagination of national sovereignty and citizenship.

In the following section, I first present the cartography of dehumanization of Kashmir and Kashmiris that effectively renders them perpetually "inhuman" within the context of sovereign India's engagement with Kashmir. Second, I sketch how right-wing, illiberal democracies like India appropriate human rights discourse to craft a renewed definition of human rights that stands apart from the "Western liberal" understanding of human beings and the rights that are deemed inherent to their existence.

This supposed decolonization of human rights provokes the question: Is a *Hindutva* theory of human rights possible? I reread the episode of the human shield used by officers of Indian armed forces to understand how *Hindutva* ideology has developed a critique of universal human rights through its mimicry of a *homo economicus* approach toward Kashmiri Muslims' lives. Here, I trace how this mathematical-utilitarian logic of *Hindutva* biopolitics interacts with the neoliberal ethics of "innovation" in Kashmir and its continued political crisis.

Cartographies of violence and dehumanization in Kashmir

Kashmir, "the Valley," or Kashmir Valley discussed here refers to the geographical region situated between the Karakoram and Pir Panjal mountain ranges in the Himalayan ranges of the Indian subcontinent. The territory of Jammu and Kashmir has been the location of intense territorial rivalry since the Partition of British India in 1947 and the creation of India and Pakistan. Since 1947, the postcolonial states of India and Pakistan have fought three wars (1947, 1965, 1999) for control of this territory. The ceasefire that was declared on January 1, 1949, left the state of Jammu and Kashmir partitioned into two territories, each governed, respectively, by the Indian and Pakistani states. The lack of a resolution acceptable to India, Pakistan, and the state of Jammu and Kashmir makes it one of the oldest standing conflicts on the subcontinent. Traditionally, India and Pakistan have remained preoccupied with concerns about territoriality, sovereignty, and principles of equality and moral legitimacy when approaching the issue (Padder, 2014). A series of wars, resolutions, proposals, summits, dialogues, and ceasefires by New Delhi, Islamabad, and the United Nations have occurred to resolve the dispute with no success.

Indian-administered Jammu and Kashmir is India's only Muslim-majority state. The Indian state has exacerbated the tragedy of the "dispute" by consistently violating human rights and sustaining an unprecedented scale of military occupation in the region. The sustainability of the military presence by the state in the name of security creates a logic of war (APDP/ITPK, 2015; Duschinski & Ghosh, 2017) that makes human rights violations a quotidian way of life. The military invests in infusing the fear of violence and consistently generates mechanisms of regulating "unruly bodies" (Parrey, 2010). Studies on military impunity show a direct relationship between the state-military-intelligence complex and the systemic violence inflicted by the Indian state in Kashmir (APDP/ITPK, 2015; Farasat, 2013; Human Rights Watch, 1993). These deeply entrenched patterns of militarization produce social suffering for local communities while simultaneously being obscured and rendered invisible through the Indian national (New Delhi-emanating) popular rhetoric of protecting national security, promoting national interests, and maintaining law and order (Duschinski, 2009, p. 693).

The history of the Kashmiri movement for self-determination is a history of struggle against these bilateral dispute resolution mechanisms, injustices, sustained human rights violations, and the failure of promised democratic principles. For Kashmiris, India's post-1947 claim to Kashmir is one more phase of occupation and colonization, premised on an instrument of accession that has never been confirmed and a promise of plebiscite that has never been fulfilled. The legal foundations of contemporary claims for self-determination are a series of UN Security Council resolutions addressing the need for a plebiscite to determine the region's political future. Since 1989, the armed resistance against the Indian state gained new momentum due to increased disenchantment with Indian rule. Ignoring the movement's indigenous anchorage, the Indian state launched a protracted counterinsurgency program that involved covert operations by networks of paid informants and renegade militants. This created a "pervasive public culture of suspicion, distrust and fear" (Kaul, 2011, p. 195).

The 1990s in Kashmir saw a decade of extreme violence against the Kashmiri Muslim inhabitants who were, and continue to be, caught between militancy, resistance, and state oppression (Mathur, 2016). Draconian emergency powers under laws like the Armed Forces Special Powers Act of 1958 (AFSPA) continue to be under operation in the present day, which gives the Indian armed forces special impunity in "a disturbed area" (Duschinski, 2009). This has meant no prosecutions for wanton violence and human rights abuses in many cases (Human Rights Watch, 1993; Kaul, 2017). Despite international condemnation, protests, and numerous judicial recommendations to repeal it, this act continues to be in force in places such as Kashmir and the Northeast, where the indigenous resistance struggles are met with human rights violations (Bhattacharya, 2016). Under the pretext of national security and quelling insurgency and terror, numerous violations have been documented, including instances of mass rapes in the villages of Kunan Poshpora in North Kashmir; well-documented evidence of routinized humiliation, torture camps, extrajudicial killings, massacres, and the presence of mass graves; detention without trials; and the widespread existence of half-widows, or women without knowledge of the whereabouts of their husbands, who may have been disappeared or most likely have been killed (Amnesty International, 2015; APDP/ITPK, 2015; Batool et al., 2016; Human Rights Watch, 1993).

Life and institutions in Kashmir are yet to recover from the war-like conditions and particularly from the military and intelligence agencies' repressive counterinsurgency strategies. The generation of Kashmiris who came of age after the 1990s have been socialized in an atmosphere surrounded by bunkers, barbed wire, extrajudicial killings, civilian deaths, routine curfews, arbitrary suspension of telecommunications, restrictions on rights and liberties, and daily news of disturbances and crackdowns (Kaul, 2017, p. 129).

Not surprisingly therefore, cycles of summer uprisings were witnessed in 2008, 2010, and 2016, primarily led by young Kashmiris, some of whom have resorted to stone pelting at the armed forces as a technique of protest and resistance to express their resentment and anger against Indian rule. The armed forces often respond to these protesting youth with bullets, metal pellets, and other lethal means that have led to permanent physical disability for many. This violence has become additionally layered with the force of neoliberalism and the ascendancy of right-wing Hindu fascist politics (Zia, 2020).

After 2014, with the advent of *Hindutva* political forces officially ruling India, targeted communal violence and normalization of Islamophobia have brought in a new era of human rights violations, subjugation, and dispossession in Kashmir. A neoliberal Indian state with a renewed zeal for *Hindutva* sentiments has enhanced the idea of enforced nationalism and patriotism, which has been brought into the fold of public culture of India. Although historically not unknown, the intensity of brutal chicaneries of law and power that embolden the arbitrary subterfuge of Indian constitutional laws for matters ranging from horrific human rights violations to issues about the status of Jammu and Kashmir within the ambit of constitutional parameters have increased manifold in recent years (Sharma, 2020a).

In a watershed moment in the recent political history of India and Kashmir, in August 2019 the Indian Parliament unilaterally revoked the semi-autonomous status accorded to India's only Muslim-majority state of Jammu and Kashmir under Article 370 of the Constitution of India by the President of India. Subsequently, the Indian Parliament also passed an act reorganizing the existing state of Jammu and Kashmir into two union territories: Jammu and Kashmir and Ladakh. This specific legal provision of Article 370 was often read with an assurance of a distinct political existence owing to the distinct political history of the state within the Indian federal structure. The conniving exploitation of presidential powers in the absence of any people's representation in the Parliament—as well as placing the state under lockdown, muzzling independent media, and banning internet and telecommunications for the entire population during the entire period of state's legal transformation—was justified on the grounds of populist promises of job creation and development aimed to "correct the historical errors" in the disputed territory (Sharma, 2020a).

The ongoing enforcement of patriotism in India, the silencing of dissent with violence, rampant arrests of political activists, unlawful arrests of human rights defenders, co-option of corporate-funded media houses, infusing vitiated atmosphere in universities, striving for revisionist historiography, the rewriting of textbooks, the appointments of right-wing hardliners to key posts, and the conspicuous miscarriages of justice in cases involving Hindu right-wing violence (Kaul, 2017; Sundar, 2005) are key processes to understand how the popular *Hindutva* politics is transforming not merely the textures of everyday life and polity in Kashmir but also legibly transforming the grammar of discourses around the politics, power, and people of Kashmir.

It is in this sense that I conceptualize how the people of Kashmir live in a landscape characterized by two simultaneous situations, both interminable. Elsewhere, I have argued that life in Kashmir is about navigating between this contemporaneous reality of continuous conflict and unrest on the one hand, and a constant struggle to achieve the desired goal of *Azadi*[5] (or freedom) on the other. This simultaneity of constant war and unrest forces Kashmir into an unsustainable position in which it can never belong. At the same time, the concrete manifestations of "normalcy" and the so-called peace projected by statist narratives appear in a manner that Kashmir finds difficult to settle for itself, thereby resulting in a continuous struggle for *Azadi*. To put it simply, to live a life in Kashmir is to be stuck between a conflict that never ends and a definition of peace that is unacceptable to the masses, thereby placing Kashmir and its people in a landscape of what I refer to as the "double interminability" (Sharma, 2020b).

Various scholars of Kashmir have interpreted India's military occupational tactics primarily through two perspectives. The first is through a feminist reading of hyper-masculinized Indian rule over a feminine Kashmiri body politic that renders voices and resistance by Kashmiris invisible and dehumanizes them yet considers them in need of disciplining and control through humiliation, torture, and domination (Batool et al., 2016; Kaul, 2017; Malik, 2018; Misri, 2014;

Figure 1. Image of human shield first circulated on Internet. Image sourced here under fair use.

Zia, 2019). The second perspective is through unpacking the political economy of neoliberal ethics embedded in military occupation and militarized humanitarianism (Varma, 2020), accompanied by the sustained dispossession and chains of dependency on the Indian state and their resources (Trisal, 2015), that convert Kashmir into a begging bowl in urgent need of economic development (Bhan, 2013, 2014). These biopolitical and legal strategies of control and extraction are manifested through the settler-colonialist processes of occupying the state (Bhan & Duschinski, 2020; Kanjwal, 2019; Zia, 2020). These practices of violence and discrimination thereby create an environment marked by a "trust deficit" among the people of Kashmir and the Indian state, forcing Kashmiris to resort to mechanisms of "reflective improvidence" to survive all forms of assault on life and livelihood in Kashmir (Saraf, 2020).

This article is thus an intervention into the consequences of epistemic definitions of "human" and its perpetual instability within the liberal discourse of rights. To me, the Indian army's use of a human shield to humiliate an individual and to violate the human rights of an entire community is therefore not only about deciphering the logics of settler–colonial instincts and the gendered overtones of patriarchal, hyper-masculine *Hindutva* violence. Rather, it is about understanding the consequences of how right-wing politics knit together an "ideology of injury and violation" in remarkably creative and malleable ways to address the "specificity of local grievances while, at the same time, operating as a meta-narrative that arouses and electrifies the sentiments of the body politic" (Govindrajan et al., 2021). In this context, the ideology of injury and violence braided with neoliberal ethics allows *Hindutva* to weave a "decolonial" framework of human rights. In the following sections, I elaborate on how the human in the human shield becomes absent in the state's attempt to articulate the Hindutva critique of "universal humanity" principles embedded in "Western" human rights discourse and its regime.

The absent human in the human shield

The viral image (see Figure 1) of a human shield used by the Indian armed forces brought shock and condemnation across the South Asian media and political landscape in April 2017. The picture showed a middle-aged man identified as Farooq Ahmad Dar, a Kashmiri shawl weaver, tied to the bonnet of an armored vehicle with a rope, displaying an indistinct placard. Media reportage that emerged from Dar's narrative expressed his terror of being shot by the officers of the armed forces at point-blank range when he was dragged amid the crowd of villagers on the day of the local election in North Kashmir.

The incident was said to have taken place mid-day, when a contingent of armed forces entered the village during the polling. According to several news reports, Dar was merely a bystander and was not among the protesting villagers who were supposedly pelting stones at the armed forces cavalry. He was nabbed, strapped onto the bonnet of an armored vehicle, and paraded through the streets of the village (Naqash, 2017). According to Dar, he was dragged and beaten up before being tied to the bonnet of the car and a sign pinned on to his shirt that said, "This is the fate that will befall stone throwers." Ironically, Dar was among the meager 7.1 percent of the eligible voters who voted in local elections (Naqash, 2017) (Figure 1).

An Indian Army officer, Major Nitin Leetul Gogoi, was leading the troops of armed officers to the polling station. According to his report, he reached the polling station after he received a request for help and assistance from the local administration in maintaining the order and safety of polling station workers. Upon confronting stone-pelting by residents near the polling station and its vicinity, Major Gogoi decided to "catch" a man from the local population, who were supposedly instigating the crowd to pelt stones at armed officers. In his words,

> In a fraction of a second, I told my boys to drag a local man from the crowd and strap into the bonnet of our Jeep, so that the crowd stops pelting stones at us and we can manage a safe passage out of the village. This plan resulted in success because by using one person as a human shield, the crowd dispersed and that did not force us to shoot at least 12 other villagers. We upheld human rights and saved the lives of at least 12 people. (see *India Today*, 2017)

It is worth mentioning *en passant* that a contingent of professionally trained, armed troops found it difficult to navigate through a village with a few stone pelters. This indicates the strategic and psychological fragility of the Indian army in Kashmir. Nevertheless, the use of human shields in any situation of war across the globe has been considered unlawful and a war crime according to Article 28 of the Fourth Geneva Convention, the 1998 Rome Statute of the International Criminal Court, and international humanitarian law.[6] Despite widespread condemnation by the media and organizations like Amnesty International, the then-chief of the Indian army, late Bipin Rawat, defended the army officer's action by arguing, "This is a proxy war, and a proxy war is a dirty war. It is played in a dirty way. That is where innovation comes in. You fight a dirty war with innovations" (Rowlatt, 2017).

After an apparent closed-door investigation conducted by the Indian Army on the incident, Major Gogoi was awarded a medal and prize money in May 2017 for his "innovative approach" of using a human shield to ensure law and order as well as the "safety" of many lives in the village. A year later, Bhartiya Janta Dal (BJP) Delhi Unit spokesperson printed t-shirts with Dar's picture as a human shield and sold them online for Rs. 495 INR (approx. $7 US), which likewise generated widespread condemnation. The t-shirt sales continued, nonetheless (*The Wire*, 2018).

For several commentators and observers, the articulation of proxy war was a signifier of change in the state's imagination and understanding of what war meant and the status of the dispute (Datta, 2017). The Indian Army's defense of its officer's violation of universal human rights, as well as the statutory commandments of the Indian constitution itself on the grounds of innovation in warfare, was considered a singular moment in the military history of the Indian Army. First, the Kashmir dispute was publicly defined as a proxy war against the neighboring enemy state of Pakistan. Second, the army overtly endorsed the twin legacies of "everything is fair in war" and the neoliberal corporate discourse of "disruption as innovation" (Kaur, 2020). Therefore, the declaration of proxy war that had to be inevitably dirty was bereft of the obligation to abide by the war conventions or ethics of warfare.

Discussion of the changing nature of modern warfare and its implications is beyond the scope of this article. Here, I focus on tracing the process of changing imaginations of the human exemplified in the human shield incident and the ethics of innovation emboldened by the *Hindutva* ideology's endorsement of violence and injury.

At the core of the response by the then chief of the Indian army is the desperation and intense desire to rearticulate the rules of the war required to reiterate the sovereignty of the nation by breaking away from the burdensome rule of law regimes obligatory to the state and its machineries. It also hints at the "latent desire for a more muscular style of politics that can tame any resistance" (Kaur, 2020) on the nation's path to becoming a "strong-modern" country that does not shy away from taking politically and ethically questionable risks. Expression of this desire overtly signals a move toward satiation of the "public desire" for "strong leadership" to deviate from the established content of laws and ethics by innovating "bold decisions" for the nation's good. This vital connection between neoliberal economy and illiberal majoritarian populism, a widespread current anxiety in many parts of the world, is often overlooked (Kaur, 2020).

Crucial to the reading of this event is the absence of acknowledgment of the humiliation, trauma, and life-long stigma infusing the personhood of a human being. The fact that the elected representatives of people in a democracy and its law enforcement officials did not consider it necessary to respond to the horror and fear expressed by Farooq Dar complicates the contemporary Indian state's imaginaries of human rights. The logic of inflicting fear, trauma, and humiliation on an individual within the geography of a community as a method to reprimand protestors and dissenters was understood as an innovative, necessary risk to tame and discipline the Muslim body politic of India, one that gained an overt mandate through the cash rewards, the sale of t-shirts, and the declaration of a war.

The supposed greater weight of "lives saved" versus the trauma and humiliation of reducing the body of an individual to a shield for trained, armed men underlines the imagination of human lives and safety along the vectors of marginal utilitarian value. It is the economics of dead vs. alive humans and their binary values, added to the minimum expenditure mode, that informs the imagination here. Despite the widespread condemnation of the action by human rights organizations across South Asia, the state and its armed forces representatives defended the action in terms of an innovation achieved by saving maximum human lives with minimum expenditure of sensitivity and infrastructure.

A key influence on this process of interweaving the neoliberal profitability of innovation and *Hindutva*'s desire for a masculine politics that undertakes "risks" to discipline the Muslim body is its understanding of justice. Rachel Wahl (2017), in her work on the distinct social and moral imageries of rights and justice among police, military, and paramilitary officials in India, discussed how the instrumentalist goal of serving justice through all means for the "public" triumphs over the ethical obligation to follow the rule of law. In the face of abject distrust in the processes of Indian judicial mechanisms to uphold law and order and anticipation of sustained political interference in the practice of enforcing law, Wahl described how law enforcement officers endorse and legitimize violence and human rights violations to attain a utilitarian justice for the larger good of the society. Therefore, not surprisingly, law enforcement officers weigh the competing rights—how they perform the mathematics of utility—in ways that rarely favor the rights of those who question the state or fall in the category of "deserving" punishment and disciplining (Wahl, 2017, p. 57).

Although human rights activists insist that human rights hold an ethical status independent of their purpose, drawing from Kantian philosophy that refutes a utilitarian understanding of human rights, they repeatedly encounter instances of a utilitarian reading of rights. In the utilitarian reading of rights (such as those done by Indian armed forces officers), desire to innovate techniques to preserve lives beckons for a secondary reading of rights: one that allows individual human rights to be treated as contingent on utilitarian conditions, thereby permitting individual human rights to become alienable. The ability to transform much-defended "inalienable" human rights to alienable human rights through the utilitarian reasoning of preservation of a specific group and their interests "legitimizes an instrumentalist conceptualization of justice" (Wahl, 2017, p. 65). This instrumentalist conceptualization of justice endorses an ends-over-means rationale to justify any violation of human rights and the ability to bypass the procedural feature of justice. Although utilitarianism shares a much longer history with liberalism as a political project, in the human shield incident in Kashmir there is an emergence of a text that allows stabilization of the relationship between utilitarianism of justice delivered and the neoliberal ethics of innovation.

Framing of a *Hindutva* critique

The human shield incident and the narrative that stabilizes and justifies it illustrate how *Hindutva* emboldens a critique of liberalism as a political project for an illiberal, majoritarian authoritarianism through the practices of a classification model. These imaginations are neither new nor absent from the institutional legal histories of India, yet its articulations have a renewed link to the understanding of national sovereignty and citizenship in India (Dyuti, 2020).

A *Hindutva* discourse of human rights goes beyond the old culturalist/communitarian critique of human rights. The discourse does not shy away from reiterating that all *humans are not equal*, grounded by a theology of caste-based stratification. Under such theological tenets, *Hindutva* ideology negates the Kantian imperative that human rights cannot be selectively applied. Therefore, principles of universal humanity and equality grounded in a moral law and ethics that inform liberal rights discourse are rendered oxymoronic by the *Hindutva* rationale.

As Wahl's ethnography (2017) pointed out, this imaginary that all people are not equal, and that to treat them equally would undermine justice, confronts the imaginaries of human rights discourse whose defenders advocate the equality of all individuals with respect to rule of law. A social imaginary in which people are grouped according to *perceived differences* in their character, and a moral imaginary that ascribes *different levels of worth and treatment* based on these differences (Wahl, 2017, p. 68; emphasis mine), are useful to decipher how the classification model of contested and uncontested occur.

Although not underlined by Wahl (2017), the imaginaries of the law enforcement officers in Wahl's ethnography find resonance within the Hindu theological and *Hindutva* ideological platforms by default. By corollary this discourse allows certain uncontested human beings with rights to view themselves as morally responsible for those considered contested humans, which in turn enables them to experiment with innovations in the torture and humiliation of contested human beings.

An illustration of the framing of this discourse was tangentially addressed by the Union Home Minister (Internal Affairs) of India two years after the human shield event in Kashmir. On October 12, 2019, the Union Home Minister of India, Amit Shah, addressed the 26th Foundation Day of the National Human Rights Commission (NHRC) and presented the need to address the matter of human rights violations from the perspective of an "Indian outlook."

In this speech, Shah denounced the application of "Western standards of human rights" when discussing the nature of human rights violations in India. He made the case for developing an Indian perspective toward human rights that was both theologically and culturally coherent within Indian reality. Interestingly, Shah acknowledged the killings of Indian armed forces personnel in various attacks by armed rebel groups in several locations within India. He underlined the gross violation of human rights of men in uniform serving the nation.

Without explaining how attacks on armed forces personnel could be reduced to an Indian outlook on human rights, Shah went on to reiterate that Hinduism as a religion and its family structures foreground the concept of care and that any form of violation was inherently absent in the Hindu way of life ("At NHRC, Amit Shah Says Don't Apply Western Norms of Rights Here," 2019). His speech addressed the "fractured publics to be mobilized—through profoundly modern calls for civic participation—into violence and into condoning violence" (Banaji, 2018, p. 3).

The Home Minister's comments sounded astonishing on the anniversary of a day when a constitutional body was founded precisely to uphold the Universal Declaration of Human Rights; however, his speech followed a clear and predictable genealogy of thought that resonated with his party colleagues and adherents of *Hindutva* politics[7]: the notion that secular and intellectual traditions in India—and tolerance toward people from many faiths—epitomize political weakness, economic decline, and a corruption of India's greatness has been propagated ceaselessly by *Hindutva* ideologues in speeches (Banaji, 2018, p. 345).

After his speech, bureaucrats who wished to remain unidentified while responding to questions from media seeking a clarification of what was meant by "Western values of human rights," argued that the Home Minister was calling for upholding traditional Hindu values that have been often ignored in "Western" discourse. However, critical political analysts in India do not see this reiteration of "traditional Hindu values" as just another moment in the long history of culturalist versus rationalist schools of thought that have influenced law and jurisprudence in Indian institutions. The genealogy of establishing a hegemonic narrative of who belongs to a nation, who can be considered human, and who deserves rights to the preservation of life has served as the point of reference for the sovereignty of India ever since the formation of the modern Indian nation-state (Kothari, 1996). In this case, the revived Hindu sovereign rule classifies Muslim bodies as those of contested human beings, the eternal "others," whose lives and destinies need to be adjudicated in terms of the prosperity of the Hindu *Rashtra* (*Hindutva* state), and to correct the historical mistakes of violence and indignity on uncontested Hindu bodies.

Two specific vectors of *Hindutva* discourse on rights emerge from here that work in tandem with the classification of contested and uncontested humans. First, the reasoning that the unit of governance is not an individual but a family reaffirms the patriarchal family headed and governed by a paternalistic state (Roy, 2018). Under such an arrangement, Kashmir and the Muslim bodies living there are viewed as unruly adolescents who fail the paternalistic Indian state of which they are an "integral" part and hence are in urgent need of reform. Dar's Kashmiri Muslim body thereby becomes part of the logical practice of a *Hindutva* masculinity trope that mandates the father to discipline one unruly son to intimidate the other undisciplined sons of the family. Both Dar and the Kashmiri spectators who witnessed him being used as a human shield are relegated to contested human beings whose bodies and psyches can be forcefully used as sites of innovation that can bring about "reforms in the Indian version of democracy that needed obedience" (Kapila, 2022; Roy, 2018).

Second, organized Hinduism and the Indian family structure in Shah's imagination are therefore beyond the realm of accountability and responsibility to address the vast spectrum of historical and structural violations, discrimination, and marginalization of individuals and communities in postcolonial India. Hinduism is imagined as "always-already-secular" because of its multiple sects (hence, tolerant by default), so any Western paradigms of secularism, ethics of coexistence, or principles of tolerance are considered unnecessary.

The deduction of "Western standards" as irrelevant and unnecessary in the Indian context was underlined by foregrounding the self-sufficiency of Hinduism as an ancient religion, which only needed redramatization and recollection in the Indian public sphere. The episteme identified draws on partial Orientalist readings of ancient Hindu texts to urge the innate modernity of various Hindu practices (Banaji, 2018, p. 345). This new episteme is derived from consistent attempts to erase the distinction between the party and the state by incrementally but systemically undermining or controlling the mechanisms that seek executive accountability (Khaitan, 2020, p. 51).

What is unique about this distinctive framing of *Hindutva* human rights discourse is not its cultural logic as a response to the hegemonic "universal" principles of equality. Rather, it reveals how the postcolonial state appropriates the language of decolonialization emerging from the neoliberal ethics of innovation to create a dystopian imagery of universal humanity endorsed by a specific reading of religious theology. Because the *Hindutva* state consistently aims to misappropriate law for its social and historical justice projects, in situations of appeals for redress of human rights violations of Muslims, the regime of human rights itself is subjected to the violence of law (Chatterjee, 2017). *Hindutva* thereby renders the ethical rationality of human rights law ineffective in favor of majoritarian ideology.

Rights, racialization, and religion

In his influential essay, "Why Has Critique Run out of Steam? From Matters of Fact to Matters of Concern," Bruno Latour (2004) alerted us to the dangers of certain practices of critique that eventually gain traction and are co-opted by ideological projects contrary to the original intentionality of the critique. In Latour's words,

> My argument is that a certain form of critical spirit has sent us down the wrong path, encouraging us to fight the wrong enemies and, worst of all, to be considered as friends by the wrong sort of allies because of a little mistake in the definition of its main target. The question was never to get *away* from facts but *closer* to them, not fighting empiricism but, on the contrary, renewing empiricism. (Latour, 2004, p. 231)

To return to the use of a human shield in Kashmir, this empirical example becomes an interesting moment to underline the changing image of the universality of human rights in the Indian polity. The postcolonial critique of Western, Enlightenment-driven understanding of universality is barely new. On the one hand, there are rationalist justifications of human rights, espoused by those who view themselves as moral and cultural universalists. On the other, there are postmodernists, communitarians, cultural relativists, and others who would argue for a more culturally sensitive, perhaps pragmatic understanding of rights discourse (Osborne, 2003).

It is understood that rights culture is neither an expressive phenomenon of a particular cultural or ideological context nor merely a late operationalization of Enlightenment-inspired rationalism or universalism but a specific rationality of innovation. What is at "stake is a sort of expanding circle of rights, always in movement away from their original contextual applications toward a kind of hypothetical universalism; but an expansion motivated as much by judicial expediency as by moral absolutism or rational principle" (Osborne, 2003, p. 524).

Similarly, Clifford Bob (2019) argued for a greater attention to the underexamined ways in which the powerful wield rights as aggressive weapons against the weak: denying the abuses they are accused of, constructing rival rights to protect themselves, portraying themselves as victims rather than violators, and repudiating authoritative decisions against them.

The *Hindutva* discourse of rights is one such sophisticated discourse. It weaves its social imaginaries of contested human beings and their worth with the neoliberal ethics of innovation enabled by *Hindutva* masculinity, all couched in the framework of rights as weapons to correct historical wrongs and discipline unruly contested human beings. The dramatization of the Hindu traditional value system on NHRC's Foundation Day also signaled the new epistemic source of a definition of human in the *Hindutva* human rights discourse in which the humans who are profiled to be underserving of rights are denied a position within any equality project crafted by it.

The argument that any rights discourse in a democracy would remain inherently unstable because democracy itself struggles with ethical mooring, and more so when tied to a regime of rule of law, is well rehearsed. The ways in which *Hindutva* is both similar to and distinct from political projects like white supremacy and others of its kind in structures and methodology has stirred passionate debates recently. Scholars like Ajay Skaria (2021) have defended the approach to understanding *Hindutva* as a racial supremacy project based on how it purports a logic of racial equality created by the Hindu permanent majority *vis-à-vis* an inferior other.

On the other hand, Cháirez-Garza et al. (2022) proposed a rethinking of the meteoric rise of *Hindutva* as a racial supremacy project as one that operates through casteist socio-spatial logics to further racial capitalism perpetuated through nationalism. White supremacy is often thought of as ideological, a constellation of ideas and values that explain social practices and boundaries, or as a system, something far more encompassing than social practice that is institutionalized and maintained throughout social life (Rana, 2020). To that end, *Hindutva* certainly shares resemblances and mimics racial supremacy projects like white supremacy. These resemblances and mimicries do indicate the role of religion and theology in upholding racial supremacy projects, and comprehending these patterns would aid anthropological theory to better conceptualize ongoing forms of racialization such as anti-Muslim racism, as well as struggles against white supremacy (Rana, 2020, p. 102).

Building a critique of Hindutva by comparing it to white supremacy and renewing our focus on empirical practices of Hindu religious theology are valuable, but it would also be an overstretch to equate *Hindutva*'s distinctive discourse with that of a white racial supremacy project. The uniqueness of a political project like *Hindutva* is that it frames a discourse of rights by interweaving both the context-specific discourse of Hindu religious theology with the appropriation of the liberal language of rights to articulate a decolonial moment.

What is needed is a renewed attention to empiricism, one that can discern how the history of Hindu theology, casteism, and colonialism converse with neoliberal economic logic to normalize a utilitarian imaginary of Muslims as threatening to Hindu majoritarian rights. In this way, the event of the human shield establishes a relationship between a changed definition of human with a renewed imagination of national sovereignty and communitarian citizenship in India, one that is distinct from the white supremacy phenomenon as it bypasses the burdens of the rule of all state laws.

Conclusion

Human rights are comprehended as legal sites of moral and political contestation over fundamental questions about structure and operation of international law (Macklem, 2015, p. 26). Although the human rights regime is international, its greatest influence has been to establish standards for state obligations *vis-à-vis* their own citizenries (Maher, 2002, p. 19).

It has been long established that human rights discourse, law, and practice are deeply governed by how we understand the human, and how humanness is experienced by contested and uncontested humans. Examining how Farooq Ahmad Dar was used as a human shield by law enforcement officers in India, and the series of responses by the state that emerged after the act, illuminates the political and contested nature of these processes. Whereas the term "human" reinscribes a natural unity (along with the boundary around a species to whom rights adhere), the term "subject" opens the question of the identity of the rights holder to scrutiny and transformation (Celermajer & Alexandre, 2020).

That said, human rights theories and institutions have not historically included all human beings within their conception of the human (Celermajer & Alexandre, 2020, p. 3). And, more than ever before, the classification of inclusion and exclusion within human rights discourse has gained prominence within every local particularism. These processes of inclusion and exclusion are actively being derived from right-wing politics of rewriting histories and myths to generate an alternative annal of individual and communitarian rights.

This article is an attempt to follow through the process of interweaving of these various vectors of the debates to underline the changing facets of human rights in India and the creative framing of a *Hindutva* discourse of rights. In the framework of these events and processes, the article insists on focusing on Hindu theological and caste doctrines and their conversation with neoliberal ethics to comprehend how the *Hindutva* discourse of human rights articulates its epistemologies about the Muslim other.

The implications of *Hindutva* discourse for the future of international human rights laws and practices are grave, primarily for their ability to render the principles of universality of human rights untenable and impotent. Much like other postcolonial and racial superiority projects' critiques of hegemonic discourses on rights, *Hindutva* exploits the vulnerability of global human rights abstractions to equivocation, mimicry, and extension through an ambiguous knowledge of one's own social power and a complete erasure of the contexts that justify why we need universal human rights (Rudy, 2020).

The mere fact that the *Hindutva* discourse enables and grounds itself on the convergence of these various moral and social imaginaries of rights, justice, power, and innovation through an absolute negation of universality and accountability offers a glimpse into the potentiality of its political force. What remains to be seen is how international human rights law responds to such decolonial critiques of universal human rights emerging from locations and times that were previously viewed only from the binaries of East and West.

Notes

1. The term is derived from the two terms "Hindu" and "Tattva" (essence), and literally translates to "Hindu Principles," which have been defined as the ideological basis of the militant Hindu nationalist movement in India (Jaffrelot, 1996).
2. *Adivasi* is the term used to refer to the indigenous people of India.
3. The Public Safety Act (PSA) is a preventive detention law arbitrarily used by the state in Kashmir to arrest human rights activists, including children, under the pretext of maintaining public law and order. PSA allows the State Police to imprison individuals without trial for up to two years. For details, see Duschinski and Ghosh (2017).
4. The Unlawful Activities (Prevention) Act (UAPA) is one of India's most stringent antiterrorism legislations. The Act is used to declare any association or a body of individuals "unlawful" if they indulged in any activity that included acts and words, spoken, or written, or any sign or representation, that supported any claim to bring about "secession of a part of the territory of India," or which questioned or disclaimed the country's sovereignty and territorial integrity. It enables law enforcement bodies like police in India to gain judicial custody of any accused person for 180 days before a charge-sheet is even filed in the court, making it impossible for the accused to gain bail or parole before the trial begins or ends.
5. The term *Azadi* is a Persian word meaning freedom. *Azadi* has been used as the clarion call for demanding the right to self-determination movement in Kashmir Valley.
6. For a detailed discussion on the jurisdiction of international humanitarian laws (IHL) regarding human shield usage by armed forces of nation-states or resistance groups in both international and noninternational conflict zones, see Vestner (2019).
7. Violence being antithetical to Hinduism has been long justified using Hindu theological explanations of a *Brahmanical* vegetarian diet as well as the concept of *Ahimsa* (nonviolence). For a detailed discussion on how vegetarianism and nonviolence underwrote the Gandhian anticolonial movement, see Devji (2021).

Acknowledgments

I would like to thank Heather Smith-Cannoy and Tricia Redeker Hepner for their patience, compassion, and generosity. I am grateful for the opportunity to have presented this paper and receive valuable comments at the virtual global conference, "Human Rights on the Edge: The Future of International Human Rights Law and Practice," organized by Arizona State University. Stimulating discussion of ideas and concepts with Malay Firoz, Sourav Roy, Haziq Qadri, Antony Pattathu, Sarah Ewald, and Max Kramer have immensely contributed to the making of this article. I would also like to thank the two anonymous reviewers for their suggestions, which helped develop the arguments of the article.

Funding

This research was funded by the National Science Foundation under Grant ID 2029490.

ORCID

Sarbani Sharma http://orcid.org/0000-0001-8877-4286

References

Amnesty International. (2015). *"Denied": Failures in accountability for human rights violations by security force personnel in Jammu and Kashmir* (Report No. ASA 20/1874/2015). Amnesty International.

Association of Parents of Disappeared Persons/International People's Tribunal on Human Rights in Indian Administered Kashmir (APDP/IPTK). (2015). *Structures of Violence: The Indian State in Jammu and Kashmir.* Srinagar. http://www.jkccs.net/structures-of-violence-the-indian-state-in-jammu-and-kashmir-2/.

At National Human Rights Commission of India. (2019, October 13). Amit Shah says don't apply Western norms of rights here [Express News Desk]. *The Indian Express.* https://indianexpress.com/article/india/at-nhrc-amit-shah-says-dont-apply-western-norms-of-rights-here-6066447/

Banaji, S. (2018). Vigilante publics: Orientalism. *Modernity and Hindutva Fascism in India. Javnost - The Public, 25*(4), 333–350. doi:10.1080/13183222.2018.1463349

Batool, E., Butt, I., Mushtaq, S., Rashid, M., & Rather, N. (2016). *Do you remember Kunan Poshpora?* Zubaan.

Bhan, M. (2013). *Counterinsurgency, democracy, and the politics of identity in India: From warfare to welfare?* Routledge.

Bhan, M. (2014). Morality and martyrdom: Dams, dharma, and the cultural politics of work in Indian-occupied Kashmir. *Biography, 37*(1), 191–224. doi:10.1353/bio.2014.0012

Bhan, M, & Duschinski, H. eds. (2020). Occupations in context – the cultural logics of occupation, settler violence, and resistance. *Critique of Anthropology, 40*(3), 285–297.

Bhattacharya, R. (2016). Living with Armed Forces Special Powers Act (AFSPA) as everyday life. *GeoJournal, 83*(1), 31–48.

Bob, C. (2019). *Rights as weapon: Instruments of conflicts, tools of power.* Princeton University Press.

Celermajer, D., & Alexandre, L. (2020). *The subject of human rights.* Stanford University Press.

Cháirez-Garza, J. F., Gergan, M. D., Ranganathan, M., & Vasudevan, P. (2022). Introduction to the special issue: Rethinking difference in India through racialization. *Ethnic and Racial Studies, 45*(2), 193–215. doi:10.1080/01419870.2021.1977368

Chatterjee, M. (2017). The impunity effect: Majoritarian rule, everyday legality, and state formation in India. *American Ethnologist, 44*(1), 118–130.

Datta, A. (2017, June 9). *D for dirty, w for war-Indian army chief's alphabet lesson.* The Raiot: Challenging the Consensus. https://raiot.in/d-for-dirty-w-for-war-indian-army-chiefs-alphabet-lesson/.

Devji, F. (2021). The return of nonviolence. *Critical Times, 4*(1), 93–111. doi:10.1215/26410478-8855243

Duschinski, H. (2009). Destiny effects: Militarization, state power, and punitive containment in Kashmir valley. *Anthropological Quarterly, 82*(3), 691–717.

Duschinski, H., & Ghosh, S. N. (2017). Constituting the occupation: Preventive detention and permanent emergency in Kashmir. *The Journal of Legal Pluralism and Unofficial Law, 49*(3), 314–337. doi:10.1080/07329113.2017.1347850

Dyuti, a. (2020). Abrogation and assertion: The fault lines of the Indian constitution with regards to Kashmir. *HAU: Journal of Ethnographic Theory, 10*(3), 758–766.

Evans, J. H. (2016). *What is a human? What the answers mean for human rights.* Oxford University Press.

Farasat, W. (2013). Understanding impunity in Jammu and Kashmir. *Economic and Political Weekly, 48*(19), 15–18.

Govindrajan, R., Joshi, B., Rizvi, M. (2021, March 16). *Majoritarian politics in South Asia.* Cultural Anthropology Hot Spots, Fieldsights. https://culanth.org/fieldsights/series/majoritarian-politics-in-south-asia

Human Rights Watch. (1993). *The human rights crisis in Kashmir: A pattern of impunity* (Report No.- 1-56432-104-5). Human Rights Watch.

India Today. (2017, May 23). *Major Nitin Leetul Gogoi explains 'human shield' incident in Kashmir, exclusive interview* [Video]. YouTube. Retrieved December 21, 2021, from https://www.youtube.com/watch?v=zkGSncecfyQ&t=34s

Jaffrelot, C. (1996). *The Hindu nationalist movement in India.* Penguin Books.

Kanjwal, H. (2019, August 5). India's settler-colonial project in Kashmir takes a disturbing turn. *Washington Post.* https://www.washingtonpost.com/opinions/2019/08/05/indias-settler-colonial-project-kashmir-takes-disturbing-turn/

Kapila, S. (2022, January 3). Sarvarkar's hindutva needs obedience. But obedience has never helped economy. *The Print.* Retrieved January 04, 2022, from https://theprint.in/opinion/savarkars-hindutva-wants-obedience-but-obedience-has-never-helped-economy/793081/

Kaul, N. (2017). Rise of the political right in India: Hindutva-development mix, Modi myth, and dualities. *Journal of Labor and Society*, *20*(4), 523–548. doi:10.1111/wusa.12318

Kaul, N. (2018). India's obsession with Kashmir: Democracy, gender, (anti-) nationalism. *Feminist Review*, *119*(1), 126–143. doi:10.1057/s41305-018-0123-x

Kaul, S. (2011). "An' you will fight, till the death of it…": Past and present in the challenge of Kashmir. *Social Research: An International Quarterly*, *78*(1), 173–202.

Kaur, R. (2020, June 2). The market hunters: Corporate masculinity and art of opening the economy. *Tasveer Ghar.* http://www.tasveergharindia.net/essay/corporate-masculinity-art.html

Khaitan, T. (2020). Killing a constitution with a thousand cuts: Executive aggrandizement and party-state fusion in India. *Law & Ethics of Human Rights*, *14*(1), 49–95. doi:10.1515/lehr-2020-2009

Kothari, S. (1996). Whose nation? The displaced as victims of development. *Economic and Political Weekly*, *31*(24), 1476–1485.

Latour, B. (2004). Why has critique run out of steam? From matters of fact to matters of concern. *Critical Inquiry*, *30*(2), 225–248. doi:10.1086/421123

Macklem, P. (2015). *The sovereignty of human rights.* Oxford University Press.

Maher, K. (2002). Who has a right to rights? Citizenship's exclusions in an age of migration. In A. Brysk (Ed.), *Globalization and human rights* (pp. 19–43). University of California.

Malik, I. (2018). Kashmiri desire and digital space: Queering national identity and the Indian citizen. In R. K. Dasgupta & D. DasGupta (Eds.), *Queering digital India: Activisms, identities, subjectivities* (pp. 180–194). Edinburgh University Press.

Mathur, S. (2016). *The human toll of the Kashmir conflict: Grief and courage in a South Asian borderland.* Palgrave Macmillan.

Misri, D. (2014). *Beyond partition: Gender, violence and representation in postcolonial India.* University of Illinois Press.

Naqash, R. (2017, April 15). 'I will never vote again': Kashmiri man used as 'human shield' describes his journey of humiliation. *The Scroll.* https://scroll.in/article/834706/i-will-never-vote-again-kashmiri-man-used-as-human-shield-describes-his-journey-of-humiliation

Osborne, T. (2003). What is neo-Enlightenment? Human rights culture and juridical reason. *Journal of Human Rights*, *2*(4), 523–530.

Padder, S. (2014). Cross-LoC trade: Peace and process. *Social Sciences Review of Pakistan*, *1*(2), 1–16.

Parrey, A. A. (2010). Kashmir: Three metaphors for the present. *Economic and Political Weekly*, *45*(47), 47–53.

Perugini, N., & Gordon, N. (2015). *The human right to dominate.* Oxford University Press.

Rana, J. (2020). Anthropology and the riddle of white supremacy. *American Anthropologist*, *122*(1), 99–111. doi:10.1111/aman.13355

Rowlatt, J. (2017, May 31). Why Indian army defended Kashmir 'human shield' officer. *BBC World.* https://www.bbc.com/news/world-asia-india-40103673

Rudy, S. (2020). 'Human Rights', 'Rule of Law', and 'Violence. In L. Vashist & J. D. Sood (Eds.), *Rethinking law and violence* (pp. 19–85). Oxford University Press.

Roy, S. (2018, April 15). The constitution of India: A national gallery of few good men. *Tasveer Ghar.* http://www.tasveergharindia.net/essay/national-gallery-constitution-india.html

Saraf, A. (2020). Trust amid 'trust deficit' war, credit, and improvidence in Kashmir. *American Ethnologist*, *47*(4), 387–401. doi:10.1111/amet.12987

Sharma, S. (2020a, August 5). *Chicaneries of power and subterfuge: Constitutional laws on Kashmir.* Academic. Speaking Justice to Power Series, Association for Political and Legal Anthropology. https://politicalandlegalanthro.org/2020/08/05/chicaneries-of-power-and-subterfuge/.

Sharma, S. (2020b). Labouring for Kashmir's *azadi*: Ongoing violence and resistance in Maisuma, Srinagar. *Contributions to Indian Sociology*, *54*(1), 27–50. doi:10.1177/0069966719890525

Skaria, A. (2021, September 10). Why Hindutva is a racist supremacy- not merely communalism and majoritarianism. *The Wire.* https://thewire.in/politics/why-hindutva-is-a-racist-supremacism-not-a-communalism-or-majoritarianism

Sundar, N. (2005). Teaching to hate. In E.T. Ewing (Ed.), *Revolution and pedagogy* (pp. 195–218). Palgrave Macmillan.

The Wire. (2018, March 28). BJP leader selling Kashmir human shield t-shirt says there's no stopping sales. *The Wire.* https://thewire.in/rights/bjp-leader-kashmir-human-shield-t-shirt

Trisal, N. (2015, November 30). In Kashmir, Nehru's golden chains that he hoped would bind the state to India have lost their lustre. *The Scroll*. https://scroll.in/article/772211/in-kashmir-nehrus-golden-chains-that-he-hoped-would-bind-the-state-to-india-have-lost-their-lustre

Varma, S. (2020). *The occupied clinic: Militarism and care in Kashmir*. Duke University Press.

Vestner, T. (2019). *Strategic security analysis: Addressing the use of human shields (December, Issue 8)*. Geneva Centre for Security Policy.

Wahl, R. (2017). *Just violence: Torture and human rights in the eyes of the police*. Stanford University Press.

Zia, A. (2019). *Resisting disappearance: Military occupation and women's activism in Kashmir*. Washington University Press.

Zia, A. (2020). The haunting specter of hindu ethnonationalist-neocolonial development in the Indian Occupied Kashmir. *Development*, *63*(1), 60–66. doi:10.1057/s41301-020-00234-4

"Legal exhaustion" and the crisis of human rights: Tracing legal mobilization against sexual violence and torture of Kurdish women in state custody in Turkey since the 1990s

Nisa Göksel and Jaimie Morse

ABSTRACT

Throughout the 1990s and 2000s, Kurdish women reported sexual violence in state custody during intense conflicts between the Turkish military and the guerrilla organization PKK. Drawing on archival research and in-depth interviews with lawyers and activists in Turkey, we trace the development of legal mobilization by human rights lawyers and activists who characterized state-led sexual violence in the Kurdish region as a war crime against women and brought cases before domestic courts and the European Court of Human Rights (ECHR). Inspired by the work of Kerem Altıparmak, we develop the concept of "legal exhaustion" to characterize the emotional and relational aspects of legal mobilization in the context of war and counterterrorism politics. Bringing together scholarship in sociolegal studies and critical approaches to human rights, we argue that legal exhaustion is productive—not just an unproductive and constraining state—prompting human rights lawyers to sustain legal mobilization in/outside courts and critique national and international laws.

Introduction

On January 24, 2019 (internationally known as the Day of the Endangered Lawyer), a crowd of lawyers gathered in the central Istanbul neighborhood of Taksim to protest recent attacks against human rights defenders, displaying a huge banner that read, "To silence the lawyer's voice is to deprive the citizen of breath" (HRW Report, 2019).

In Turkey, human rights lawyers have increasingly been subject to criminalization, threats by state actors, beatings by the police, and even assassinations—generally instigated by charges brought against them for terrorism-related crimes. Lawyers have related a feeling echoing the banner, of being "unable to breathe" because of an exhausting crisis of human rights in Turkey. The crisis is not new; it dates to the 1980 military coup and the early 1990s' intensification of the war between the Turkish state and the Kurdish guerrilla organization PKK (*Partiya Karkerên Kurdistan*, or Kurdistan Workers' Party). At the time, state atrocities were extensive and the use of sexual violence as a tool of torture was common. Human rights lawyers and activists have mobilized to expose the use of sexual violence as a systematic instrument of torture and war. In this article, we examine this legal mobilization by lawyers and activists to condemn state-perpetrated sexual violence against Kurdish women in domestic courts in Turkey and at the European Court of Human Rights (hereafter ECHR or Strasbourg Court).

Human rights defenders have demonstrated that state and military forces perpetrated sexual violence and torture against Kurdish women taken into custody as "terrorism suspects" from the 1990s to the early 2000s, supposedly to reveal ties between Kurdish women and the PKK as part of the state's "fight against terrorism." Common torture techniques included rape under custody, strip searches, harassment, and verbal and psychological violence. The categorization of state activities as "counterterrorism" has allowed the state to intentionally fail to record 99 percent of detentions in which sexual violence was used (KHRP, 2003, p. 28), so even when victims overcame barriers to reporting, they faced difficulties proving they were even detained.

It is important to note that state-perpetrated sexual violence is never an isolated incident, but often accompanies and is entwined with other human rights violations, including displacement, intimidation and racism, and extrajudicial killings and assassinations of family members. Therefore, mobilization around sexual violence, a particularly intractable harm for human rights lawyers to address in court, provides a unique window into the human rights movement and the broader crisis experienced by lawyers seeking justice for state atrocities.

Despite limited legal grounds for charges of rape in the 1990s, victims and lawyers had recourse to domestic laws against torture and international treaties ratified by Turkey. Among the latter was the European Convention for the Protection of Human Rights and Fundamental Freedoms. In 1987, for the first time, Turkish citizens gained the right under Turkish law to file lawsuits at the ECHR related to violations (Kurban et al., 2008). In the 1990s, lawyers began to bring many cases of state-perpetrated sexual violence before the Strasbourg Court, with Turkey found guilty in some cases. However, Turkish authorities have continued to deny wrongdoing, accusing victims and their lawyers of spreading "terrorist propaganda" in domestic courts and at the ECHR. Impunity prevails for perpetrators. Still, however limited the actual implementation of these rulings, international law has remained a key locus of local legal and human rights struggles, in part to connect with transnational struggles.

Given this context, we examine two related questions: How have lawyers and activists mobilized to seek legal redress for state-led sexual violence against Kurdish women? How do they maintain their legal struggle in the face of state persecution under counterterrorism laws and an escalating global crisis in human rights post-9/11? To explore these questions, we draw on archival research and 15 in-depth interviews with lawyers and activists to trace the development of legal mobilization to seek justice for state-led sexual violence against Kurdish women in domestic courts and at the ECHR since the 1990s.

Inspired by the work of human rights lawyer and scholar Kerem Altıparmak (2019), we develop the concept of "legal exhaustion" to characterize the emotional and relational dimensions of legal mobilization by lawyers seeking legal redress for torture and rape of Kurdish women in state custody. Altıparmak (2019) described the law in Turkey as a site of desperation for victims and human rights defenders, moving from one court to another seeking justice. In a similar vein, we use the notion of legal exhaustion to capture the collective experiences of lawyers and victims who are caught between show trials in domestic jurisdictions and the growing reluctance of the ECHR to hear cases on state-perpetrated sexual violence. We also employ the concept of legal exhaustion, in part, as a play on the legalistic notion of exhaustion of all domestic remedies before petitioners have standing before supranational courts. We thus demonstrate that intensifying persecution under state counterterrorism laws and increasing barriers to case adjudication at the ECHR have led to a profound state of exhaustion, as lawyers and activists experience arbitrary detention, criminal charges, and public assassinations in retaliation for their human rights advocacy.

Yet lawyers do not respond to this condition by abandoning their struggle. Rather, legal exhaustion, we suggest, prompts a search for new ways of navigating the broader human rights crisis when change is not forthcoming. Lawyers and victims seek ways of retaining normative commitments to law and human rights through which they can continue—discursively if not always materially—to challenge state violence. Bringing together scholarship in sociolegal studies and critical approaches to human rights, we therefore argue that legal exhaustion is productive—not just an unproductive and constraining state—enabling human rights lawyers to sustain legal mobilization in and outside courts and to critique national and international laws.

This study contributes to advancing our empirical and theoretical understanding of the dynamics and processes of legal mobilization in authoritarian and violent settings by analyzing the emotional and relational aspects of mobilization in the context of counterterrorism politics. Theoretically, we expand on the literature on legal mobilization and human rights in authoritarian contexts by addressing an understudied domain, which is *microprocesses* of legal mobilization (see Viterna 2013), encompassing day-to-day struggles and relational and emotional engagements of lawyers and activists. This case further speaks to the constraints and potential of human rights law by examining the role of local activists and lawyers in broadening the scope of law in and beyond courtroom battles through their conversations on the contested future of international law.

In what follows, we first develop our analytical framework of legal exhaustion and describe the data and methods on which we draw. We then turn to the history of war and violence in Turkey *vis-à-vis* sexual violence under detention targeting Kurdish women and examine processes of legal mobilization in domestic courts and before the ECHR since the 1990s. We conclude with a discussion of the broader crisis of human rights that has prompted new resistance strategies and sites of mobilization.

Mobilizing through law in authoritarian times: Conceptualizing legal exhaustion

To conceptualize legal exhaustion, we bring together two broad areas of scholarship that are rarely put in conversation with one another: (1) scholarship on law and social movements, with a focus on legal mobilization in authoritarian regimes; and (2) scholarship on critical approaches to human rights.

Historically, scholarship on legal mobilization was developed largely based on case studies in the United States. Extending studies of legal mobilization to new contexts, an emerging area of scholarship considers how human rights activists and lawyers in authoritarian states and settings of armed conflict invoke human rights and appeal to courts for legal redress, even under conditions of political repression and regime capture of the judiciary (e.g., Chua, 2018; Hajjar, 2005; Kurban, 2020; Lemaitre & Sandvik, 2015; see Chua, 2019 for a review).[1] In authoritarian regimes, litigation may also provide an opportunity for lawyers and activists to forge ties with transnational social movements that, in turn, can petition national governments to end state abuses and meet activists' demands—captured in Keck and Sikkink's (1998) terminology of the "boomerang effect" of transnational advocacy networks (TANs).

Counterterrorism politics pose unique challenges to legal mobilization for racialized and minoritized groups accused of having ties to terrorist organizations. To our knowledge, processes of legal mobilization in the context of counterterrorism politics remain an understudied topic even within emerging scholarship on legal mobilization in authoritarian contexts and conditions of war (for exceptions, see Kurban, 2020; Negrón-Gonzales, 2021; Prabhat, 2016). Comparatively, interdisciplinary scholarship on critical approaches to human rights has paid greater attention to the role of counterterrorism and global security politics in the retrenchment of the postwar global human rights regime (e.g., Allen, 2013; Hajjar, 2013; Puar & Rai, 2002). However, this scholarship has largely not placed legal mobilization at the center of analysis.

We bring together these two broad areas of scholarship to analyze legal mobilization in authoritarian conditions characterized by "lawfare" (Comaroff & Comaroff, 2007) waged by states in the name of counterterrorism: namely, "the resort to legal instruments, to the violence inherent in the law, to commit acts of political coercion, even erasure" (p. 144). Under counterterrorism laws, lawyers and activists become targets of the very forms of state violence they seek to redress, including legalized forms of criminalization and imprisonment as "terrorists" in retaliation for their legal aid work, as well as extralegal acts of torture and public assassinations.

In this context, those mobilizing to resist the state form intimate—even familial—ties that are pivotal in catalyzing and sustaining legal mobilization in the face of extreme state repression. In our analysis, we draw on Chua's (2018) framework of "human rights practice as a way of life" to examine the emotional and relational aspects of legal mobilization under these conditions, with a focus on what we term legal exhaustion: an overarching affective state that lawyers, activists, and victims experience as they seek legal redress for state-led human rights violations over many years in courts known to be dysfunctional and allied with state perpetrators of violence. In this article, we trace the evolution and intensification of legal exhaustion from initial encounters between lawyers, activists, and victims in the aftermath of human rights violations to the evidentiary challenges they face in corroborating victim testimony to the shifting political climate post-9/11 in Europe and globally that has limited the number of cases that can be heard at international courts, including the ECHR.

In cases of sexual violence, barriers to victim disclosure of abuse and case adjudication are particularly acute. Victims (as in the case of Kurdish women) may fear being ostracized by their families and communities. Often domestic penal codes require corroborating evidence in the form of clinical findings from a medical forensic exam conducted by a state medical examiner that, in effect, impedes case prosecution, particularly in cases of war crimes and state-led torture, in which such evidence is unlikely to be available (Can, 2016; Morse, 2021). This is particularly difficult when state medical examiners collude with the accused to undermine victim credibility or issue false reports to cover up state crimes.

In the 1990s, the international criminal tribunals for Rwanda (ICTR) and the former Yugoslavia (ICTY) removed consent and corroboration requirements typical of domestic jurisdictions as part of the ICTR/ICTY rules of procedure and evidence, enabling landmark convictions on the basis of victim and witness testimony that established sexual violence as a war crime, a crime against humanity, and an act of genocide under international criminal law (de Brouwer et al., 2013). Although similar procedural protections were adopted by the International Criminal Court, subsequent success in charging and prosecution has been uneven (Inder, 2013; SáCouto & Sellers, 2018–2019). Lawyers and activists in Turkey have faced similar challenges in substantiating cases of state-led sexual violence. The difficulty in securing evidence to corroborate victim testimony has become a key site of legal exhaustion for lawyers, activists, and victims in their decades-long struggle to achieve public recognition of state crimes of sexual violence against Kurdish women.

We contribute to the scholarship on legal mobilization by attending to the emotional and affective dimensions of what Viterna (2013) has called "micro-level processes of mobilization" in the context of counterterrorism and the global crisis in human rights post-9/11. This understudied side of legal mobilization offers insight into the daily processes of resistance involved in pursuing the law in risky conditions in which chances of legal redress are low and lawyers and defendants alike are criminalized under counterterrorism laws. Lawyers and victims become entangled in what Altıparmak (2019) has called a "labyrinth of law" that forestalls justice and extends legal cases for months if not years, leading to a state of legal exhaustion.

In our analysis, we call attention to the following characteristics of legal exhaustion: (1) the multiple positionalities lawyers occupy as both human rights advocates and victims of state persecution; (2) the articulation of law as simultaneously a site of resistance and a site of violence, as states use counterterrorism politics and emergency law to justify state violence; and (3) the pursuit of legal mobilization as a form of daily resistance, in response to increasing authoritarianism and counterterrorism politics. In this context, we contend that legal mobilization becomes "a way of life," to borrow Chua's (2018) phrase: a life-long struggle against a state that persecutes and criminalizes lawyers and activists defending Kurds amid an escalating global crisis in human rights. Legal exhaustion as an unproductive state constrains the mobilization of human rights movements locally and transnationally. Yet, in spite of these challenges, lawyers and activists do not give up on the emancipatory potential of international human rights law. Instead, they search for new sites of struggle outside courts to reclaim the potentiality of law to uphold human rights protections.

Methods and data

In the summer of 2014, we interviewed 15 human rights defenders, including lawyers, activists, and doctors working at human rights associations in Turkey and the Kurdish region.[2] This article draws primarily from the accounts of six lawyers and six activists who have raised sexual violence under custody as a human rights issue in national and international courts since the 1990s. Alongside the lawyers, many activists function like legal experts in supporting victims in the process of legal mobilization.

All participants had Kurdish or Turkish ethnic backgrounds. Most interviews took place in Turkish, and we later translated them into English. In addition, we assembled an original archive of published and unpublished documents to trace processes of legal mobilization over three decades, including human rights reports, feminist newsletters, and case-law documents of the ECHR. We also brought together insights from our respective projects on the Kurdish women's movement (Göksel, 2019) and the use of medical forensic exams to document sexual violence in humanitarian emergencies (Morse, 2021) to contextualize our findings within broader historical developments in human rights law.

When we conducted our study in the summer of 2014, it was a relatively peaceful period, as the "peace process" between the Turkish government and PKK was ongoing. However, in 2015 that process collapsed, and a *coup* attempt in Turkey followed soon after. In order to capture the recent context of rising authoritarianism and state violence since 2015, we conducted follow-up research, including observation of pandemic-era virtual conferences. We conducted content analysis of interview transcripts and written documents to identify common themes.

Our data cover two major historical periods: the first began in the early 1990s, when human rights defenders mobilized national and international laws to sanction the rape of Kurdish women in state custody. The second one followed changes in geopolitics in the 2000s in reaction to the terrorist attacks of 9/11, which transformed the scope of transnational advocacy networks and the functioning of the ECHR. By tracing legal mobilization during these two historical periods, we demonstrate the emergence and intensification of legal exhaustion through four stages of legal mobilization: (1) formation of intimate ties and solidarities between lawyers and activists and the initial stages of legal mobilization; (2) crises of evidence collection and courtroom battles of lawyers and activists; (3) expansion of legal mobilization from Turkish national courts to the ECHR; and (4) predicaments of legal mobilization and the opening of new sites of struggle outside courtrooms. In each section, we analyze the microprocesses of struggle, in the day-to-day legal and extralegal forms, in which legal exhaustion emerges as a collective experience of lawyers and victims. In what follows, we examine the promises and pitfalls of law and legal mobilization inside and outside the courts in the face of counterterrorism politics in a violent, authoritarian state.

The origins of legal mobilization against war, torture, and sexual violence under detention

For four decades, serious human rights violations have been a consistent feature of political life in Turkey. The military *junta*'s rule in Turkey, beginning with the 1980 *coup*, is considered a major turning point for human rights. Across Turkey, the *junta* regime employed rape, sexual humiliation, and harassment as a systematic tool of torture in detention centers and prisons.

A well-known center of torture and brutality was in the Kurdish region, at the Diyarbakır military prison, or Prison No. 5 (*Diyarbakır Cezaevi*). There, Kurdish men and women from various sociopolitical backgrounds, mostly leftists, were tortured and detained under notoriously poor conditions (see Abiral, 2016).

After their release from the Diyarbakır military prison, many Kurdish men and women held at the prison joined the guerrilla organization PKK, which took up arms against the Turkish state in 1984. The resulting war has continued sporadically ever since. The Turkish state has framed this war as a "fight against terrorism" (*terörle mücadele*, in Turkish)—listing the PKK as a terrorist organization and targeting Kurds as "potential terrorists" or "supporters of terrorism."

Raids on Kurdish villages by Turkish military forces during the intense conflicts of the early 1990s caused the politics of war to peak. The military forces detained both men and women, claiming women arrestees had provided "support," mostly in the form of shelter and food, to the PKK. Sexual violence was used as a tactic of war by the state against female detainees to force them to reveal political affiliations within their families as well as to destroy their "families, culture and community" (KHRP, 2003, p.28). Human rights activists and lawyers introduced the notion of "sexual violence under custody" (*gözaltında cinsel taciz*, in Turkish) to capture this phenomenon.

The range of Kurdish women targeted for sexual violence has included civilians, guerrillas, political activists, political party representatives, human rights advocates, and members of women's organizations. Sexual violence by agents of the state has taken place not just in the Kurdish region but in urban centers across Turkey, where the Turkish military forced Kurds to migrate in large numbers in the 1990s. Forced migration was another common tactic of war used by the state. In this context, state-sponsored sexual violence has also gone beyond violence under custody, as it occurs in public spaces and women's own homes.

The field of human rights as well as legal mobilization developed in this context of war and human rights violations in the early 1990s. Associations and activist groups, most of them with leftist political agendas and ideological backgrounds, initially dominated the field.[3] The first human rights association in Turkey, *Insan Hakları Derneği* (IHD, Human Rights Association), was founded in 1986, in the wake of the 1980 military coup. The IHD was originally established through the efforts of relatives of political prisoners who had been arrested, disappeared, or tortured across Turkey. Four years on, in 1990, the IHD partnered with a group of activists, doctors, and lawyers to found *Türkiye Insan Hakları Vakfı* (TIHV, Human Rights Foundation of Turkey). The TIHV aimed to uncover human rights violations and violence in prisons, to provide treatment and rehabilitation services to survivors of torture and their relatives, and to document the events with alternative reports to be used as evidence in court.

As the war ramped up in the early 1990s, the IHD and the TIHV began raising issues of wartime violations, but those rarely included sexual violence. It was in this context that a small group of lawyers and activists established the *Gözaltında Cinsel Taciz ve Tecavüze Karşı Hukuki Yardım Bürosu* (Legal Aid Bureau Against Sexual Harassment and Rape in Custody) in 1997. It was the first organization to bring sexual violence under custody into the public eye by providing legal assistance to those sexually tortured by state and military authorities under custody or during war, and it still operates today in Istanbul. All of these associations have continued to be key platforms of legal struggle in the 2000s, fighting against state atrocities in the context of increasingly authoritarian Turkey. In this way, lawyers' and activists' legal actions around state-perpetrated sexual violence in Turkey initially developed as part of the larger human rights movement.

To explore the initial stages of mobilization, in the next section we examine what it means to be a human rights lawyer and activist under the extreme conditions of war and violence, and how lawyers' mobilization around state-perpetrated sexual violence builds on their personal biographies and encounters with victims.

The intimate ties of legal mobilization

For many Kurdish lawyers and activists, their legal mobilization began long before their courtroom battles. As recounted in the interviews, they and their families were exposed to various forms of state atrocities. Indeed, some had already mobilized with their families beginning in their childhood. Therefore, for many of these lawyers, lawyering is a personal and intimate matter as much as a political one.

More importantly, we suggest that, over the course of their protracted, years-long legal struggles, human rights lawyers and defenders form lasting and intimate connections with the victims with whom they work; their struggles extend beyond courtrooms, and they all experience and share frustration in a way that creates a common affective ground. This is what we call the collective experience of legal exhaustion. In order to explain this collective experience, we explore the formation of intimate ties with victims because it is partly on the basis of these encounters that both lawyers and victims face legal exhaustion.

Zehra's and Eren Keskin's stories illustrate the significance of personal biographies and encounters with victims as initial pathways of mobilization as well as roots of legal exhaustion.

Zehra is a Kurdish human rights lawyer with more than 15 years of experience in human rights advocacy. At the time of the 1980 military coup, Zehra was six years old and had traveled with her family to try to visit relatives in the notorious Diyarbakır prison. After witnessing the discrimination and violence against her relatives and other prisoners, she made up her mind to become a lawyer to fight against state atrocities. She defined her and other human rights defenders' struggle as based on 100 percent commitment and voluntary engagement. Before taking their struggle to courts, many lawyers' first goal, according to Zehra, was to leave behind "written accounts of the witnesses" of the early 1990s. However, keeping and leaving witness accounts was the most difficult part of their legal struggle, as there were no official records to document the accounts of victims.

Many activists and lawyers told us that they frequently visited various parts of the Kurdish region in the early 1990s, with the primary purpose of documenting human rights violations. When they initially began speaking with victims, women's accounts of state-perpetrated sexual violence were quite unexpected. For instance, in our conversation with Eren Keskin, one of the key founders of the Legal Aid Bureau, she related her own personal story and her shocking encounter with the reality of state-perpetrated sexual violence.

A member of the IHD in the early 1990s who worked on trials of dissidents, Keskin regularly represented torture victims in court. But in 1995, the court sentenced her to two years in prison after claiming that she was a "separatist" for uttering the word "Kurdistan" and referencing military atrocities in a newspaper op-ed. While in prison, she told us, she was surprised when a fellow political prisoner approached her to tell her story of sexual violence under custody. It was the first time she had heard such violence spoken of that openly. Keskin began talking to her fellow prisoners about their experiences in custody, and she found that almost all of the women with whom she spoke had been sexually harassed and tortured under custody. This inspired Keskin to participate in founding the Legal Aid Bureau Against Sexual Harassment and Rape in Custody after her release, and to begin traveling with her colleagues to various prisons and Kurdish villages to collect women's stories.

While Keskin and her legal team were gathering Kurdish women's experiences of sexual violence, hearing and recording these accounts meant more than evidence collection for them. It involved attending to and caring for the most traumatic experiences of each victim; in turn, lawyers gradually formed intimate relationships with the victims. In other words, the act of sharing the most closely held secrets, the unspoken knowledge about stories of sexual violence, rendered the relationship between lawyers and victims *intimate*. Many victims sought familial support from the lawyers, because victims of state-perpetrated sexual violence were at times forced out of and marginalized by their families due to gendered stigma. Zehra related this as follows: "We become both lawyers and psychologists. We became their confidantes and friends. We are the ones rehabilitating them. All of a sudden, we have become their everything. This is the main issue."

Zehra's words allude to multiple positionalities that human rights lawyers occupy, and this situation generates a sense of exhaustion lawyers experience beyond the courtrooms, as they struggle on a day-to-day basis to support the victims. Because the victims share the most secret traumas of their lives, Keskin similarly expressed, the victims would expect the lawyers to solve all their problems (Keskin & Yurtsever, 2006, p. 20). Such expectations created a heavy sense of responsibility with which lawyers were not able to cope. In the process of collecting victims' testimonies, often lawyers like Zehra and Keskin became not only "confidantes" and "friends," but also firsthand witnesses of torture. In one instance, for Zehra, this meant digging up the unmarked mass graves of the tortured and disappeared with her own hands: "I carried the bodies of those tortured and murdered people. I dug those mass graves with my own hands ... with my own nails. I mean, I really did it, and digging with my own nails—that is something that I really, physically had to do."

Since the early years of their mobilization, human rights lawyers like Zehra have played key roles in discovering and excavating the mass graves of tortured and disappeared individuals across the Kurdish region. Their continuous involvement in the investigation of torture and disappearance cases put human rights defenders at a day-to-day risk of facing terrorism charges and the threat of death and violence. Zehra related, "in the 1990s, when Kurdish lawyers began to take cases to national courts and the ECHR, they experienced very serious human rights violations—for instance, 22 executive leads of the IHD were murdered in extrajudicial killings."

In the face of losing their friends and colleagues, lawyers like Keskin and Zehra feel they have a debt (Alp & Yarkın, 2015) to their friends who have suffered and died in the same struggle as well as to the victims they represent, one they seek to repay through their advocacy in and beyond the courts. We therefore suggest that legal mobilization around sexual violence emerges as an intimate and emotional, yet also dangerous, field of advocacy, from which they cannot simply distance themselves. This situation produces a state of legal exhaustion that arises from the lasting intimate ties lawyers and activists form with victims as well as their risky involvement as witnesses of state violence. Hence, the law turns into the ground of legal exhaustion for human rights lawyers, whose experience of lawyering is multidimensional and requires full-time commitment over the course of a lifetime, bearing risks such as facing criminal charges and threats to their lives. We next turn to lawyers' daily struggles around evidence collection and their efforts to exhaust all national and international legal means.

Crisis of human rights: Revealing the facts, struggling to collect evidence

Human rights violations against Kurds—and particularly state-led sexual violence against Kurdish women—escalated in the early 1990s under conditions of war and counterterrorism politics in Turkey. The increasing human rights violations and warfare constituted a crisis of human rights that was reinforced by legal and medical institutions. This crisis of human rights created another layer of crisis, in which lawyers and activists strove to collect and present evidence to prove state atrocities in and outside of court. In this context, when Keskin and other lawyers founded the Legal Aid Bureau, the primary obstacle to their mobilization was turning women's accounts of sexual violence into legal evidence to demonstrate the reality of state-led sexual violence against Kurdish women in national and international courts.

As Keskin noted in our conversation, the Legal Aid Bureau did not charge victims and therefore did not earn legal fees. Via a founding member based in Germany, Keskin and her colleagues established connections with lawyers from Amnesty International in Germany who agreed to provide funding. This enabled Keskin and her colleagues to organize visits to prisons across Turkey and the Kurdish region to talk to women who had experienced state-perpetrated sexual violence.

However, in their visits to prisons, women were often hesitant to talk about their experiences, particularly those who feared being disowned by their families and political organizations more than they feared the state, should they acknowledge that they had been raped.

As advocacy continued in the late 1990s, increasing numbers of women overcame their fears to relate their experiences of state-perpetrated sexual violence. In collecting these accounts, lawyers and activists had three goals: (1) establishing a systematic record of sexual violence to explain how this violence occurred and which groups were targeted (the record showed that Kurdish women were the primary victims of this form of violence); (2) proving that sexual violence was a systematic state tool and demonstrating the link between the war and state-perpetrated sexual violence; and (3) generating evidence to take cases to domestic and international courts. Keskin and her colleagues began working to gather statistics and publish reports based on the data they could gather, given that the majority of cases went unreported. The Legal Aid Bureau received 393 applications related to state-perpetrated sexual violence between 1997 and 2013. Most applicants were self-identified Kurdish women, and the most common reasons listed for their detention were "political-related" and "war-related."

The scope of the law that might allow redress for these women was quite limited at the time. As Keskin pointed out in our interview, the 1926 Turkish Penal Code (*Türk Ceza Kanunu*, TCK) made no description of sexual abuse of any kind; the only portion that could be described as relevant addressed "crimes against public morality and family order." For a long time, the Supreme Court (or Court of Cassation; *Yargıtay*, in Turkish) rulings defined rape as "the penetration of the female genitalia by the male genitalia," which excluded penetration with objects, which was the more common form of sexual violence against Kurdish women. Only in 2004 did the new Turkish Penal Code categorize rape as a crime against "sexual inviolability." However, lawyers told us this changed nothing in practice.

These are the conditions in which Keskin and her colleagues faced a major problem of generating evidence. More importantly, prosecutors and domestic courts would accept only medical forensic reports prepared by the Forensic Medicine Institution (*Adli Tıp Kurumu*, or ATK), a state agency. As Keskin explained, this state-run institution has never in its history prepared a report about a soldier or a police officer committing rape, so lawyers can rarely present any evidence beyond victim testimony. Can (2016, p. 345) stated that since the 1980 *coup*, "denial of torture through a series of medico-legal apparatuses, instruments, and epistemologies has emerged as an important performative and constitutive act for the Turkish state." In this context, the ATK provided a medical and institutional ground for erasing traces of state violence and, by extension, for supporting state torture and counterterrorism politics. The Turkish state completely denied all incidents of rape and torture throughout the 1990s, and this politics of denial and impunity continued in courtrooms when human rights lawyers began to file lawsuits in domestic courts and later at the ECHR.

Impunity is reinforced by charges of terrorism brought against victims, which they must refute to have their testimony heard. Yet refuting terrorism charges is generally an impossible task, as Turkish state authorities easily justify any suspicions of terrorism in court, and even "potential terrorists" can be criminalized and punished. Kamile,[4] for instance, was detained in 1992 and 1993 based on the accusation that she had supported PKK terrorists and was interrogated about the location of PKK hideouts. She was brutally tortured and raped many times over 33 days in detention (Aşan, 2010). The Legal Aid Bureau brought a criminal complaint against the police officers who had tortured her to the Mardin High Criminal Court in 1999. The trial was prolonged until the statute of limitations for the crime had been exceeded, permitting an easy dismissal, and the Supreme Court denied Kamile's appeal. Over the course of the protracted legal struggle, Kamile faced further human rights violations and violence, leading to a state of desperation. She left Mardin for Istanbul, then left Turkey altogether (Aşan, 2010). Kamile's case is one among many trials that go on for years and have, without exception, ended in impunity for perpetrators. Such cases give lawyers and victims little reason to expect a fair trial and generate a state of legal exhaustion.

During their legal struggles, charges of terrorism have frequently been brought against lawyers as well. In prosecuting lawyers and activists as terrorists, the Turkish courts, we contend, often have three main objectives: first, to disrupt the intimate ties and solidarity relations between the lawyers and victims of state violence; second, to undermine the solidarities that human rights lawyers build with national and transnational organizations and legal bodies; and, third, to prevent the lawyers from defending their clients and themselves and also from publicly revealing state atrocities.

Keskin, for instance, has been sued many times for various criminal offenses, including "making propaganda for a separatist organization [i.e., the PKK]" and "insulting the state and military officials." In February 2021, she received a prison sentence of six years, three months on charges of being a "member of an armed organization." She has recently appealed to the Supreme Court for the charges to be dropped; as of this writing, her case is still awaiting a final verdict. Although she may be among the more prominent of human rights lawyers seeking redress for sexual violence by state actors, others have suffered a similar fate, which has produced a profound state of legal exhaustion. In this context, lawyers and human rights defenders have had no choice but to pursue transnational advocacy networks and bring litigation to the ECHR, as we next examine.

Forging transnational networks of advocacy: Legal exhaustion at the ECHR

Beginning in the early 1990s, international legal platforms such as the ECHR became central sites for human rights defenders to advocate for policy changes and seek justice for Turkish state atrocities against Kurds. At the time, Kurdish activists and lawyers filed numerous petitions at the ECHR, which they saw as an opportunity to save lives and address atrocities (Kurban, 2020, p. 199). The ECHR thus came to be an effective mechanism of legal mobilization in the 1990s. However, after the 2000s, it also turned into a site of legal exhaustion for lawyers and activists.

In the early 1990s, the Kurdish Human Rights Project (KHRP) provided a stable complaint-filing process to take Kurdish cases to the ECHR and played a key role in the formation of transnational advocacy networks between human rights organizations based in Turkey and Europe. The KHRP project was founded in 1992 in London by Kerim Yıldız, a Kurdish human rights lawyer and political refugee, and two British law professors with the primary objective of offering *pro bono* services for Kurdish cases at the ECHR.

According to KHRP reports, between 1996 and 2002, 400 individuals from Turkey filed criminal complaints at the ECHR (Yıldız & McDermott, 2004, p. 13). Among these, Yıldız identified *Aydın v. Turkey* (1996) as a landmark case, because the ruling redefined torture to include rape (Yıldız & McDermott, 2004, p. 13). This was the first case in ECHR history that acknowledged rape as a form of torture (see McGlynn, 2009). Many lawyers we interviewed mentioned the case and expressed their admiration for victim Şükran Aydın's courage in speaking publicly about her experience of state-perpetrated sexual violence during a period of extreme state atrocities.

Şükran Aydın was 17 years old when the *gendarmerie* raided her home in 1993. She was detained, along with her father and sister-in-law, in Derik, Mardin province, near the Turkish–Syrian border, for three days, during which military forces raped her. She filed a criminal complaint with the Derik prosecutor after her release. She was then sent to the hospital and experienced repeated invasive "virginity checks." Aydın's family later married her to her cousin. Although her complaint incited harassment by state authorities against them and their relatives, she did not withdraw it.

One of the actions Aydın had taken with the help of IHD and KHRP was to apply to the ECHR. Her application was accepted in 1995. The Turkish authorities accused her of being a

PKK militant using the ECHR for "propaganda purposes" (Kurban, 2020, p. 173). With Turkish authorities maintaining their denial of her account, the European Commission decided to hold fact-finding hearings in Turkey (see also Çalı, 2010). When three judges from the ECHR arrived in Ankara for the hearings in July 1995, Aydın and her husband had disappeared to escape the harassment by state authorities (Kurban, 2020, p. 173). However, the IHD members found her and convinced her to continue with the ECHR case, over her husband's objections (Kurban, 2020, p. 173). Following the hearings, Aydın traveled to Europe to testify in court, and in an interview conducted by Göksel, a Kurdish human rights lawyer recalled Aydın's case as a success story,

> In court, cross-examination began. … She was so ashamed; she could not even raise her voice. She was unable to speak. I was defending her with two other lawyers. She just said, "They did dirty things to me." Concerning the UN and the Court, rape was not considered torture at the time, but we made the Court accept the rape as torture, and we won the trial.

As he pointed out, they "won" the trial. The Court did rule the rape to be a form of torture, and it declared Turkey in violation of both Article 3 of the European Convention, which prohibits torture, and Article 13, the right to an effective remedy. The Court ordered Turkey to pay financial compensation to Aydın in the amount of 25,000 pounds. The case made the ECHR a significant legal domain for seeking justice for the victims of sexual violence under detention and for uncovering and challenging arbitrary policies on terrorism.

However, the Court did not hold Aydın's attackers responsible for violation of the European Convention, and has never held individual perpetrators responsible. There is no indication that Turkey has changed its policies to avoid further legal enjoinders. Although throughout the 1990s, bringing cases to the ECHR offered activists and lawyers hope of transformation, perpetrators have continued to enjoy impunity, and the impact of ECHR rulings in Turkey has remained limited.

In the absence of other international legal mechanisms for lawyers and victims in Turkey, they continued to file complaints at the ECHR in the 2000s. However, many lawyers mentioned that they no longer had faith that the European Court can create change in Turkey. They emphasized the inadequacy of international laws, especially with respect to addressing sexual violence under detention. In our interview, Keskin described international law as having a male-dominated mentality. She described how the European Court asks for an unreasonable standard of evidence for cases involving rape. Indeed, many cases at the ECHR have been deemed "inadmissible" or dismissed for lack of evidence because victims' testimony is the only available evidence. The ECHR case-law judgments, as Keskin described in our interview, overlook the systematic nature of sexual violence. Nor have they acknowledged that most of the women who have applied to the ECHR for relief following state-perpetrated sexual violence are Kurdish.

Lawyers and activists' distrust can also be attributed to major transformations in both transnational advocacy networks and the structure of the ECHR in the wake of rising counterterrorism politics post-9/11. First of all, Kurban laments that the "golden age" (referring to the 1990s) of transnational legal mobilization ended in the 2000s, not least because the KHRP ceased operations in 2010 (Kurban, 2020, p. 222). More importantly, the ECHR stopped its fact-finding hearings in Turkey in the 2000s, lowered its compensation amounts, and applied rigid rules concerning which cases it would hear and the standards of evidence that would allow a case to go forward (Kurban, 2020, p. 223). It has rejected many cases on the grounds that the victims had not exhausted national legal remedies, referencing Article 35 of the European Convention. Lawyers and activists spend years in the Turkish courtrooms seeking to satisfy this requirement and thus, if and when they get to the ECHR, they are already experiencing a state of legal exhaustion. In this context, the ECHR has exacerbated the state of legal exhaustion by making the lawyers and activists spend years and years in Turkish courts as if their requests for legal redress would find resonance.

Under these conditions, many lawyers and scholars from Turkey have become increasingly critical of the decisions and functioning of the European Court by pointing to a "crisis at the ECHR" as well as to a broader international crisis of law and human rights (see Altıparmak, 2009; Kurban, 2020). One of the main critiques addressed in our conversations is that, rather than functioning as a supranational mechanism to hold states accountable for the human rights crimes they have committed, the ECHR now functions like "the court of states."

Lawyers and advocates also cite the rising global politics of counterterrorism in the 2000s as a factor in the ECHR's failure to protect them and their clients (see Kurban, 2020; Yıldız & Breau, 2010). Less than a month after 9/11, the European Council declared the "fight against terrorism" a priority objective and began publishing a list of "persons, groups and entities [supposedly] involved in terrorist acts," including the PKK as of 2002 (Kurban, 2014, p. 18). In this context, Altıparmak (2020) and many other lawyers suggested, the ECHR has gradually reified antiterrorism politics and related domestic laws that form the foundation of human rights violations instead of serving as a supranational legal platform for the protection of human rights.

These factors have created a multilevel crisis of human rights that stretches from national courts in Turkey to international courts, intensified with the global politics of counterterrorism after 9/11. It has become increasingly difficult for lawyers and victims to bring cases of state violations to the ECHR. Terrorism accusations have been arbitrary and have expanded to include most Kurdish politicians and activists, as well as human rights defenders. The domain of law has thus become ineffective in addressing state-perpetrated sexual violence, which has produced an acute state of legal exhaustion. This state of legal exhaustion has led activists and lawyers to become more critical of the ECHR and the prospects of international law.

It is crucial to note that their critiques do not necessarily mean they completely reject the significance of the ECHR. We consider their critiques to be part of their activist struggle to turn the ECHR into a more effective mechanism of legal mobilization. Likewise, we approach their public critiques primarily as activist acts that call on international legal platforms to be more involved in national politics to implement changes. This activist strategy enables them to further advocacy networks beyond the courtrooms and ultimately to reclaim the potentiality of law to sanction state-led human rights violations.

Beyond the courtrooms: Navigating crisis and legal exhaustion

We have so far examined how legal mobilization around state-perpetrated sexual violence in the 1990s hinged on intimate ties and transnational advocacy networks, but persistent barriers to case adjudication in national and international courts led to a pervasive state of legal exhaustion.

In the 2000s, the arbitrary politics of counterterrorism expanded, and legal exhaustion intensified. The targeting and jailing of an increasing number of lawyers since 2015[5] based on the widening legal definition of terrorism has made legal exhaustion rampant. Whether in Turkey or at the ECHR, courtroom struggles now yield very little.

Under the increasing politics of authoritarianism and counterterrorism, legal exhaustion, we propose, emerges simultaneously as a productive and an unproductive collective experience. On one hand, this experience of exhaustion restrains the scope of legal mobilization, as lawyers and victims find themselves in a far-reaching cycle of violence and intimidation, stigmatized at every turn as "terrorists." On the other, persecution under counterterrorism laws has prompted them to move their struggle into the activist realm on the streets and through protests, conferences, and press releases, as they search for new sites of action and debate the future of human rights and international law.

More and more lawyers have taken their struggle from the courtrooms to the streets, while backlash and attacks against them mount. A recent Human Rights Watch report (2020) entitled, "Lawyers on Trial," laid out the conditions that force lawyers out of the courtrooms. First, terrorism charges and other forms of harassment and intimidation lawyers face make it impossible for them to defend themselves or their clients in the Turkish courtrooms. More specifically, the report described the courts ignoring lawyers' demands to have evidence examined and tested in trials. In some cases lawyers are not permitted in courtrooms; in others, they are violently forced out. Their communication with their clients (detained or imprisoned) has been restrained. A lawyer quoted in the report described eight-hour "purely symbolic" trial hearings and added, "if a lawyer defends a Kurd these days that makes him a Kurdish nationalist" (HRW, 2020, p.6).

This is not to mention the charges many lawyers themselves face. As mentioned, Keskin was recently charged with six years, three months imprisonment; she stated that she never felt as "hopeless" as she did after 2016 (Köse, 2016). What is surprising is that lawyers still act "as if" the law functions properly (see Allen, 2013), and this raises the question as to why and how lawyers can keep fighting state abuses in the courtrooms and beyond.

Lawyer and scholar Feyzi Erçin articulated this "as if" condition in a public/online lecture by emphasizing the importance of expanding legal mobilization into the political realm:

> Because the ones who are against us violate the law and are against the law, an opposition is created here. We need to trust the law; if we lose the law, we will have nothing left. … We need to keep our belief in law. Law is also a historical document, in world history prominent defense documents and petitions have a historical significance. … The legal struggle is not always undertaken to win and reach a conclusion. Sometimes it is undertaken just to make a declaration, to make our historical location and our [political] sides clear. … I believe that the expansion of law into public space and political struggle is very significant. (Erçin, 2021)

Erçin made two key points with this statement. First, the opposition that he highlighted is not just between state officials and human rights defenders, but also between two registers of law: the law as a tool of social control and violence, and the law as a means of justice and human rights. Although lawyers experience the law as a tool for social control and repression, which in turn generates a state of legal exhaustion, they also uphold the seemingly conflicting and abstract notion of the law as a tool of justice and human rights and believe in its universality.

Second, this statement demonstrates that we cannot reduce the "success" of the mobilization to "winning" cases in national or international courts. This legal struggle, he stated, cannot be limited to the courtrooms and must be moved to public spaces and turned into a political struggle. In this way, we argue that the microprocesses of mobilization have extended beyond courts to include extralegal spaces of mobilization that are central to day-to-day resistance.

One of these spaces of struggle is press releases and protests where lawyers and activists deliver public speeches to resist state violence discursively. In the context of ongoing legal exhaustion and harassment, in which lawyers are not allowed to perform as lawyers, they feel compelled to open up new spaces of mobilization outside the courts primarily through their speeches. Just as Erçin alluded to the symbolic and political significance of defense documents, legal defense outside the courtroom also has an historical and political meaning in the struggle against state violence.

For example, in the case of state-perpetrated sexual violence, in which women's narratives are constantly marginalized, lawyers repeat their stories at every opportunity. In particular, Keskin has committed to defending herself and victims of violence by turning each speech into an act of legal defense that the courts have barred. In each public speech she delivers, she invites the public—not only the Turkish one but also the international public, including the ECHR—to take action against Turkish state atrocities. She becomes the voice of victims, and her speeches record unaccounted narratives of sexual violence in history. The communication of these accounts to the wider public fosters the creation of a collectivity that would care for and attend to these victims' voices. This form of visibility and vocality provides human rights lawyers with a space to continue their act of lawyering beyond the courts, where lawyering becomes a heavily emotional and political engagement at once.

Other crucial spaces of struggle to advance legal mobilization beyond the courtrooms are conferences and panels organized by legal and human rights organizations. These conferences generate spaces of dialogue and critique and build national and transnational networks to continue the work for justice amid these conditions. For instance, Turkey's Human Rights Foundation (TIHV) organized an event in 2020 with the title of, "Confronting the Global Human Rights Crisis: Towards a Novel Human Rights Movement," and raised many critiques, as it stated in the Symposium Proceedings:

> [A]s of today, we are confronted by the fact that human rights protection mechanisms are seriously worn out and have become dysfunctional in various ways. The abusive practices of states and the imposing needs of capitalism increasingly undermine human rights as the global benchmark of justice. Still worse, the institutions of the international human rights regime seem to have become part and parcel of the problem, [rather than] responding to it effectively. … Hence there is a pressing need for a critical assessment of the current crisis, and a debate on how to move on. (Symposium Proceedings, 2020, p. 3)

Human rights activists in Turkey have concluded that the international human rights platforms and institutions are not just limited but in fact hinder legal mobilization at the national level. This suggests that the problem is not solely based on the lack of proper response mechanisms by the ECHR, as addressed in the previous section. Rather, the Proceedings point to a more pervasive crisis of international law and human rights.

Furthermore, at the event, Nilgün Toker, a scholar and a human rights defender, raised another key question: "What do we mean by crisis? Are we talking about the crisis of the human rights regime or the crisis of human rights movement[s]?" (2020, p. 7). She noted that whenever a regime faces a crisis, a movement relying on that regime also faces the same crisis, and she asked if there was a human rights movement that has the capacity to transform this regime (Toker, 2020, p.7).

Through questions like these, Turkey's human rights defenders have created a platform of discussion, critique, and self-reflection, not only about the ongoing global crisis of human rights but also about the capacity of human rights movements to navigate this crisis. Because many human rights defenders emphasize action, they are not sure how and where to begin a "new" mobilization and to build a "new" regime of human rights. In the midst of the global crisis of human rights, these dialogues are an example of a conversation emerging from a community living in a state of legal exhaustion.

Conclusion

Since we began conducting research in 2014, state violence and torture (including sexual violence) have been on the rise. Lawyers and human rights activists have increasingly moved their struggle from the courtrooms to the streets, while they continue to be criminalized on terrorism charges. It is under these conditions that Keskin and other lawyers like her have continued to fight for acknowledgment of state-perpetrated sexual violence as a form of state violence and a war crime in Turkish and European courts. Examining this protracted struggle here, we developed the concept of legal exhaustion to capture the legal and extralegal struggles of both lawyers and victims of violence, as they move from one court to another, navigating distinct but related aspects of a multilayered crisis of human rights.

Human rights defenders in Turkey have responded to three transformations since the 1990s: first, the intensification of war in the Kurdish region, including increased reports of rape of Kurdish women in state custody; second, the impacts of what many have referred to as the "crisis of human rights" in Europe, as the once-strident ECHR grew more conservative; and, third, the recent increasing criminalization of human rights defenders themselves as "terrorists" amid rising authoritarianism in Turkey. Early on, the ECHR condemned the Turkish state, with the landmark 1996 ECHR case *Aydin v. Turkey* recognizing rape in custody as a form of torture for the first time. But the tide began to turn as counterterrorism initiatives gathered speed in post-9/11 Europe, and institutions like the ECHR, once considered beacons of the post-World War II human rights regime, began to privilege conservative notions of state security over individual human rights violations.

This study provides a unique perspective on the limits of the law as well as the possibilities for legal mobilization by examining legal struggles as day-to-day battles, an emotional and risky domain amid rising authoritarianism and counterterrorism politics. The concept we advance, legal exhaustion, takes inspiration from Altıparmak (2019), who addressed the contemporary state of legal and human rights violations by invoking the feeling of desperation.

Here we suggest that this experience of legal exhaustion is not limited to domestic courts but also continues at the level of the ECHR, particularly since 9/11. We argue that lawyers' continued efforts show that legal exhaustion is productive, not just an unproductive and constraining state. However unproductive and limiting legal exhaustion may seem, it prompts lawyers and activists to create new modes and sites of mobilization and to search for alternative ways to cope with the ongoing crisis of human rights. This search is one to watch closely, as it may drive human rights defenders to bridge the conventional divide between political and legal struggles and to generate new transnational networks and dialogues around the prospects of international law and human rights.

Notes

1. Chua (2019) argued that democratic states may have regions or territories of authoritarian rule. For this reason, she included early scholarship on legal mobilization during the 1960s civil rights movement in the United States in her review of legal mobilization in authoritarian regimes.
2. In order to protect the confidentiality of interviewees, we use pseudonyms throughout the article for participants, except for Eren Keskin, whose written permission was obtained. The research protocols were approved by the Northwestern University Institutional Review Board.
3. For a detailed account, see Babül's works (2017, 2020).
4. For the detailed accounts of other victims and lawyers, see Keskin and Yurtsever (2006).
5. In 2015 and later, human rights violations have surged in Turkey after the PKK-state peace process collapsed and the 2016 coup attempt, along with renewed wartime conditions in the Kurdish region and government authoritarianism (see Darıcı & Hakyemez, 2019; Göksel, 2018).

Acknowledgements

We would like to thank the anonymous reviewer and the editors of this special issue, Heather Smith-Cannoy and Tricia Redeker Hepner, for their insightful and encouraging reviews. We would like to thank the organizers and participants of the conference titled, *Human Rights on the Edge: The Future of International Human Rights Law & Practice*, organized in 2021 by the ASU's Global Human Rights Hub. The conference was funded by the National Science Foundation. Special thanks to our discussants, Malay Firoz and Genevieve Bates, for their valuable feedback. We are also grateful to Caroline McKusick and Imge Oranlı for commenting on drafts of this article. We would also like to thank John Hagan for supporting this project as faculty sponsor for the MacArthur Summer Research Grant that funded our fieldwork.

Funding

This work was supported by the MacArthur Summer Research Grant by Northwestern University Sociology Department.

References

Abiral, B. (2016). Silencing sexual violence and vulnerability: Women's narratives of incarceration during the 1980-1983 military Junta in Turkey. In A. G. Altınay & A. Peto (Eds.), *Gendered wars, gendered memories: Feminist conversations on war, genocide and political violence* (pp. 93–109). Routledge.

Allen, L. (2013). *The rise and fall of human rights: Cynicism and politics in occupied Palestine*. Stanford University Press.

Alp, R., Yarkın, G. (2015). Ölülerimize Olan Borcumuz: Devletle Hesaplaşmak, Eren Keskin ile Röportaj [Our debt to our dead: Coming to terms with the state, an interview with Eren Keskin]. *Toplum ve Kuram Lêkolîn û Xebatên Kurdî*, 10, 59–75. Retrieved June 12, 2021, from http://zanenstitu.org/uploads/dosyalar/Kitaplar/Toplum%20ve%20Kuram/TKD-10.pdf

Altıparmak, K. (2009). The European system for the protection of human rights in crisis: The end of the road? *Journal of European Criminal Law*, *3*(4), 4–23. https://ssrn.com/abstract=1471402

Altıparmak, K. (2019, January 25). *OHAL'de Hak İhlalleri Paneli [Rights violations in the state of emergency]-[Panel discussion]*. Retrieved January 5, 2021, from https://www.youtube.com/watch?v=zWNXGtLHikQ

Altıparmak, K. (2020, December 10). Promise of Justice & International Law / Kerem Altıparmak & Małgorzata Szuleka [Online Event]. *Hafıza Merkezi Berlin*. Retrieved December 15, 2020, from https://www.youtube.com/watch?v=ieB3jYYYLXI

Aşan, E. (2010, November 1). Cinsel Saldırı, Tecavüz Davaları Üzerine Eren Keskin'le Söyleşi [An Interview with Eren Keskin about the Cases of Sexual Violence and Rape]. *Artizan*. Retrieved January 6, 2021, from http://www.art-izan.org/artizan-arsivi/cinsel-saldiri-tecavuz-davalari-uzerine-eren-keskinle-soylesi/

Aydın v. Turkey. (1996). Application no. 23178/94, Commission Report, 7 March 1996.

Babül, E. M. (2017). *Bureaucratic intimacies: Translating human rights in Turkey*. Stanford University Press.

Babül, E. M. (2020). Radical once more: The contentious politics of human rights in Turkey. *Social Anthropology*, *28*(1), 50–65. doi:10.1111/1469-8676.12740

Çalı, B. (2010). The logics of supranational human rights litigation, official acknowledgment, and human rights reform: The Southeast Turkey cases before the European Court of Human Rights, 1996–2006. *Law & Social Inquiry*, *35*(02), 311–337. doi:10.1111/j.1747-4469.2010.01187.x

Can, B. (2016). Human rights, humanitarianism, and state violence: Medical documentation of torture in Turkey. *Medical Anthropology Quarterly*, *30*(3), 342–358. doi:10.1111/maq.12259

Chua, L. J. (2018). *The politics of love in Myanmar: LGBT mobilization and human rights as a way of life*. Stanford University Press.

Chua, L. J. (2019). Legal mobilization and authoritarianism. *Annual Review of Law and Social Science*, *15*(1), 355–376. doi:10.1146/annurev-lawsocsci-101518-043026

Comaroff, J., & Comaroff, J. (2007). Law and disorder in the postcolony. *Social Anthropology*, *15*(2), 133–152. doi:10.1111/j.0964-0282.2007.00010.x

Darıcı, H., & Hakyemez, S. (2019). Neither civilian nor combatant: Weaponised spaces and spatialised bodies in Cizre. In B. Bargu (Ed.), *Turkey's necropolitical laboratory: Democracy, violence and resistance* (pp. 71–94). Edinburgh University Press.

de Brouwer, A., Ku, C., Römkens, R., & Van Den Herik, L. (2013). Interdisciplinary approaches to recognizing, investigating and prosecuting sexual violence as an international crime. In A. de Brouwer, C. Ku, R. Römkens, & L. Van Den Herik (Eds.), *sexual violence as an international crime: Interdisciplinary approaches* (pp. 3–13). Intersentia.

Erçin, F. (2021, March 31). Boğaziçi Üniversitesi - Haklar 101 Açık Dersi - Öğretim Görevlisi/Avukat Feyzi Erçin [Bogazici University- Rights 101 Public Class-Scholar/Lawyer Feyzi Erçin]. *Vimeo*. Retrieved April 29, 2021, from https://vimeo.com/531382047

Göksel, N. (2018). Peace and beyond: Women's activist alliances under Turkey's 'regime of emergency'. *Critical Times*, *1*(1), 149–157. doi:10.1215/26410478-1.1.149

Göksel, N. (2019). Gendering resistance: Multiple faces of the Kurdish women's struggle. *Sociological Forum*, *34*(1), 1112–1131. doi:10.1111/socf.12539

Hajjar, L. (2005). *Courting conflict: The Israeli military court system in the West Bank and Gaza*. University of California Press.

Hajjar, L. (2013). *Torture: A sociology of violence and human rights*. Routledge.

Human Right Watch (2019). *Lawyers on trial: Abusive prosecutions and erosion of fair trial rights in Turkey* (report). Retrieved February 3, 2021, from https://www.hrw.org/report/2019/04/10/lawyers-trial/abusive-prosecutions-and-erosion-fair-trial-rights-turkey#

Inder, B. (2013). Partners for gender justice. In A. de Brouwer, C. Ku, R. Römkens, & L. Van Den Herik (Eds.), *Sexual violence as an international crime: Interdisciplinary approaches* (pp. 315–338). Intersentia.

Keck, M. E., & Sikkink, K. (1998). *Activists beyond borders: Advocacy networks in international politics*. Cornell University Press.

Keskin, E., & Yurtsever, L. (2006). *Hepsi Gerçek: Devlet Kaynaklı Cinsel Şiddet* [All is real: State-perpetrated sexual violence]. Punto Yayınları.

Köse, H. (2016, August 20). Eren Keskin: Bu kadar umutsuz olmamıştım [Eren Keskin: I have never been this hopeless]. *Cumhuriyet*. Retrieved March 4, 2021, from https://www.cumhuriyet.com.tr/haber/eren-keskin-bu-kadar-umutsuz-olmamistim-587846

Kurban, D. (2014). *Europe as an agent of change: The role of the European Court of Human Rights and the EU in Turkey's Kurdish Policies* (SWP Research Paper). Stiftung Wissenschaft und Politik -SWP- Deutsches Institut für Internationale Politik und Sicherheit. Retrieved January 4, 2021, from https://nbn-resolving.org/urn:nbn:de:0168-ssoar-411409

Kurban, D. (2020). *Limits of supranational justice: The European Court of Human Rights and Turkey's Kurdish conflict*. Cambridge University Press.

Kurban, D., Erözden, O., & Gülalp, H. (2008). *Supranational rights litigation, implementation and the domestic impact of Strasbourg Court jurisprudence: A case study of Turkey*. JURISTRAS project by the European Commission.

Kurdish Human Rights Project (2003). *Trial observation Report: Turkey's shame: Sexual violence without redress: The plight of Kurdish women*. Retrieved September 6, 2020, from http://www.khrp.org/component/docman/cat_view/32-2003-publications.html

Lemaitre, J., & Sandvik, K. B. (2015). Shifting frames, vanishing resources, and dangerous political opportunities: Legal mobilization among displaced women in Colombia. *Law & Society Review*, *49*(1), 5–38. doi:10.1111/lasr.12119

McGlynn, C. (2009). Rape, torture and the European Convention on Human Rights. *International and Comparative Law Quarterly*, *58*(3), 565–595. doi:10.1017/S0020589309001195

Morse, J. (2021). The geopolitics of 'rape kit' protocols: Historical problems in translation as humanitarian medicine meets international law. *Osiris*, *36*, 200–218. doi:10.1086/713425

Negrón-Gonzales, M. (2021). Countering counterterrorism: Defending human rights and challenging curfews in Turkey. *Turkish Studies*, *22*(5), 723–743. doi:10.1080/14683849.2021.1884550

Prabhat, D. (2016). *Unleashing the force of law: Legal mobilization, national security, and basic freedoms*. Palgrave Macmillan.

Puar, J. K., & Rai, A. (2002). Monster, terrorist, fag: The war on terrorism and the production of docile patriots. *Social Text*, *20*(3), 117–148. doi:10.1215/01642472-20-3_72-117

SáCouto, S., & Sellers, P. V. (2018–2019). The *Bemba* appeals chamber judgment: Impunity for sexual and gender-based crimes? *William & Mary Bill of Rights Journal*, *27*(3), 599–622.

TIHV Symposium Proceedings (2020, October 3–7). *Confronting the global human rights crisis: Towards a novel human rights*. TIHV Akademi.

Toker, N. (2020, October 3–7). Düzenleyicilikten Dönüştürücülüğe: İnsan Haklarının Siyasal Ufkunu Unutmak / Hatırlamak [From Being Organizers to Transformers: Forgetting and Remembering the Political Vision of Human Rights]. In *TIHV symposium proceedings: Confronting the global human rights crisis: Towards a novel human rights movement*. TIHV Akademi.

Viterna, J. (2013). *Women in war: The micro-processes of mobilization in El Salvador*. Oxford University Press.

Yıldız, K., & Breau, S. (2010). *The Kurdish conflict: International humanitarian law and post-conflict mechanisms*. Routledge.

Yıldız, K., & McDermott, J. (2004). *Torture in Turkey: The ongoing practice of torture and ill-treatment*. Kurdish Human Rights Project.

The boundaries of religion in international human rights law

Shanna Corner

ABSTRACT
Intergovernmental institutions constitute "ecological" settings in which international human rights laws and norms are developed and shaped over time. Yet understandings of these settings remain limited. Notable feminist scholars of international law have argued that uncritical reliance on gendered dichotomies—such as objective/subjective, legal/political, and binding/nonbinding—has stunted knowledge of these spaces. I extend this critique by arguing reliance on yet another gendered dichotomy—the secular/religious—has further limited knowledge in this area. Moving past this unreflective reliance provides needed space to identify previously unrecognized ways supposedly local and global factors intersect to shape human rights norm-making within intergovernmental legal institutions. I demonstrate this using data collected as part of a qualitative study that examined how UN officials who work with women's rights conceptualize the meaning of religion and its relationship to the human rights legal standards they work to interpret, monitor, and advance.

Introduction

Intergovernmental institutions constitute "ecological" settings in which international human rights laws and norms are developed and shaped over time (Block-Lieb & Halliday, 2017). Yet empirical and theoretical understandings of them remain limited. Notable feminist scholars of international law have argued that uncritical reliance on gendered dichotomies—such as objective/subjective, legal/political, and binding/nonbinding—has stunted understandings of these spaces (Charlesworth & Chinkin, 2000, p. 49). I extend this critique by arguing reliance on yet another gendered dichotomy—the secular/religious dichotomy (Cady & Fessenden, 2013; Scott, 2007, 2012, 2013, 2018)—has further limited knowledge about people and dynamics present in these settings.

Increasing efforts are being made to investigate the role religion plays in international human rights law and global governance (Carrette & Miall, 2017; Stensvold, 2018). Still, as with these other dichotomies, moving past reliance on the secular/religious dichotomy in investigations of international human rights institutions is crucial (e.g., Årsheim, 2018; Carrette & Miall, 2017; Hurd, 2012, 2015). This is needed to develop more accurate understandings of these spaces, including the "transnational professionals" working within them (Harrington & Seabrooke, 2020), the micro-interactive processes they use to engage in law and norm-making (Block-Lieb & Halliday, 2017), and the gendered dichotomies "structur[ing]" and "stabiliz[ing]" the broader international legal system in which they are embedded (Charlesworth & Chinkin, 2000, p. 49).

I extend knowledge in this area through investigation of the CEDAW Committee—the 23-member treaty body overseeing the United Nations' (UN) main convention on women's rights—and its monitoring procedure. This convention is the Convention on the Elimination of All Forms of Discrimination against Women (CEDAW). Its monitoring procedure constitutes the United Nations' primary legal mechanism for interpreting women's human rights and encouraging states to protect them.

For this project, I collected and examined semistructured interviews with current and former CEDAW Committee members,[1] fieldnotes based on ethnographic observations of four multiweek CEDAW sessions at the United Nations Office at Geneva (UNOG), transcripts of dialogues between committee members and state representatives during these sessions, and documents produced as part of these reviews. I supplemented these data with reflections committee members have published about their work within the committee.

I show members of this treaty body vary in their religion-related identities[2] and contextually grounded "personal knowledge" (Polanyi, [1962]1958, [1983]1966)—knowledge based on lived experience—about religion and religion-state relationships. Further, I show their differing religion-related identities and personal knowledge critically influence three micro-interactive processes I uncovered through my investigation.

These micro-interactive processes are (1) conceptualization of CEDAW Committee members as religion-related sub-area "experts" and the use of these experts to facilitate the committee's informal division of labor, (2) use of members' "personal knowledge" (Polanyi, [1962]1958, [1983]1966) to inform and filter their understandings and discussions of issues they review, and (3) treatment of members' consensus—despite their internal religious and cultural diversity—as confirmation of the cross-cultural legitimacy of positions they take. Tied to this third process, committee members similarly use their abilities to point to differences in religious interpretations and legal positions taken by states with similar religious characteristics to bolster the legitimacy of their interpretations and to delegitimize religious-based counterarguments.[3]

These processes help to orient how the CEDAW Committee works to develop shared understandings of women's rights outlined in CEDAW and to promote acceptance of their meaning and legitimacy through its monitoring procedure. They are "strategies of action" (Spillman, 1995; Swidler, 1997) this treaty body employs in both the internally and externally focused dialogues and communications central to its work. More specifically, they are tools through which this treaty body contributes to the ongoing, labor-intensive work of shaping and spreading global norms about women's rights and their relationship to religious factors within the transnational level (Krook & True, 2012, referenced by Zwingel, 2016).

I use these findings to demonstrate that identifying and critiquing—rather than simply taking for granted and relying on—the gendered secular/religious dichotomy embedded in the international human rights legal system can draw attention to characteristics of these settings and dynamics within them that this dichotomy obscures. Focusing attention on silences created by the gendered secular/religious dichotomy and its taken-for-granted status can advance needed knowledge about international legal institutions, people who work within these settings, and mechanisms through which norm-making take places within them. This expansion of our knowledge is critical to our abilities to accurately conceptualize and assess the future of international law and its practice.

Embedded gendered dichotomies

International relations scholars and those in related disciplines have built a rich literature focused on the multilayered nature of the negotiation of human rights norms and laws (Finnemore & Sikkink, 1998; Risse et al., 1999). Case-based studies within this literature have unpacked aspects of the nuanced framing happening within intergovernmental treaty body monitoring procedures, conferences, and other intergovernmental settings (Friedman et al., 2005). Still, further work is needed to extend knowledge of intergovernmental legal spaces and the dynamics through which international laws and related norms are constructed, negotiated, and spread within them (Block-Lieb & Halliday, 2017; Harrington & Seabrooke, 2020).

Feminist scholars have done heavy lifting in these areas (Calgar et al., 2013; Charlesworth & Chinkin, 2000; Charlesworth et al., 1991; Friedman et al., 2005). One way they have done this is by identifying and focusing attention on gendered dichotomies built into the structure of international legal discourse and institutions (Charlesworth, 1999; Charlesworth & Chinkin, 2000). According to Charlesworth and Chinkin (2000), these dichotomies include, "objective/subjective, legal/political, logic/emotion, protector/protected, independence/dependence, binding/non-binding, international/domestic, intervention/non-intervention, sovereign/non-self governing" (p. 49, referencing Cohn, 1993). They are "gender cod[ed]" with "the first signifying 'male' characteristics and the second 'female'" (Charlesworth, 1999, p. 382).

Recognizing the gendered nature of these dichotomies is critical. Why? First, they constitute taken-for-granted hierarchies. These hierarchies naturalize and bolster emphasis, expression, and weight placed on their masculine-coded sides while "silencing" expression and recognition of their feminine-coded sides in discourse within international legal settings (Charlesworth, 1999; Charlesworth & Chinkin, 2000). Second, they "structure" and provide "stability" to "the international legal order" and "[i]international legal discourse" (Charlesworth & Chinkin, 2000, p. 49).

Taken-for-granted employment of these hierarchical dichotomies is visible in discourse and approaches of both human rights practitioners and scholars. Smith's (2006) study of the internal work within the United Nations illustrated such limitations in international relations scholarship. As he showed, this scholarship disproportionately focuses on the formal, legal "outputs" produced by UN bodies, whereas the internal—often informal—interactions, processes, and decisions through which they are created have received much less attention.

As noted, researchers are increasingly working to counter this tendency by investigating internal dynamics within intergovernmental setting and the multi-level nature of relevant negotiations (Friedman et al. 2005). Block-Lieb and Halliday (2017), for instance, have shown the "ecological" nature of intergovernmental legal settings and the need to examine ways these settings influence the micro-interactive processes through which "lawmaking" and "normmaking" take place within them. Other recent research has highlighted the need for attention to characteristics of "transnational professionals" and their influence on work within transnational settings (Harrington & Seabrooke, 2020).

Neither of these growing strands of scholarship has focused on gendered dichotomies in their critiques. Still, their arguments illustrate the need to question long-standing tendencies to center attention on the male-coded side of several relevant dichotomies.

Another gendered dichotomy: Secular/religious

I extend this type of critique by arguing that reliance on yet another gendered dichotomy—the secular/religious dichotomy (Cady & Fessenden, 2013; Scott, 2007, 2013, 2018)—has further limited knowledge of the people and dynamics present within international human rights legal arenas.

Evidence abounds that a secular/religious dichotomy is built into international human rights legal system (e.g., Årsheim, 2018; Hurd, 2013, 2015; Carrette & Miall, 2017). We can see this in core UN documents. Both the United Declaration of Human Rights (UDHR) and the framework through which it was constructed incorporated a diverse range of views (Waltz, 2004). Still, as Stensvold (2018, p. 7) pointed out, this document "sees religion as a part of the general good but implicitly defines it as belonging elsewhere—apart from the UN context." Similarly, the UN Handbook for Treaty Body Members acknowledges that UN treaty body members hold "personal views and convictions" including "religious convictions," but instructs them to keep them from "adversely affect[ing] their official duties or the interests of the United Nations" (UN OHCHR, 2015, Regulation 2(d)). These instructions fit within the United Nations' broader framework which, as Miall and Carrette (2017, p. 220) explained, "upholds a distinction between the secular public sphere of international relations" and "a private sphere in which people have rights as individuals to practice religion alongside other fundamental freedoms."

Scott (2007, 2012, 2013, 2018) has masterfully articulated the inherent entwinement of gender and "the discourse of secularism". Drawing on Asad's (2003) theorizing of "secularism [...] as a 'myth of liberalism'" and "his call for attention to [secularism's] discursive construction" (Scott 2018, p. 6), she argues that central distinctions in the "discourse of secularism"—including the public/private divide—overlap with the "men"/"women" and "masculine"/"feminine" dichotomies (Scott 2018, p. 4–6). In this discourse, religion has been pushed into the "private" side of this divide (Scott, 2013, 2018). As such, it is further overlapped with characteristics such as sex (vs. reason), traditional (vs. modern), subjective (vs. objective), and local (vs. global), each of which have also become associated with the private—feminine—side of the public/private divide in this discourse (Scott, 2018, p. 6; Cady & Fessenden, 2013; Scott, 2013, 2018).

Scholars such as Hurd (2013, p. 212) have begun to use Scott's (2012, 2013) theorizing to "discuss ... the implications of a gendered critique of secularism for the study of domestic politics, foreign policy, and international human rights" (see also Cady & Fessenden, 2013). Hurd's (2013) scholarship fits within a broader interdisciplinary body of work that builds on Asad's (2003) theorizing of secularism and the secular/religious binary—theorizing on which Scott (2007, 2013, 2018) also has drawn.

This scholarship has made critical contributions on which I build (e.g., Årsheim, 2016; Hurd, 2008, 2012, 2015; Mahmood, 2015, 2018). In particular, it interrogates ways state and intergovernmental authorities construct and employ political power through their abilities to define and regulate the category of "religion" (vs. "the secular") and legitimate religious expression. Likewise, it identifies researchers' tendencies to underestimate ways secularity and secularism come into play in international politics and law, including international human rights.

Yet, as Omer (2015, 2018) critiqued, relevant scholarship in this area has limitations. It tends to limit its focus to state and intergovernmental-level actors and use a "power-reductionist" approach. As such, actors' definitions and engagement with "religion" and "religious freedom" are reduced to enactments of abstracted political power. This scholarship also tends to "re-inscribe" (Omer, 2015, p. 51) the secular/religious dichotomy and interconnect it with related dichotomies such as "liberal/modern vs. traditional/nonmodern" (Omer, 2015, p. 39). This creates a bifurcation limiting "authentic" religious identities and actions to traditional-local vs. modern-global actors and settings (Omer, 2015, 2018).

Thus, further investigation and theorizing that builds on and critiques this scholarship is needed. Specifically, additional work needs to connect Scott's (2013) theorizing of the gendered character of the secular/religious dichotomy to feminist legal scholars' critiques of gendered dichotomies within the international human rights legal system. In particular, we need greater investigation into "silences" fostered by uncritical reliance on a gendered secular/religious dichotomy within this system. This is important to interrogate and move past oversimplifications in the ways international legal settings and people working within them are often characterized.

Focus on the CEDAW Committee and its monitoring procedure is particularly useful for examining the character and relevance of the secular/religious dichotomy. Claims conflicts exist between religious factors and human rights are frequently identified as particularly knotty challenges for efforts to advance support for human rights standards and their protection (Hopgood, 2015). Within UN settings, such claims are disproportionately used to contest women's rights and those focused on sexuality (Freeman, 2009; Friedman, et al., 2005). Thus, "CEDAW has attracted the greatest number of reservations with the potential to modify or exclude most, if not all, of the terms of the treaty" (Clark, 1991, p. 317, quoted in Wade, 2013, p. 223). References to religion are often used to justify these reservations, as illustrated in reservations to CEDAW's Article 16, which focuses on women's equality in marriage and the family (Freeman, 2009).

Although CEDAW does not directly reference religion, the committee has delineated guidelines regarding it. General Recommendation 29, for instance, identifies reservations to Article 16 as "incompatible" with CEDAW (UN CEDAW, 2013).

The CEDAW Committee and its monitoring procedure

The CEDAW Committee is charged with interpreting the meaning of the rights outlined in CEDAW and overseeing the procedure through which states party to this convention report on their protection of these rights. Through this, committee members help to refine shared understandings of specific women's rights and encourage UN member states to "realize" their protection.

The heart of the CEDAW Committee's work is carried out during three- to four-week CEDAW sessions. These sessions center on the committee's review—on a rolling basis—of member states' reports on their implementation of CEDAW. States that have ratified CEDAW agree to participate in this procedure every four years. State representatives submit reports about their state's progress in implementing CEDAW's central articles. They then participate in day-long, in-person "constructive dialogues" with the committee.

These "constructive dialogues" make up the "backbone of the Committee's work" (Zwingel, 2016, p. 80, capitalization and italics removed). CEDAW Committee members and other UN officials identify them as one of the United Nations' main instruments for conveying the meaning of women's rights standards—including their relationship to religious factors—and encouraging their acceptance (Merry, 2006; Schöpp-Schilling & Flinterman, 2007; Zwingel, 2016).

Compounding their centrality, the points raised during these constructive dialogues determine the range of concerns and recommendations the committee includes in the 10- to 15-page "concluding observations" it creates in response to each member-state review (Boerefijn, 2012, p. 501). These documents make up one of the committee's two primary written outputs for guiding member states in the meaning and implementation of the convention (Chinkin & Freeman, 2012, pp. 20–23). The committee's less-frequently-produced "general recommendations" make up the other.

Along with these constructive dialogues, the majority of CEDAW Committee members' time surrounding CEDAW sessions is spent in internal meetings. During them, they review state-report-related documents and develop documents such as those mentioned above. These documents outline the committee's jointly agreed upon interpretations of convention articles and assessments of individual member states' progress in implementing these rights. Developing these written communications requires internally focused dialogue and negotiation to foster consensus. As committee members I interviewed reiterated, this consensus development during their internal meetings is critical: It is a central mechanism through which the committee agrees on and produces its recommendations and other decisions.

Data and methods

I collected and analyzed three types of data. First, I conducted 19 semistructured interviews with nine current and 10 former members of the CEDAW Committee. Between 1982, when its first members began working, and 2021, 151 people served as CEDAW Committee members. I interviewed 39 percent of the people serving on the committee at the time I collected data for this project and, as of 2021, 12.6 percent of the people who have served on this committee since its inception. Since most CEDAW Committee members have been female, I use feminine pronouns when referencing all interviewees.[4]

Second, I observed the daily state-report-review meetings of four CEDAW sessions at the UN Office at Geneva. I did not attend the committee's closed-door internal meetings. However, I gained a rich understanding of them through my interviews, my analysis of committee members' written reflections about their work within the committee, and my broader ethnographic observation of CEDAW sessions. Thirty-five member states were reviewed during these sessions.[5] I produced and analyzed fieldnotes about the discourse used by CEDAW Committee members and state representatives involved in their constructive dialogues. I then used publicly available videos of these meetings to transcribe portions of these dialogues.

Third, for each state reviewed during these sessions, I analyzed the state's report and related documents, "summary reports" of the state delegation's dialogue with the CEDAW Committee, and the committee's concluding observations.

I coded and examined the discourse present in these three forms of data. I then triangulated these data, which provided varying vantage points for assessing the formal and informal discourse CEDAW Committee members used to discuss religion individually and as a formal body. Finally, I compared my findings with written reflections several members have published about their experiences working as part of the committee.

Previous investigations of the CEDAW Committee and related intergovernmental bodies have delineated aspects of their members' characteristics—such as their gender compositions and typical professional backgrounds—and pointed out ways these characteristics have influenced these bodies' credibility or decision making (Calgar et al., 2013; Charlesworth et al., 1991; Merry, 2006; Zwingel, 2016). Notably, in her recent study, Zwingel (2016, pp. 76–80) outlined CEDAW Committee members' differing regional backgrounds and briefly identified their belief in the importance of their regional and cultural diversity to the committee's knowledge and sense of competence.

My identification of the processes outlined below was bolstered by this earlier investigation. However, my examination and theorizing move past descriptions included in previous studies.

Maintaining a secular space

"It's true," one religious CEDAW Committee member I interviewed highlighted, "we have a full[y] secular position." CEDAW Committee members identify the CEDAW monitoring procedure as a legal procedure in which their roles are defined by, as many of them explained to me, "their mandate." By this they meant their authority and roles were defined by the convention. Thus, in our interviews, they emphasized the expectation they felt—and held—that their dialogues and decisions be oriented and defined by the formal wording of the convention and their systematic—presumably rational and objective—interpretation and application of it.

CEDAW Committee members I interviewed differed in the degree to which they thought issues of religion came up in or were important to their work. Still, several I interviewed explained that a key reason the committee does not talk more about religion—at least explicitly—in its decision-making and assessments is because, as one explained: religion is not mentioned in the CEDAW Convention. Thus, "if you look at concluding observations from the CEDAW Committee, you will hardly find anything about religion."[6]

Related to this, some committee members I spoke with also expressed the belief that, to fulfill the role of CEDAW Committee members, they and their colleagues must bifurcate personal religious beliefs they may hold from their committee work. One member who identified as religious articulated this. Committee members, she explained, are "really professional in these respects, and they may be deeply religious themselves, but they are quite professional in terms of implementing the Convention and only the Convention. So the questions asked are never colored by anyone's personal [*sic*] as such."

Such comments echo expectations for treaty body members' behavior outlined in the UN Handbook for Treaty Body Members and the Addis Ababa Guidelines (UN OHCHR, 2012; 2015). They also illustrate the existence and influence of the secular/religious dichotomy built into the CEDAW monitoring procedure's institutional structure. This dichotomy, I argue, discourages attention to and expression of some topics and identities—coded as religious—while supporting the discussion and expression of others—coded as secular.

Yet simply identifying these spaces and the people who work within them as "secular" or as oriented by a "secular culture" is inadequate (Merry, 2006). As Charlesworth and Chinkin (2000) argued, taking for granted the naturalness of the emphasis on and visibility of the masculine side of dichotomies built into the international human rights legal system can stifle our understandings of international human rights legal settings.

Regarding the secular/religious dichotomy, this can leave unrecognized and underappreciated the boundary work and related power dynamics that take place over this dichotomy and how they shape and limit discourse and actions within these settings (Asad, 2003; Dressler & Mandair, 2011; Hurd, 2008, 2015). Likewise, it can leave unexamined the ways people working within these spaces draw on and use aspects of their religion-related identities and experience-based knowledge about religion in ways that affect their work.

Diversity within the CEDAW Committee

UN professionals are commonly identified as "global" and "secular" (Bush, 2007; Merry, 2006). Yet, as outlined in CEDAW, the differing backgrounds and characteristics of CEDAW Committee members are key components of their qualifications to serve as part of this treaty body. Article 17(1) of CEDAW highlights this, stating, "The experts shall be elected by States Parties from among their nationals, ... consideration being given to equitable geographical distribution and to the representation of the different forms of civilization as well as the principal legal systems" (UN General Assembly, 1979). Merry (2006) noted these regional differences in her well-known ethnography. However, she downplayed their importance, arguing that, despite their differing backgrounds, CEDAW Committee members and other "elites" who participate in CEDAW monitoring procedures are primarily oriented by a shared, secular, transnational culture.

Yet, along with their regional differences, I found CEDAW Committee members also differ significantly in their religious, spiritual, and nonreligious identities. Committee members I interviewed showed evidence of this: 58 percent (11) identified as religious, 10.5 percent (two) identified as spiritual but not religious, 26 percent (five) identified as nonreligious, and 5 percent (one) chose not to respond. Of the five who identified as nonreligious, three said they had grown up within specific religious traditions.

Additionally, whether they identified as religious, spiritual, or nonreligious, I found CEDAW Committee members' perspectives about religion, about religion-state relationships, and human rights were influenced by their "personal knowledge" (Polanyi, [1962]1958) about religion and religion–state relationships. This means I found their development of knowledge about human rights and conceptualizations of religion and religion–state relationships in their work had similarities with the ways Polanyi ([1983]1966) argued scientists develop understanding of modern science.

He theorized that people—including scientists—do not develop their understandings of science strictly, or even primarily, through "detached, objective knowledge" (Polanyi, [1983]1966, p. 20, quoted by Smith, 2011, p. 171, note 98). Rather, scientific knowledge is filtered through "experiential knowledge" people gain through lived, embodied experiences within physical, context-specific locations (Smith, 2011, p. 296). This includes "tacit knowledge," or the knowledge people have as a result of living in the world which they cannot consciously articulate (Polanyi, [1983]1966, p. 4).

In line with Merry's (2006) theorizing, CEDAW Committee members share some personal knowledge as a result of shared "transnational" experiences, such as their shared work on the committee. At the same time, they also have differing personal knowledge about religion and religion–state relationships based on their divergent past and current identities and experiences of living and working within different geographically anchored communities and state contexts.

Illustrating this, one committee member I spoke with identified differences she perceived among members in their viewpoints about religion and linked these differences to their varying lived experiences with religious factors:

> We have one or two people who are adamant against [religion]. They used to be believers, they were born in a [religious tradition] family, and they are fed up. And now they become completely against [whereas] the majority is more respectful without being [religious and] some are, believers, practitioners, and very keen.

She summarized:

> So we have sort of three categories of them. Minority is those who are against [whereas] most of the others are people who live with the faith [and] don't think that it clashes with their evolution, development, *et cetera*. The proof is that they are here as women and they are active.

Process 1: Members and religion-related sub-area 'experts'

UN treaty body members and others who work in key roles within intergovernmental settings are frequently identified as "experts" in their area (Carraro, 2019). Thus, CEDAW Committee members are formally identified as women's rights experts. Additionally, however, the committee also conceptualizes its members as sub-area experts, and members use their varying sub-areas of "expertise" to "unofficial[ly]" divide their tasks (Kapalata, 2007, p. 104).

In a published reflection, one committee member recounted learning about this micro-interactive process:

> During the first few days of my membership, I burned a lot of midnight oil trying to catch up with a rigorous examination of the reports. I later found out that, because members of the committee come from different disciplines, it is possible for each expert to concentrate on her or his area of expertise in the examination of states parties' reports while at the same time acquiring new knowledge of the country. This 'unofficial distribution of expertise' enriched the debates and produced a comprehensive examination of the reports before the committee. (Kapalata, 2007, p. 104, italics removed)

This strategy of identifying members as sub-area experts and unofficially dividing tasks based on this "distribution of expertise" significantly shapes how members actually carry out the enormous body of tasks they must complete (Kapalata, 2007, p. 104). Similarly, it influences which members feel qualified and motivated to take the lead in voicing views about specific issues and the deference other members give them.

As Kapalata (2007) noted, committee members identify one another's professional backgrounds as sources of expertise. In addition, I argue CEDAW Committee members' personal religion-related identities and contextually-shaped knowledge about religion are also treated as key sources of expertise. This includes experience-based knowledge of particular religious traditions, as well as of religious institutions and dynamics within their home countries or regions. This matters because members of this treaty body use their different areas of expertise to unofficially divide aspects of the dialogues and the other tasks they use to interpret the convention and assess its implementation (Kapalata, 2007; Acar, 2007).

The two main groups of religion-related experts

Two overlapping groups of CEDAW Committee members are disproportionately identified as religion-related sub-area experts in this division of labor: Muslim committee members and those from countries with plural legal systems,[7] especially when they have experience working within these legal systems.

This division of labor was illustrated in patterns I observed in the questions CEDAW Committee members asked during CEDAW sessions I attended. In line with my observations, a member described this division of labor in a published reflection she wrote about work within the committee. She explained: "[I]n its efforts to reach diverse audiences, the Committee has often thought long and hard on how best to word its comments, particularly when those [are] on discriminatory practices associated with religion or sacred beliefs."

She continued:

> [I]n the unspoken division of labor among Committee members, directing questions on personal status matters to representatives of Muslim countries, or voicing criticism of such discriminatory practices as polygamy or unequal inheritance assumed to stem from religious dictates, often fell on the shoulders of Muslim members. (Acar, 2007, p. 343, italics removed)

Here, this committee member directly identified a "division of labor among Committee members" regarding which of them asks "questions on personal status matters" based on their differing religion-related identities. Her reflection also gave voice to the fact that—in this division of labor—Muslim committee members and those with experience within countries with plural legal systems shoulder a disproportionate amount of this work.

In addition to their own sense of religion-related expertise, other committee members similarly conceptualized particular committee members within these two groups as sub-area experts who played important roles in the committee's work related to religion. Illustrating this, one member I interviewed explained, "We have experts who are, how should I say, who come from Muslim countries, and who feel comfortable enough to engage in these kinds of questions." In contrast:

> Committee members who are not coming from countries that employ this situation of plural legal systems or who do not have anything to do with religion, probably feel a bit restrained from bringing up these issues. For not wanting to be seen as critical, as Western, you know, domineering, and, because, well, everybody understands that, this is a very, very delicate and sensitive matter.

As this suggests, members conceptualize their own and other members' identities and knowledge related to religion and religion–state relationships as areas of expertise, some of which are seen as more relevant than others to the committee's work. They then use this expertise to help them divide aspects of their dialogues and other tasks.

Muslim committee members and those from countries with plural legal systems are not the only members recognized as holding religion-related expertise within the committee. However, I found them to be disproportionately identified as sub-area experts in this area upon whom the committee relies. Patterns in states' use of explicitly religious justifications for not implementing aspects of the convention make up one likely reason for this (Freeman, 2009).

Process 2: Personal knowledge as resources

The CEDAW Committee also employs a second micro-interactive processes: It uses its members' personal knowledge about different areas—including religion and religion-state relationships—as filters and resources in their efforts to understand, agree on, and engage in dialogue about how religious factors should be understood in relation to particular women's rights.

This second micro-interactive process is closely related to the first, but is distinct. The first—identification of religion-related sub-area experts—is a tool the committee uses to informally divide its labor. The second—use of religion-related personal knowledge—is a tool both individual committee members and the committee as a whole use to justify this division of labor, to delineate the positions they should take regarding different issues, and to articulate these positions.

This personal religion-related knowledge is not alone in informing members' perspectives. However, scholars have downplayed the fact that their varying knowledge in this area—and in others—provides important filters and sources of insight the committee and its members use to inform the arguments and decisions they make.

Resources for framing dialogues

During my fieldwork, I observed the committee's day-long reviews of 35 countries. Most of the time state delegations did not use religion-based arguments to challenge the application of aspects of CEDAW. However, when they did, the committee typically pushed back. Likewise, committee members also brought up issues related to religion or religious claims. In both cases, the questions were disproportionately raised by members who could draw on their personal religion-related identities or their lived, context-based knowledge about relevant factors, such as the religion–state relations in their countries. Sometimes they specifically used their identities and knowledge to frame their questions.

This was illustrated in an exchange I observed between CEDAW Committee members and delegates from a country under review. As part of this exchange, one member questioned the country's newly adopted *Sharia* penal code reinstating the death penalty, which the state's delegation justified using a religious argument. In response, this committee member said:

> I do share the views that Islam is a religion of *rahma*, of mercy, and that life is extremely precious, that this is a sacred right to life by *Allah* [phrase in Arabic]. However, I feel I have a certain, you know, problem understanding some of the recent development. … [A]s a Muslim woman myself … I'm also very much surprised that this penal code would apply to Muslim and non-Muslims, after all this is a Sharia penal code.

Continuing, another member interjected:

> [W]hile reading the report of [country] I also felt that there are areas where it … may at times conflict with Islam. Madame Minister, I'm a Muslim, and I come also from a country which is Muslim majority, [her country]. I can understand the challenges, but I would beg to differ that, you know, there is no way I see Islam as a contradiction to a promotion of rights of women. And I'd also recommend, if I could, through you that [country] should be able to see the best practices in different Muslim countries where there have been changes. The changes may have been incremental, but there have been changes towards the betterment of women, because Islam has in fact provided a lot of rights to women when we compare to pre-Islamic times, but even then, you know, we can be progressive towards that.

Both of these members made arguments focused *not* primarily on the wording of different UN human rights conventions or resolutions. Rather, they used their own personal identities and lived knowledge as Muslims and as people from countries with specific religious demographics and legal systems to orient their arguments. They used their personal understandings of Islam and Islamic texts to challenge the interpretation presented by the delegation and to advocate for the existence—and correctness—of an alternative way of understanding Islamic teachings that aligned with the committee's understanding of how specific practices relate to women's equality. They also used their knowledge to ground the legitimacy of their claims and, as several members I interviewed explained, to help state representatives "relate" to the committee.

Resources for individual members' perspectives

Committee members' abilities to use their personal knowledge as a strategy to connect with and challenge state representatives are important. They help to shape how they articulate and work to spread support for the legitimacy of their interpretations of the convention. However, their varying personal knowledge also works at a deeper level: It provides fundamental building blocks constructing their perspectives and influences the actions the committee must take to reach internal agreement about their recommendations.

For instance, as one Christian member explained, the committee holds the view that it can (and must) work with member states with differing legal systems to implement the standards outlined in CEDAW. However, she had concerns about this position. Personally, she believed the protection of women's rights standards laid out in CEDAW could not realistically be achieved in countries with plural legal systems allowing people to be held to different legal requirements.

This view, she explained, was rooted in her experience living and working to protect women's equality within her country with this type of legal system. Although the committee tries to work with countries with plural legal systems, her ongoing, first-hand experience limited the conditions in which she believed women's rights can be supported and legally enforced. It bounded the range of meanings and religion–state frameworks she could imagine as capable of providing the conditions needed for governments to enforce protection of these rights.

As another example, I spoke with another religious committee member from a country with a plural legal system. As she explained, being a member of her religious tradition and working to advance women's equality "from within" has informed how she thinks about the relationship between religion and gender inequality. I asked her how she thinks about the relationship between religion and women's rights. She replied:

> It could actually be the greatest challenge of all in terms of gender inequality. I think … men's control of religion is what we're facing now. And the key is simply … to have women enter the religious world. The way is not to fight religion, religion is here to stay. It's not going to go away, and I don't think we want it to go away. And, you know, as a religious person myself, I really believe in the value of spirituality and what religion can offer to humanity. Sadly, in today's world, religion plays a terrible role in … ongoing conflicts. [References her own country.] … So, all these are, in my view, distortions of religion.

She then connected her perspective with the actions she thinks the Committee should take in this area:

> What we have to fight for, is to enable as much as possible—more than possible—to have space for women's voices within religion. So, that when delegations tell us, "Yes, we are engaging with religious leaders to see the scope of harmonization possible," so on and so forth, the question to ask is, "Are women part of this process?"

Likewise, another committee member who identified as spiritual but not religious told me: "[R]eligion is a private matter and should be dealt with in private." This, she continued, "has a lot to do with … nondiscrimination of women." To explain, she talked about her knowledge of religion in her country and in other countries in her region: "[W]e [all] have cultures. … I mean, religion has been everywhere and religion has suffused our countries." Referencing things she had seen while traveling within her region, she explained:

> The paintings, the music, everything, this has been influenced by religion. I don't want to lose this. This is part of what has shaped the landscape, the physical landscape, this is part of what has shaped our mental landscapes. … But, what I'm saying is religious views should not dominate public discourse and should not dominate the legal forces too.

She then connected her knowledge of changes over time in her own country regarding women's use of religious clothing to her perspective about government veil banning, an issue relevant to the committee:

> I'm not one of those who feels you have to impose that women should not be veiled from day one to the other. I know from my country and from the evolution of my country that … when I was a child in certain parts of my country, women wore [forms of religious apparel]. And when they would not have gone to [religious institutions] without [religious apparel]. I don't see one single woman wearing [religious apparel] now. So, and this has changed without people coming from outside to tell our people, "Hey, remove those [religious apparel]."

As she suggested, a government may not need to make a strict ban on wearing religious clothing or other forms of public religious expression in order for these types of religious expression to decline from the public sphere over time.

Like her, regardless of their religion-related identities, many committee members I observed and interviewed drew on their experiences with religious traditions, organizations, and religious–-state frameworks to help explain how they thought, personally, about the relationship between religion or religious institutions and the advancement of women's equality.

In line with previous scholarship, as members work within intergovernmental institutions, they gain "transnational experiences" that enable them to recognize commonalities across countries and religious traditions (Merry, 2006). However, perspectives and discourse they use to talk about these dynamics are not only products of exposure to "transnational culture" or "transnational experiences" (Merry, 2006). Rather, they also draw on their lived experiences in particular religiously and secularly identified communities and legal systems to recognize commonalities and differences between their experiences and those they learn about through their work.

Resources for committee consensus-building and recommendation-making

Committee members differ in their viewpoints about how to approach religious issues, including religion–state relationships. As one explained, "the challenge," for the committee, "is how to create synergy between the rights-based approach and the faith-based approach. I don't know the answer because the committee is not always of the same opinion." As an example, she referenced her perspective about the approach the committee had taken when engaging with a particular state about its government's relationship with the Vatican.

Individual CEDAW Committee members' varying personal knowledge about religion and religion–state relationships can impact the committee's internally-focused dialogues and the resulting positions it takes in its constructive dialogues and formal documents in a couple of ways. First, it can impact how the committee talks internally—particularly, in its effort to avoid talking about religion, especially in broad terms. Second, it can also influence members' consensus-building efforts, both the recommendations they develop and the actions needed to reach consensus.

On one hand, committee members' differing personal knowledge can influence decisions the committee makes. For instance, regarding another situation, a member recounted an internal exchange in which several members were conferring about how to address an issue present in specific Latin American countries. During this discussion, concerns were raised about the role of the Catholic Church regarding this issue. She explained:

> [T]he committee discussed the situation of women in [region] Latin American countries, and the Western European members wanted to adopt a resolution or concluding observation in particular mentioning … [that] the Catholic Church [was] absolutely the culprit behind the-the discriminatory practice. [However,] the Latin American members of the committee opposed that. And argued it. [They said under] no circumstances can we mention the Catholic Church in [this document]. … [T]he interesting thing was that it was the Western European … members coming from a Catholic, Roman Catholic country who argued in favor of it. But the Latin American members […] strongly did refuse to accept that.

As this exchange illustrates, committee members can develop concerns about religious institutions or other religious factors they feel they need to address. In these situations, members' differing contextually grounded, experience-based knowledge about religious traditions, religious institutions, and religion–state relationships can influence how these issues are understood and discussed.

Here, committee members from European and Latin American countries conversed about whether or not the committee should make a statement about the role of the Catholic Church in perpetuating a particular issue. These members used their first-hand knowledge and experiences living in countries where the Catholic Church plays important roles to shape their viewpoints. Other members then took their perspectives seriously as they made their decision. Thus, as a group, committee members used the combination of their own and other members' personal knowledge about religious traditions and religion–state relationships within particular regional contexts as a meaning-developing strategy. This strategy informed their conceptualization of specific issues they addressed and how they develop arguments about them in both their internal and externally focused interactions.

On the other hand, committee members' differing personal perspectives can also impact the committee's internal consensus-building efforts. I asked one member if, within the committee, people's personal religious and nonreligious identities and backgrounds vary quite a bit or tend to be fairly similar. In response, she explained that members are: "Very different. Very different." Elaborating, she explained: "We have Muslims among us. We have Catholics, we have [unclear], we have several different—everybody's different. And we find that most of the time, religious issues come to play and can delay decision-making."

To illustrate, she explained:

> I remember when [the committee was] coming out with a general recommendation on women [and broader issue]—and we were talking about [a specific practice] and so on, and this held up the, the certification of that document. ... Because a group of us [committee members] who are [religious tradition] said they would never—in fact, some people did not sign that document. I think one or two did not sign that document. Did not sign, because of her personal belief, you know.

Similarly, in the view of another member who identified as spiritual but not religious, differences in committee members' religious beliefs have influenced the committee's stance on abortion. I asked: "How does the issue of religion tend to come up, if it comes up at all, among the committee?"

"Well, it's there. ... For me, it was quite an issue when I found out, for example, abortion" is an "issue in CEDAW Committee itself."

She identified four cases—"rape [...] incest [...] life or health"—on which committee members agree about abortion, but added that they do not agree on it more broadly. She continued, "And only in these four—these four cases—all [of the] committee is there [agreed]."

In her view, members' differing perspectives on this issue are influenced by their personal religious beliefs. She explained, "So we have [disagreement] even within committee toward [this] issue. And under this approach is a religious [pause] religious beliefs and faith."

As these examples illustrate, differences within the committee can impact actual negotiations that take place to develop country-specific recommendations and general recommendations, the committee's two primary written outputs, as well as its position on less settled issues, such as abortion.

Process 3: Comparison among committee members

CEDAW Committee members use their ability to reach consensus—despite their internal religious, cultural, and regional diversity—as evidence, for themselves and others, of the cultural legitimacy of the interpretations and recommendations it develops. Zwingel (2016, pp. 79–80) highlighted this with regard to regional and cultural diversity in her recent study. I build on her analysis here.

I found committee members often used "region" as a catch-all term that includes their context-specific understandings of religion–state relationships. Likewise, when communicating with particular states and their representatives, members use knowledge they have developed about different states in their communications with states representatives and their governments. They use their knowledge of different ways countries with similar religious characteristics are taking steps to implement the convention to challenge religious-based arguments for why particular states are unwilling or unable to implement the committee's recommendations.

In other words, the committee uses consensus across people with different religious, cultural, and regional backgrounds they encounter through their work as evidence of the legitimacy of their interpretations (Zwingel, 2016). Similarly, they use diversity in interpretations and legal approaches taken by governments with similar regional, cultural, or religious characteristics as a wedge to challenge the adequacy and unquestionable nature of a particular government's arguments when they do not align with the committee's interpretations (Årsheim 2018, p. 246).

In our conversations, CEDAW Committee members highlighted their internal consensus-building as the key way they develop interpretations and recommendations (Chinkin & Freeman, 2012). In line with Zwingel's (2016) investigation, they then use their ability to do this—despite their internal diversity and knowledge of different religious and regional contexts—as evidence of the cultural legitimacy of these decisions and their abilities to be applied to specific contexts.

Illustrating this, I asked one member how she knew committee decisions can be applied across contexts. She pointed out the committee's regional diversity and then explained that the committee develops its recommendations through consensus, explaining, "now sometimes we do have differences of opinion, as you know. Twenty-three individuals are not easy to get them all to come to the same understanding. But in our chambers we are able to persuade one another."

Another similarly highlighted members' high level of internal diversity, including their religious diversity, saying, "You know, even the Islamic people within the CEDAW think differently." But, despite these differences, "we *try*, we try to harmonize our thinking" to find "the least common denominator" in which they agree to "come up with something *constructive*."

This ability to reach consensus, even if it is "the least common denominator," she believed to be productive and valuable. Furthermore, she and other members believed this consensus-developing ability illustrates the cross-cultural validity and applicability of these decisions (Zwingel, 2016). Thus, as another explained, "[The] CEDAW Committee is represented by women from all over the world, so there is no scope to say that this is the Western talks" that cannot apply across contexts.

Discussion and conclusion

CEDAW constructive dialogues make up a primary avenue through which the CEDAW Committee shapes global norms about women's rights and wrestles over their meaning with state representatives. These norms and related indicators are also delineated within documents the committee creates, including the concluding observations it produces after each member state review. The recommendations the committee provides a member state in its concluding observations delineate guidelines it expects this state to strive to implement before its next review.

The three micro-interactive processes I identified also influence these formal documents. One way this happens is that the questions and issues raised during the committee's constructive dialogue with a state delegation help to determine the range of issues and recommendations the committee includes in its concluding observations to that state.

We can see this in the concluding observations produced after the committee's constructive dialogue with the state delegation mentioned above.[8] In this document, the committee stated it was "gravely concerned" about the government's "restrictive interpretation of *sharia* law and at the adverse impact on women's human rights of the recently adopted [law name]." It then made the following recommendations.

First, it "urges the State party" to "immediately review the new [law name] with a view to repealing its direct and indirect discriminatory provisions affecting women." Second, it recommended the government "compile information on the best practices of States parties with similar legal systems and cultural and religious backgrounds, where more progressive interpretations of Islamic law have been codified in legislative reforms." Finally, it encouraged the member state, "To undertake law reform to eliminate all discrimination against women, including through partnerships and collaboration with Islamic legal research institutions, women's non-governmental organizations and community leaders."

As one can see, these written concerns and recommendations parallel portions of the critiques members made during their meeting with this state's delegation about the way it used references to Islam to justify discriminatory practices conflicting with the convention.

Using analysis of the CEDAW Committee and its monitoring procedure, this article connects Scott's (2007, 2013, 2018; also Cady & Fessenden, 2013) theorizing of the gendered nature of the secular/religious dichotomy with feminist legal scholars' theorizing about gendered dichotomies structuring the international legal system (Charlesworth, 1999; Charlesworth & Chinkin, 2000).

This theoretical linkage and the resulting knowledge it affords provide several insights for expanding our understandings of the future of international human rights law and its practice.

Expanding knowledge of international legal settings

Developing more accurate understandings of the characteristics of international human rights legal settings is critical to our abilities to understand the future of international human rights law. Together, the bodies of feminist scholarship combined in this article provide needed footing for identifying a gendered secular/religious dichotomy embedded in international human rights legal institutions. Likewise, they enable us to see that attention to this dichotomy and to ways it is linked to other gender-coded dichotomies, such as the global/local dichotomy, fosters space for examining and expanding understanding about the characteristics of these institutional settings. This includes the people who work within these spaces and the micro-interactive processes through which they engage in norm-making within them (Block-Lieb & Halliday, 2017).

The CEDAW monitoring procedure, like other international legal settings, is typically conceptualized as a secular—or secularist—space (e.g., Årsheim, 2016; Merry, 2006). Likewise, when relevant scholarship gives attention to people working in central roles within international legal settings, they are often identified using the broad-brushed categorizations "secular" and "global" "elites" (Bush, 2007; Merry, 2006). Or, as Merry (2003, p. 945) illustrated, they are identified as professionals primarily oriented by shared transnational experiences and a shared "transnational culture … rooted in a secular transnational modernity." However, these types of characterizations leave much unexamined.

These characterizations obscure ways the secular/religious dichotomy—as part of the CEDAW monitoring procedure's institutional structure—shapes and limits the types of discourse, identities, and actions expressed within it and how they are perceived. However, the secular/religious dichotomy—like other gendered dichotomies feminist legal scholars have identified (Charlesworth & Chinkin, 2000)—helps to constitute the boundaries of the "ecological setting" (Block-Lieb & Halliday, 2017) in which the CEDAW monitoring procedure is situated and the "discursive field" it produces (Spillman, 1995). Thus, this dichotomy significantly shapes the range of discourse and micro-interactive processes through which law and norm-making take place within them.

In addition, these characterizations obscure the existence and influence of identities, discourse, and actions within associated with the religious side of the secular/religious binary within this and other similar settings (Charlesworth & Chinkin, 2000). This aligns with Bush's (2007, p. 1659) observation that, even if an "expanding, rationalist world culture" permeates global society, "claims about world culture's relationship to secularism [remain] overdetermined … while the capacity of religion to thrive in rationalized environments [remains] underestimated."

Countering this tendency, my analysis demonstrates that people who work in central roles within the heart of supposedly rationalized, secular international legal bodies can hold varying religion-related identities and knowledge. Likewise, their varying identities and knowledge can inform the micro-interactive processes through which they do their work.

Explaining limitations in scope of past scholarship

Why, despite increasing attention to dynamics within intergovernmental legal settings, has more investigation and weight has not focused on human-level, religion-related identities and knowledge present within them? The combined feminist scholarship employed in this article helps to answer this (Cady & Fessenden, 2013; Charlesworth & Chinkin, 2000; Scott, 2007, 2013, 2018).

Drawing on these strands of scholarship, we can identify a gendered secular/religious dichotomy embedded within the international legal system. As Charlesworth and Chinkin (2000; Charlesworth, 1999) theorized, the feminine side of gendered dichotomies built into the international legal system are often silenced and obscured. How? First, groups of people, language, and actions coded as feminine are disproportionately marginalized from participation or expression within international legal settings (Charlesworth & Chinkin, 2000, p. 48). Second, their existence and influence is disproportionately devalued, downplayed, or ignored (Charlesworth & Chinkin, 2000, pp. 49–50).

Recordings of many of the meetings held as part of CEDAW sessions are publicly available on the United Nations' website, as are a wide range of documents produced by the committee as part of these sessions. Nevertheless, in line with Charlesworth and Chinkin's (2000) theorizing, identities, discourse, and action associated with the religious side of the secular/religious binary are unlikely to be given the same level of attention, recognition, or weight as those associated with the secular side.

Furthermore, both religion-related identities and knowledge and aspects of related micro-interactive processes are also obscured. First, their expression is limited by the confines of the CEDAW monitoring procedure's institutional structure. Second, use of some aspects of these micro-interactive processes are obscured because they are more commonly employed in the non-public aspects of the committee's work. This is true of some ways the committee uses religion-related personal knowledge as a resource in its internal meaning-making, decision-making, and consensus-building. Finally, scholarly analysis has focused less attention on the discourse and actions expressed in the committee's interactive constructive dialogues and related meeting than on its formal written documents.

Relatedly, this article' ability to uncover and examine its central findings was made possible through the combination of the fine-grained qualitative data, including interviews and ethnographic data, it examined. Aspects of the characteristics, perspectives, dialogues, informal interactions, and interactive strategies I was able to investigate are not visible in sources of data, such as formally worded UN documents, more commonly used to research the ways international legal bodies approach and engage factors such as religion.

Understanding and bridging tensions

Challenges to the legitimacy of international human rights, especially women's rights, are often framed as clashes between secular international human rights and local religious communities and cultures (Friedman et al., 2005; Hopgood, 2015). This article's findings provide resources for better understanding and engaging with these challenges in ways that can be used to advance support for women's equality.

In her theorizing, Scott (2007, 2012, 2013, 2018) argued that the secular/religious dichotomy has become overlapped with other gendered dichotomies associated with the public/private. This includes the global/local (Charlesworth & Chinkin, 2000, p. 49). As I noted, reliance on this type of overlapping linkage is common, even in secular studies scholarship building on Asad (2003), which aimed to critique the secular/religious dichotomy (Omer, 2015). Thus, this scholarship tends to rely on and perpetuate a "liberal/modern vs. traditional/nonmodern binary" (Omer, 2015, p. 39).

This overlapping of dichotomies is common in broader arguments about religion and human rights as well. In line with Omer's (2015) critique of relevant scholarship building on Asad (2003), "authentic" religion is conceptualized as "traditional/nonmodern" (p. 39), whereas states and transnational legal authorities are reduced to "faceless impos[ers]" of secularist legal or political power (p. 39). Thus, people working in central roles within intergovernmental legal bodies are sharply contrasted with "everyday" people, who are rooted in domestic contexts and may engage in authentic "lived" religion (Hurd 2015, see critiques by Omer 2015).

This contributes to the sharp distinctions that are then drawn between the overlapping dichotomies Omer (2015; 2018) identified. As a result, dynamic, interactive ways people work within these settings and draw on their shared and differing identities and knowledge are glossed over or characterized as "inauthentic" (Omer, 2015, 2018).

My investigation challenges these overlapping dichotomies pitting global-inauthentic-secular human rights against local-authentic religion (Omer, 2015, 2018; Terman, 2016). People working within a high-ranking UN treaty body hold varying religion-related identities and draw on experience-based knowledge about religion that is not limited only to their transnational experiences. Rather, it is also influenced by geographically situated—"local"—experiences. Furthermore, ways CEDAW Committee members use their varying religion-related identities and experience-based knowledge to find solutions and consensus can provide useful insights for feminist efforts to bridge tensions over the relationship between religion and the use of international human rights law to advance women's well-being.

As this illustrates, moving past uncritical reliance on the gendered secular/religious dichotomy within these types of setting can enable us to better understand the characteristics of these settings and the internal dynamics, tensions, and opportunities present within them. Through this, we can better comprehend the future of international human rights law and practice.

Notes

1. Interviews were also conducted with other relevant UN, state, and NGO officials. These interviewed were not analyzed as part of this article.
2. I use "religion-related identities" to refer to committee members' identities as religious, nonreligious, and spiritual but not religious, as well as to their identification with particular religious traditions.
3. Aspects of this third micro-interactive process have been identified in previous research. Zwingel (2016) uncovered CEDAW Committee members' identification of their cultural and regional diversity as a source of their competence. Årsheim (2018, p. 246) noted the committee's use of cross-national comparison. My analysis increases empirical evidence of these findings and extends theorizing about them.
4. Interview respondents' names have been omitted to protect their privacy, in accordance with the researcher's approved Internal Review Broad (IRB) project proposal. When needed, other identifying markers have also been omitted or changed to protect their privacy. Both current and former CEDAW Committee members were interviewed as part of this study in part to obscure the identities of those interviewed. This article also includes quotes by committee members and state delegates made during public portions of CEDAW sessions I observed. Most were transcribed using publicly available recordings of these meetings. Nevertheless, the names and state affiliations of those quoted have been omitted to limit unneeded identification of those involved in these meetings.
5. Given the small and visible nature of the CEDAW Committee and of the state delegations involved in CEDAW sessions, I have not included the names of the states reviewed during CEDAW sessions I observed to further obscure the identities of the people involved in these sessions.
6. Analysis of the frequency with which references to "religion" and related terms were used during the CEDAW meetings I observed is outside of the scope of this article. However, as Årsheim (2018, p. 67) argued, "the frequency with which the selected terms [e.g., "religion"] have been used by the committees" is of limited utility. It "would entail an acceptance that every deployment of religion or … other associated terms … be equally important in mapping the religion-making of the committees" which "would not problematize the religion-secular binary" (p. 67, note 3). Still, for context, we can look at the frequency with which the CEDAW Committee produces statements on issues such as legal pluralism that involve factors commonly identified as religious. Here, Årsheim's (2016) analysis of CEDAW concluding observations created between 1993 and 2010 is useful. He found the committee included comments about "legal pluralism" in its concluding observations to "66 [state] reports, an average of two for each [CEDAW] session" (p. 177).
7. Plural legal systems have more than one system of law. They often include one or more religion-based legal systems.
8. The citation for this concluding observation has been redacted to obscure the identities of the people involved in this session. Bolding removed.

Funding

This work was supported by the Association for the Sociology of Religion, Helen Kellogg Institute for International Studies, University of Notre Dame, the Global Religion Research Initiative at the University of Notre, National Science Foundation (Award Number: 2029490), Nanovic Institute for European Studies, Society for the Scientific Study of Religion and Center for the Study of Religion and Society, University of Notre Dame.

References

Acar, F. (2007). Thoughts on the Committee's past, hopes for its future. In H. B. Schöpp-Schilling & C. Flinterman (Eds.), *The circle of empowerment: Twenty-five years of the UN Convention on the Elimination of All Forms of Discrimination Against Women.* (pp. 340–345). The Feminist Press.

Årsheim, H. (2016). Secularist suspicion and legal pluralism at the United Nations. *Religion and Human Rights, 11*(2), 166–188. doi:10.1163/18710328-12341303

Årsheim, H. (2018). *Making religion and human rights at the United Nations.* Walter de Gruyter. doi:10.1515/9783110478068

Asad, T. (2003). *Formations of the secular: Christianity, Islam, modernity.* Stanford University Press. doi:10.1515/9780804783095

Boerefijn, I. (2012). Article 17. In M. A. Freeman, C. Chinkin, & B. Rudolf (Eds.), *The UN Convention on the Elimination of All Forms of Discrimination Against Women* (pp. 475–487). Oxford University Press.

Block-Lieb, S., & Halliday, T. C. (2017). *Global lawmakers: International organizations in the crafting of world markets.* Cambridge University Press. doi:10.1017/9781316941508

Bush, E. L. (2007). Measuring religion in global civil society. *Social Forces, 85*(4), 1645–1665. doi:10.1353/sof.2007.0063

Cady, L. E., & T. Fessenden (Eds.). (2013). *Religion, the secular, and the politics of sexual difference.* Columbia University Press.

Calgar, G., Prügl, E., & Zwingel, S. (Eds.). (2013). *Feminist strategies in international governance.* Routledge. doi:10.4324/9780203094969

Carrette, J., & Miall, H. (Eds.). (2017). *Religion, NGOs, and the United Nations: Visible and invisible actors in power.* Bloomsbury.

Carraro, V. (2019). Electing the experts: Expertise and independence in the UN human rights treaty bodies. *European Journal of International Relations, 25*(3), 826–851. doi:10.1177/1354066118819138

Charlesworth, H., & Chinkin, C. (2000). *The boundaries of international law: A feminist analysis.* Manchester University Press. doi:10.2307/2661427

Charlesworth, H. (1999). Feminist methods in international law. *American Journal of International Law, 93*(2), 379–394. doi:10.2307/2997996

Charlesworth, H., Chinkin, C., & Wright, S. (1991). Feminist approaches to international law. *American Journal of International Law, 85*(4), 613–645. doi:10.2307/2203269

Chinkin, C., & Freeman, M. A. (2012). Introduction. In M. A. Freeman, C. Chinkin, & B. Rudolf (Eds.), *The UN Convention on the Elimination of All Forms of Discrimination Against Women: A commentary* (pp. 2–32). Oxford University Press.

Cohn, C. (1993). Wars, wimps, and women. In M. Cooke & A. Woollacott (Eds.), *Gendering war talk* (pp. 227–246). Princeton University Press.

Clark, B. (1991). The Vienna convention reservations regime and the Convention on Discrimination against Women. *American Journal of International Law, 85*(2), 281–321. doi:10.2307/2203063

Dressler, M., & Mandair, A. (2011). *Secularism and religion-making.* Oxford University Press.

Friedman, E. J., Hochstetler, K., & Clark, A. (2005). *Sovereignty, democracy, and global civil society: State-society relations at UN world conferences.* SUNY Press.

Freeman, M. A. (2009). *Reservations to CEDAW. Division of policy and practice.* UNICEF.

Finnemore, M., & Sikkink, K. (1998). International norm dynamics and political change. *International Organization, 52*(4), 887–917. doi:10.1162/002081898550789

Harrington, B., & Seabrooke, L. (2020). Transnational professionals. *Annual Review of Sociology, 46*(1), 399–417. doi:10.1146/annurev-soc-112019-053842

Hopgood, S. (2015). *The endtimes of human rights.* Cornell University Press.

Hurd, E. S. (2008). *The Politics of secularism in international relations.* Princeton University Press.

Hurd, E. S. (2012). International politics after secularism. *Review of International Studies, 38*(5), 943–961. doi:10.1017/S0260210512000411

Hurd, E. S. (2013). Rescued by law? In L. E. Cady & T. Fessenden (Eds.), *Religion, the secular, and the politics of sexual difference* (pp. 211–228). Columbia University Press.

Hurd, E. S. (2015). *Beyond religious freedom: The new global politics of religion.* Princeton University Press.

Kapalata, C. (2007). Personal reflection: Persistent discrimination. In H. B. Schöpp-Schilling & C. Flinterman (Eds.), *The circle of empowerment: Twenty-five years of the UN Convention on the Elimination of All Forms of Discrimination Against Women.* (pp. 104–105). The Feminist Press.

Krook, M. L., & True, J. (2012). Rethinking the life cyles of international norms: The United Nations and the global promotion of gender equality. *European Journal of International Relations, 18*(1), 103–127. doi:10.1177/1354066110380963

Mahmood, S. (2015). *Religious difference in a secular age: A minority report.* Princeton University Press. doi:10.2307/j.ctvc77k82

Merry, S. E. (2003). Constructing a global law—Violence against women and the rights system. *Law Social Inquiry, 28*(4), 941–978. doi:10.1111/j.1747-4469.2003.tb00828.x

Merry, S. E. (2006). *Human rights and gender violence: Translating international law into local justice.* University of Chicago Press.

Miall, H. and J. Carrette (2017). Conclusion: Diplomacy, state power and irrational religion. In J. Carrette & H. Miall (Eds.), *Religion, NGOs and the United Nations* (217–234). Bloomsbury.

Omer, A. (2015). Modernists despite themselves: The phenomenology of the secular and the limits of critique as an instrument of change. *Journal of the American Academy of Religion, 83*(1), 27–71. doi:10.1093/jaarel/lfu081

Omer, A. (2018). When "good religion" is good. *Journal of Religious and Political Practice, 4*(1), 122–136. doi:10.1080/20566093.2017.1396089

Polanyi, M. [1962](1958). *Personal knowledge: Towards a post-critical philosophy.* University of Chicago Press.

Polanyi, M. [1983](1966). *The tacit dimension.* Peter Smith.

Risse, T., Ropp, S. C., & Sikkink, K. (Eds.). (1999). *The power of human rights: International norms and domestic change.* Cambridge University Press. doi:10.1017/CBO9780511598777

Schöpp-Schilling, H. B., & Flinterman, C. (2007). *The circle of empowerment: Twenty-five years of the UN Convention on the Elimination of All Forms of Discrimination Against Women..* The Feminist Press.

Scott, J. W. (2007). *Politics of the veil.* Princeton University Press.

Scott, J. W. (2012). *The fantasy of feminist history.* Duke University Press. https://doi.org/10.1215/9780822394730

Scott, J. W. (2013). Secularism and gender equality. In L. E. Cady & T. Fessenden (Eds.), *Religion, the secular, and the politics of sexual difference* (pp. 35–47). Columbia University Press.

Scott, J. W. (2018). *Sex and secularism.* Princeton University Press.

Smith, C. B. (2006). *Politics and process at the United Nations: The global dance.* Lynee Rienner Publishers.

Smith, C. (2011). *What is a person?* University of Chicago Press.

Spillman, L. (1995). Culture, social structures, and discursive fields. *Current Perspectives in Theory, 15*(1), 129–154.

Stensvold, A. (2018). *Religion, state, and the United Nations: Value politics.* Routledge. doi:10.1093/jcs/csy071

Swidler, A. (1997). *Talk of love: How culture matters.* University of Chicago Press.

Terman, R. (2016). Islmophobia, feminism, and the politics of critique. *Theory, Culture & Society, 33*(2), 77–102. doi:10.1177/0263276415590236

UN CEDAW. (2013). *General recommendation on article 16 of the Convention on the Elimination of All Forms of Discrimination Against Women.* Economic consequences of marriage, family relations and their dissolution. CEDAW/C/GC/29.

UN General Assembly. (1979). *Convention on the Elimination of All Forms of Discrimination Against Women.* 1979. G.A. res. 34/180. 34 U.N. GAOR Supp. (No. 46) at 193. Entered into force 1981. A/34/46.

UN OHCHR. (2012). *Addis Ababa Guidelines on the independence and impartiality of members of the human rights treaty bodies.* HRI/MC/2012.

UN OHCHR. (2015). *Handbook for human rights treaty body members.* HR/PUB/15/2.

Wade, C. M. (2013). Government respect for gendered rights: *The UN Convention on the Elimination of All Forms of Discrimination Against Women,* 1991–2004. *International Studies Quarterly, 57,* 233–249.

Waltz, S. (2004). Universal human rights: The contributions of Muslim states. *Human Rights Quarterly, 26*(4), 799–844. doi:10.1353/hrq.2004.0059

Zwingel, S. (2016). *Translating international women's rights: The CEDAW Convention in context.* Palgrave Macmillan.

Disentangling gendered peace: Observing gendered peace in policy

Anntiana Maral Sabeti

ABSTRACT

Understanding where and how to bolster human rights is arguably the underlying motivation of most research in human rights and the greater field of political science. Increasingly, an emphasis on gender has been shown to prevent conflict and reinforce peace, thus demonstrating how a reinforcement of women's rights benefits the sustainment of peace. Despite increasing evidence for this phenomenon, scholars have not fully explored the mechanisms through which a focus on women fosters and preserves peace. Using extant literature on women and peace, I identify two sets of policy instruments that may be more effectual than others in establishing gendered peace and preventing states from relapsing into conflict. I further categorize the policies into high-level and targeted policies and hypothesize that, contrary to intuition, high-level policies could be more effective at generating gendered peace. I test the models for each instrument using an updated version of the PAX-Gender database and find that more high-level gender policies are linked to longer-lasting peace treaties.

Presenting women as the keystone of peace is not a novel concept. The notion that women are more inclined to create peace and more adept at cultivating it is a narrative that has presented itself across time and cultures (Charlesworth, 2008). From Queen Esther's mythic ability to temper Ahasuerus's genocidal tendencies to Athena's mitigating influence on the Trojan war, there are embedded cross-cultural foundations for the perception that women have unique capabilities in resolving conflict and fostering peace. In practice, the relationship between gender inclusivity and resolving conflict has been so routinely observed that it has earned the label of "gendered peace" by political scientists (Early, 1995; Peterson & Tickner, 1993). In assigning a specific term, scholars and peace practitioners have formally recognized the gender-based phenomena linking women to the facilitation of peace and also the relationship between overall gender equality and resilient peace in societies (Björkdahl, 2012; Ellerby, 2013; Peterson & Tickner, 1993; Tickner, 1992).[1]

Over time, this relationship between women and peace has been formally institutionalized by the international community. Beginning with the Beijing platform in 1995 and reaffirmed as a priority in the Millennium Development Goals, the benefits and necessity of including women in conflict resolution and postconflict reconstruction were cemented with UN Security Council Resolution 1325, 21 years ago (Porter, 2003). Today, it is almost universally agreed on that incorporating women, physically through gender balancing[2] or thematically through gender mainstreaming,[3] results in a more resilient and robust peace in postconflict settings (Basini, 2013; Caprioli, 2000, 2005; Ellerby, 2013; Gizelis, 2009, 2011; Gizelis & Pierre, 2013).

Although the anecdotal, historical evidence indicates support for gendered peace theory, quantitative evidence is still limited. This is generally a consequence of limited data availability in conflict databases. Because gender is still considered a niche variable and not a standard indicator, it is sparingly recorded in most conflict databases, if at all. Scholars interested in delving past the observational evidence for gendered peace theory and looking to establish quantitative relationships are hard-pressed to find data for their intended research (Charlesworth, 2008; Gizelis, 2011; Tickner, 2005; Wood & Ramirez, 2018). Due to this limited availability, studies exploring the effect of women and gender often have little choice but to rely on proxy measures to evaluate the influence of women on peace (Nagel, 2021; Shair-Rosenfield & Wood, 2017; Wood & Ramirez, 2018). Such research is then handicapped in its explanatory capabilities, and this restriction has curbed quantitative exploration into the capacities of gendered peace theory.

However, unpacking this relationship is important to the academic and policy worlds. As it stands, we still do not have a clear understanding of the underlying mechanisms of this relationship. The inclusion of women seems to bolster peace efforts, but what is it that women specifically bring to the table that reinforces peace following conflict? How does gender peace manifest itself and, more exactly, what types of policies help to facilitate it? To answer this question, this article considers the various ways gendered peace can be applied to peace treaties. Using an updated version of the University of Edinburgh's Gender-PAX database, I test what type of gender inclusive policies implemented postconflict are associated with longer-lasting peace treaties and may be effective policy mechanisms to leverage the capacities outlined in gendered peace theory. This article thus contributes to the growing understanding of the capacities of gendered peace by exploring which particular gender variables matter in the durability of peace treaties. It does this by identifying what gendered peace would look like as a policy instrument, and this operationalization then allows me to test if these policies are indeed correlated with longer-lasting peace treaties that avoid conflict relapse.

Literature review

Gendered peace theory

Setting aside cross-cultural oral traditions about the ability of women to cultivate peace over the more bellicose instincts of their male counterparts, feminist scholars across a multitude of disciplines in the 1980s looked to move beyond anecdotes and uncover systematic evidence of these intuited capabilities (Early, 1995). Feminist historians such as Barbara Steinson, Harriet Alonso, Sandi Cooper, and Amy Swerdlow began rediscovering the ways women interact with conflict by revisiting the work of early women's groups that formed in the nineteenth century to champion humanitarian issues, including abolitionism and women's suffrage (Early, 1995). In particular, these historians found that, during the interwar period, idealism and the pacifist beliefs espoused by the newborn League of Nations proved amenable to the inclusion of women because of the demonstrated ability of earlier women's groups to enact change (Early, 1995). This formal recognition of the international community resulted in the development of an institution highlighting the relationship between women and peace in 1919: the Women's International League for Peace and Freedom (WILPF). WILPF and other interwar women's peace organizations shared common roots in Marxist–feminism and the conviction that women hold unique capabilities when it comes to conflict prevention and deescalation. Drawing on traditional gender roles, these groups branded themselves the "mother-half of humanity," and sought to exploit their exclusive endowments for peace (Early, 1995).

Later, political scientists including Ann Tickner (1992) and Cynthia Enloe (1990) continued this line of research by exploring the concept feminist peace within the discipline of international relations. This new spotlight on women did not occur by chance. Scholarly attention to women and conflict followed two decades of advancements in women's rights in both the Global North and South. It also reflected new institutional attention toward gender equality, including the UN designation of the Decade for Women (1975–1985; see Early, 1995; Peace Women, 2002). Furthermore, a series of decolonialization and Cold-War-related conflicts provided ample case studies for scholars to explore the novel ways in which women interact with conflict (Early, 1995; Tickner, 1992). Enloe (1990) and Tickner (1992) set the stage for the discussion on women and conflict by positing that, in order to genuinely understand conflict and approach peacebuilding in a comprehensive way, both scholars and policymakers must consider the experiences of women. By overlooking this relationship, experts and decision makers hold only a limited understanding of the field that is unreliable because of the lopsided representation bias.

Theorizing gendered peace theory

Scholars have generally hypothesized three ways in which the inclusion of gender positively reinforces peace: (1) Social gender equality reduces violence against women and thus calms more bellicose urges toward violence of society at large; (2) women's inclusion into positions of power provides for alternatives to the gendered "warrior" role of the state and allows governing bodies to consider alternative forms of action in *lieu* of conflict; and (3) gender inclusivity relaxes firm gender roles that prioritize traditional, masculine warrior approaches over nurturing mother ideals (Karim & Hill, 2018; Nagel, 2019).

Each hypothesis attempts to theorize and operationalize the ways in which women affect peace, but there is a lack of clarity. The theories overlap significantly and are nebulous in their generalized arguments, which do not clearly disentangle what women precisely bring to the table that buttresses peace efforts. Without research that more precisely operationalizes instruments of gender inclusivity, research on the subject is scattered, with empirical investigations using anything from fertility rates, political representation, to education levels to measure gender for the sake of measuring women's influence on conflict and peace (Gizelis & Pierre, 2013; Nagel, 2019).

The absence of more precise theorization and operationalization for measuring the capacity of gendered peace presents a challenge for drawing broader conclusions about the relationship between women and peace. To that end, qualitative and quantitative political science literature has increasingly documented the association between women, women's groups, women's rights, and the cultivation of peace, particularly in postconflict contexts. With the rise in intractable ethnic conflicts and civil wars in the 1990s and 2000s—most notably in Rwanda, Syria, and the Former Yugoslavia—scholars have been able to consider the different geographic areas, contexts, and ways in which women—and a focus on women's rights—incubate peace.

Participation

The most straightforward explanation for women's influence on the resiliency of peace is simply their participation and presence. A growing body of research indicates the importance of giving women ownership of postconflict peace processes. Apart from this human rights argument that suggests women who have equitable input and access to the decision-making process in postconflict settings contribute to more durable peace, functionalist arguments also exist to justify women's participation because of the beneficial outcomes they produce, most notably in maintaining peace.

Early scholars in the field noted the fact that women generally are excluded from political decision-making processes (Porter, 2003). Yet despite this limitation, women outside of formal peace processes still routinely insert themselves into the process and ultimately play dynamic roles in peacebuilding in civil society. Indeed, the presence of women in informal, or "Track II," peace processes is quite notable. Nearly three-fourths of identifiable informal peace processes have clear evidence of involvement from women's groups (Dayal & Christien, 2020). Through Track II participation, women access informal channels to the United Nations and other organizations, work to legitimatize formal negotiations, organize peace efforts, advocate for the inclusion of women's rights issues in final peace agreements, monitor and deliver information on human rights violations to actors in the formal peace process, engage in local conflict resolution, and act as general advocates of peace (Dayal & Christien, 2020).

This informal but critical intervention on the part of women has been observed in a variety of conflicts and played a substantial role in drawing warring factions to the table. In Liberia, it was not the United Nations or regional organizations that facilitated peace talks between the authoritarian government and rebels but, rather, the Women in Peacebuilding Network (WIPNET), an organization that developed as a natural progression of the existing work women were doing in Liberia prior to the conflict, under the banner of authority as "wives" and "mothers" of society (Basini, 2013; Gizelis, 2011).

Paffenholz (2016) also observed the power of women's informal participation in peace processes. In her cross-sectional study, she found that women make substantial contributions to peacemaking and constitution-making negotiations. Women also play a key role in securing the implementation of final agreements—even when their participation is challenged or met with indifference by negotiating parties and mediators (Paffenholz et al., 2016). In fact, the participation of women is positively correlated with agreements being reached and implemented. More specifically, where local women's groups are able to exercise strong influence on a negotiation process, the chances of a final agreement being reached are much higher than in those cases in which women's influence is moderate, weak, or nonexistent (Paffenholz et al., 2016).

Evidence from key field cases support these findings. In the now defunct Afghan peace agreement, informal women's groups and female civil society leaders played a significant role in the creation of the new Afghan government following the US invasion (Barr, 2020; Ferguson, 2019; Sultan, 2005). The agency of Afghan women and their ability to carve out a space for themselves in the peace process was particularly remarkable given the dramatic gender inequalities they faced in Afghan society. However, it was from this deep disparity that women were able to organize and impose themselves into the international process.

The barring of women by the Taliban from most employment and secondary education paradoxically had the effect of creating Afghan women activists and groups under the Taliban. The underground schools and literacy programs these women established to side-step Taliban prohibitions on women and girls evolved into many of the nongovernmental organizations (NGOs) in Kabul that helped secure the cooperation of diverse factions and create a power-sharing government through the Bonn Agreement (Barr, 2020; Mckay, 2004). Although this government has now collapsed, the ability of Afghan women to participate and help procure peace despite their virtual nonexistence in Afghan politics during the decades prior is noteworthy.

Women are not always relegated to the informal space: Their formal participation in government has also been found to foment peace. Melander (2005) found that more equal societies with higher proportions of women in parliament are less likely to experience violence against personal integrity rights by the state (i.e., fewer political imprisonments, torture, killings, and disappearances). Bjarnegåd and Melander (2011) suggested that the participation of women may be a keystone for establishing successful democracies. The authors found that democracy can facilitate peace but only through an interaction with political gender equality, such that more democratic societies are more peaceful only if they are accompanied by efforts to augment gender equality. They hypothesized this is because the introduction of gender equality abates cultures of militarized masculinity that can persist within democratic institutions (Bjarnegård & Melander, 2011).

Gizelis (2009) also agreed that states in which women experience greater political representation are less likely to become involved in conflict. She argued that this is a function of the United Nations having more sources of social capital to draw on when implementing peace processes. More acutely, in societies in which women have relatively higher status, women wield more opportunities to have a say in the peacemaking process as well as generate broad domestic support for exogenous peacekeeping operations. The higher level of participation produced by women in turn means that UN peacekeeping operations have a larger body of social capital they can tap into and suggests greater prospects for success missions (Gizelis, 2009).

Shair-Rosenfield and Wood (2017) similarly suggested that increasing female participation helps maintain peace. Moreover, augmenting the proportion of female representatives in a national legislature prolongs peace following a negotiated settlement. The authors credited this finding of increased female representation in legislature securing such an outcome through two mechanisms. First, female legislators will prioritize social welfare spending over military spending. This both mitigates the militarized masculinity of the state and bolsters the well-being of society by stymying socio-economic pitfalls that may lead to conflict relapse. Second, the inclusion of women increases public perceptions of good governance and the credibility of political elites (Funk et al., 2021; Hinojosa & Kittilson, 2020; Shair-Rosenfield & Wood, 2017).

Yet the physical presence of women alone may not be enough to inject gendered peace into a society, and we may need to look beyond participation to gauge the influence women actually hold. Bjarnegård and Melander (2013) cautioned that the ideology of a state can confound understandings of gendered peace. For example, many East Asian states reflect high levels of women in the legislature but do not necessarily have more peaceful societies. The authors suggested that this does not indicate the inefficacy of the influence of women or gendered peace at large, but is the result of vestiges of communist ideologies in the foundations of these governments that place women into office without permitting them any true power to influence, because social norms on gender equality are still lagging (Bjarnegård & Melander, 2013).

Indeed, how women are included seems to matter significantly to the magnitude of their influence. Ellerby (2016) corroborated this intuition. Women's presence alone is not enough to ensure the fruits of gendered peace. She found that the efficacy of women "at the table" is conditioned by the agenda and the advocacy capabilities they have to act on behalf of women in a process that sees women's issues as central to larger objectives (Ellerby, 2016).

Violence against women

Levels of violence against women in society is another factor that has been suggested to indicate the manifestation of gendered peace theory. Here, researchers have found a connection between the experience of women in a society and the inclination of a state to preserve peace (Hudson et al., 2009). Research has found a positive relationship between the physical security of women and state peacefulness, independent of a state's level of democracy, level of economic development, and civilizational identity (Hudson et al., 2009). This infers that where women's rights and physical security are ensured, the state will be less likely to engage in conflict and more likely to exercise peaceful strategies (Hudson et al., 2009). Furthermore, the security of women is a vital factor in maintaining the security of the state, implying it is in the best interest of the state to protect and promote the status of women in order to preserve the security of the state (Hudson et al., 2009). Correspondingly, states in which women experience higher levels of gender-based violence naturally impede the expression of women. Therefore, gendered peace is unlikely to appear in such settings because the conduits through which it would manifest itself are under attack.

Equality

General levels of gender equality in a society have also been shown to have an impact on the ability of the state to maintain peace. Caprioli and Boyer (2001) found that states characterized by higher levels of gender equality use less violence during crises than those with lower levels of gender equality. Moreover, Caprioli (2005) found that domestic gender equality has an impact on the level of violence employed by a state in international conflict. The pattern holds within states as well: States characterized by higher levels of gender inequality are more likely to experience intra-state conflict.

Nagel (2021) unpacked this relationship further and found that micro-level gender relations may shape state preferences. States that exhibit more patriarchal gender relations in daily society will give preference to masculine approaches over feminine approaches (Nagel, 2021). This exclusion of women from full participation in public life institutionalizes violence as the preferred method of managing conflict, and this behavior creeps into the propensity of the state to negotiate with rebels (Nagel, 2021). States with more patriarchal attitudes are less likely to engage in nonviolent negotiations with rebels and are, instead, more likely to employ violence as a means of conflict resolution.

Although less concrete, social levels of gender equality seem to influence the attitudes of a state and its likelihood to maintain peace over conflict. This relationship makes sense because it reflects the nature of the state and the breadth of the spectrum of approaches the state is able to use when facing issues of national security. States with less gender equality are more likely to perpetuate masculine behaviors and have a more limited problem-solving toolbox than those that have expanded to include women and to employ more feminine approaches.

Development

The status of development with respect to women is another salient argument for explaining the mechanisms behind gendered peace. Many scholars have linked higher levels of socio-economic status for women, achieved through a focus on their socio-economic development, to the capacity of women to imbue peace within government policies (Collier, 2007; Sen, 1999). This argument was supported by Gizelis (2009), who suggested that societies in which women have higher social and economic status and greater political representation are less likely to relapse into conflict. In these societies, women have greater opportunities to express a voice in the peacemaking process and to activate broader domestic cooperation for exogenously led peace processes (Gizelis, 2009). UN and NGO actors can then tap into these expansive resources of support to ensure their peacemaking and peacekeeping efforts become anchored rather than break down from a lack of domestic support (Gizelis, 2009). The level of development women experience in a society would seem to affect their agency in society, and in turn affect their ability to influence peace.

Implementation: Signatory and ratification

Finally, some authors have suggested that women perpetuate more resilient peace when they have an active role in its implementation. Including women in society does not necessarily empower them to inject gendered peace into a society (Ellerby, 2016). In fact, there are a litany of reasons why female participation may exist *prima facie* but face severe obstacles in practice (Bjarnegård & Melander, 2013; Paffenholz et al., 2016; Shair-Rosenfield & Wood, 2017). To circumvent possible institutional obstacles, Krause, Krause, and Bränfors attempted to isolate and identify a role that would indicate substantive female influence in peace processes—acting as signatories to peace treaties. The authors found that peace treaties with female signatories tend to last longer than those without. Rather than demonstrating the power of a signature, the research underscores that how women participate matters. Being in positions of power that permit them to execute substantive influence on state behavior and actions may be the mechanism that most effectively allows states to employ gendered peace and experience its beneficial effects (Krause et al., 2018).

Case study: Gendered peace—Capacities and challenges

A series of decolonialization and post-Cold War related conflicts provides ample case studies demonstrating instances of gendered peace theory in action (Early, 1995; Tickner, 1992; Enloe

(1990; Tickner, 1992). To illustrate the capacities of women as well as some of the many obstacles they face, I include include a case study on the participation of women at the local and international levels.

Liberia

During and after the Liberian civil wars, which took place from 1989 to the early 2000s, Liberian women leveraged their role as the flagship of family permanence and expanded into the field of peacekeeping. Drawing credibility from their traditional role in society, they sought to instill in their recovering postconflict communities the same appropriate moral, ethical, cultural, and societal values they fostered in their own families (Shulika, 2016). These efforts were then formalized with the creation of women's peace organizations that tasked themselves with the rebuilding and reconciliation processes of peacekeeping (Shulika, 2016; Basini, 2013; Gizelis, 2011).

A notable example of this peacekeeping took place during the second Liberian civil war. Liberian women's organizations such as the Women in Peacebuilding Network (WIPNET) mobilized women from the outset of the conflict, fostering collective action in order to advocate for a peaceful resolution. WIPNET was able use the extensive social networks of its members to lobby national leaders for peace talks. Their effort was enormously successful, as WIPNET was able to bring rebel groups and authoritarian leader Charles Taylor to the negotiating table and facilitated the ultimate brokering of a peace deal between the two groups (Gizelis, 2011). After the negotiations, WIPNET shifted its attention to reconciliation—focusing on disarmament, demobilization, and reintegration (DDR) efforts that would help soothe the vestiges of war, reintroduce militants back into civilian life, and revive a collapsed economy. During this effort, WIPNET and the Liberian Women's Initiative (LWI) punctuated the need for women's engagement, both as tailors and as targets of peacebuilding. They stressed that Liberian women needed to be included in the mapping of peace building due to their local knowledge and noted position as existing stewards of peace.

Despite female civil society's noteworthy success in Liberia, external actors disregarded their role when it came to postconflict peacebuilding. The most notable negligence was committed by the United Nations and various ways in which it failed to impose a gender lens. First, the United Nations did not analyze the Liberian case independently when designing its postconflict program. Instead, it copied the peacekeeping plan from neighboring Sierra Leone, which experienced its own distinct conflict a few years prior (Basini, 2013; Gizelis, 2011). Because of this, the organization opted not to hire a gender expert and instead recycled policy prescriptions from Sierra Leone. As a result, postconflict programming was unprepared to deal with the unique context of the Liberian conflict. More pointedly, it overlooked the needs of women, underestimating the magnitude of exposure they had to the conflict and the DDR support they would require.

In the Liberian case, women had a notable presence in the conflict. Although participating in the conflict as combatants and combat auxiliaries, these women rarely carried weapons. As a result, nearly all women were unable to meet the principle requirement placed by the United Nations in order to participate in DDR programs, surrendering a weapon, as they never carried one in the first place (Basini, 2013; Gizelis, 2011). Second, the absence of a gender expert aware of the needs of people in postconflict Liberia meant that the DDR programs that were created significantly underestimated the number of women who needed their services. As a result, women's DDR programs had to be reevaluated repeatedly to address shortcomings, with funding and capacities being increased several times to meet overwhelming demand (Basini, 2013). Even after increasing budgets, the expanded program was still unable to meet demand because not enough was earmarked for women's DDR.

Similarly, because the UN plan was not tailored for the Liberian case, well-meaning gender-focused programming missed the mark in meeting the needs of Liberian women. One example of this is the professional training the United Nations provided, intended to help reintegrate female combatants into the workforce and jumpstart the economy. However, the training provided was centered around stereotypical female vocations such as hairstyling and sewing (Basini, 2013). These fields were low paying and already oversaturated in the Liberian economy. Such oversights called into question the knowledgeability of the peacemakers and the credibility of the peace effort overall in the eyes of local Liberians (Basini, 2013).

The experience of postconflict Liberia outlined the ways in which the United Nations surprisingly failed to meet its own self-imposed requirements. Basic efforts toward incorporating women and gender were overlooked, even after the organization's formal commitment to a gender focus, and precluded many of the positive benefits attributed to the participation of women in the establishment of peace following conflict.

Bosnia

The ability of women to abate conflict is not limited to the Global South. Following the dissolution of Yugoslavia and the subsequent war, Bosnia required massive postconflict reconciliation and reconstruction. The war left behind deep social and economic wounds, with women being particularly vulnerable in the postconflict period. Because of the conflict, many women lost spouses and therefore their sources of income in the traditional economy of Bosnia, where men acted as breadwinners (Björkdahl, 2012). Moreover, traditional patterns of property rights in the Balkans meant that women were usually not the owners of the land and homes they occupied. With their partners dead or missing, women were left unable to prove ownership and often lost their homes and the capital they held. The Dayton Accords—the most extensive and costly peacekeeping accords in history at the time—failed to consider the disproportionate ways in which the conflict affected women and how this would influence the overall peace effort (Björkdahl, 2012).

Interestingly enough, this was not an unintentional oversight. The exclusion of women was due to the desire of international actors to establish a liberal peace in the region as quickly as possible following an especially violent ethnic war. Reorganizing gender roles in the traditional Bosnian society was deemed unimportant and possibly destabilizing for the peace effort (Björkdahl, 2012; Gizelis, 2009).

The exclusion of Bosnian women and gender from the brokering of the peace process is particularly concerning. This period presents a unique window of time when social norms can be exogenously introduced into a society and anchored by new institutions (Porter, 2003). Although not the most organic way to foster social development, it is a critical juncture in which to fast-track social development norms in struggling societies. In fact, Porter (2003) presented the idea that a peace settlement was not solely charged with ending war, but also responsible for establishing the conditions for a new just polity. The justification for this is not entirely idealistic but based on the assumption that a peace treaty that supports equality and human rights norms will reciprocally be reinforced by these norms.

Porter further specified that should norms such as universal rights to equality be in conflict with local customs, then rights to equality should take normative priority over the conservation of traditions in the reconstruction effort (2003), underscoring the importance of these norms. Yet in the Bosnian case, the United States, United Nations, and their allies proved myopic. They placed more importance on the short-term priority of installing a liberal peace as quickly as possible than on engaging in the more arduous process of establishing norms of inclusivity, despite the long-term benefits. Instead, the preconflict *status quo* was maintained and participation in peacebuilding was an activity reserved for men (Björkdahl, 2012). International peacemakers forfeited any benefits of including women and gender in the process, and this misstep has been a source of ongoing instability to the fragile Balkan peace to this day (Akyol, 2019).

At the local level, Basini (2013), Gizelis (2011; Gizelis & Pierre 2013), and Paffenholz (2015) reported how programs intended to serve local women following conflict systematically underestimate demand. Take, for example, how the United Nations' failure to invest in a gender expert in the Liberian case resulted in multiple problems, failing to meet the needs of women. Yet such mistakes are not limited to the hectic environment of the field; they can also be observed at the organizational level.

Gender-inclusive efforts at the international organization (IO) level also suffer from a lack of political will that impedes their ability to produce desired outcomes. Despite recognizing the value female peace officers can bring to maintaining security, researchers have found little evidence that IOs have made noteworthy efforts to carry out their formal declarations to incorporate women in international peacekeeping (Olsson & Möller, 2013; Schjølset, 2013). Schjølset (2013) found that within NATO's international operations, women's participation had increased by only a few percentage points since efforts toward gender balancing began in the early 2000s, and has yet to exceed 11 percent of NATO forces for any of its member countries (Schjølset, 2013). Olsson and Möller (2013) discovered similar findings in their investigation evaluating female participation not only in peacekeeping missions but in UN, EU, and OSCE settings.

Both investigations expressed concern with the insubstantial increases in female officers despite vocal declarations by organizations regarding gender balancing. The authors also underscored that *where* the limited number of female peacekeepers are being assigned is also concerning and seemingly counterintuitive. They found that, despite no increases in numbers, female peacekeeping officers are still given posts far from the front lines of conflict, making their placements gender-biased and preventing their intended influence in these fragile zones.

This pattern is curious for the authors because a principal motivation for increasing the number of female officers was the perceived impact they would have on conflict zones. Female soldiers are better able to connect with local communities than their male counterparts (Nordås & Rustad, 2013; Olsson & Möller, 2013; Schjølset, 2013; UNSC, 2012). The inclusion of women and gender expertise is also expected to increase the legitimacy of peacekeeping efforts by reducing sexual abuses and other violence inconsistent with the intentions of peacekeeping operations (Olsson & Möller, 2013; Schjølset, 2013).

War pushes gender power imbalances to extremes, where hypermasculinity leads to upticks in violence, including sexual violence, by peace officers against local communities (Mckay, 2004). Female officers are expected to act as watchdogs against such violations, preventing crimes that would deeply discredit international involvement and cause more harm to already traumatized populations (Olsson & Möller, 2013; Schjølset, 2013).

Finally, female peace officers are expected to act as diffusion mechanisms for gender inclusivity in postconflict societies (de Jonge Oudraat, 2013; Olsson & Möller, 2013; Schjølset, 2013). The presence of female officers is expected to influence local perceptions by normalizing gender equality and showcasing women in positions of power. Such role modeling is anticipated to encourage a cascade of norms and address gender imbalance in societies (Finnemore & Sikkink, 1998; Olsson & Möller, 2013; Schjølset, 2013). Omitting women from the roles and spaces where they are thought to be most needed is vexing because it contradicts the spirit of inclusivity and precludes the desired outcomes of their participation.

Each of these scenarios demonstrates the ways in which gender-related programs have been underserved and even self-sabotaged by peacebuilding programs. As a result, any measurement and evaluation of these efforts would likely misreport the effect of women and gender. The compromised execution of these programs means any evaluation would fail to capture their true potential, had they been carried out adequately.

High-level vs. targeted inclusion

A review of the extant literature indicates a variety of ways gendered peace is thought to be introduced into a society and reduce the likelihood of conflict. These include increasing women's participation, higher overall levels of social gender equality, the adoption and recognition of international human rights laws that protect women,[4] the creation of new institutions to empower women, a focus on reducing violence against women in society, institutional reform that would aim to include women more substantively in government decision-making processes, focusing on the socio-economic development of women, and placing women in positions of power to implement peace.

These hypothesized mechanisms that foster gendered peace seem to be divided by the scope of their action. Greater levels of social gender equality, the adoption and recognition of international human rights law, and reforming institutions reflect more high-level changes by the state. They indicate a shift in government behavior and the adoption of new norms. Introducing norms into society is an unclear and imprecise process but a necessary first step for social change (Finnemore & Sikkink, 1998). As a consequence, the policies that seek to introduce these norms and nurture them may be more imprecise and shapeless than specific norms aimed at creating more precise outputs, such as the increase in economic subsidies for women.

Alternatively, increasing women's participation, creating new institutions for promoting women, reducing violence against women, focusing on the socioeconomic development of women, and placing women in positions to implement peace treaties reflect more targeted ways to incorporate women and foment gendered peace. These policies embody more tangible and measurable steps that can be taken to cultivate gendered peace. For example, a new institution for women can be created—or not. Observing the implementation and execution of such policies is clearer and more straightforward than that of high-level policies. Even when they may seem similar in their goals, there are significant differences between high-level and targeted policies. For instance, the creation of new institutions for women and reforming institutions to incorporate women are seemingly two similar tasks. However, the creation of an institution is a type of policy whose success is more easily observed because it has a targeted output—the new ministry. On the other hand, reforming institutions to incorporate women and gender is a hazier task. How to go about it and how to measure when the task is successfully completed is far less clear.

Although the tangibleness of more targeted tasks may make them seem more suited to fostering gendered peace, this may not be the case. Targeted policies for inclusion would usually arise organically following significant norm shifts in societies. For example, if societies increase their levels of gender equality, it is likely that targeted policies—such as laws protecting women from gender-based violence—would arise naturally from these societal transformations. Imposing such policies without the value shifts preceding them may make them less potent instruments for fostering gendered peace and even increase the likelihood of conflict (Huntington, 1993). Applying exogenous norms to a state that are diametrically alien to existing social norms can threaten the credibility of the new government by implying that it is beholden to outside influences of foreign states. Such suspicion can be particularly damaging to the fragile and vulnerable governments that are usually in place following conflict.

On the other hand, high-level policies, although at times a bit ambiguous, may be more powerful instruments for cultivating postconflict peace. These policies entail a more exhaustive shift of intricate systems by beginning with the introduction of ideas. Because of the nature of ideas, they can be introduced into society through a variety of avenues and less bluntly than a single targeted policy. The planting of ideas via high-level policies serves two important functions. First, it allows for the slow introduction of norms that the state can take ownership of. Permitting the state to take control of and adapt to these norms is important to increasing the credibility of the state and also building the foundation for norms. Second, any subsequent introduction of targeted policies will then seem less abrasive and more coherent to a society because the state has already established justification for them.

As such, I hypothesize that of the theorized mechanisms behind fostering gendered peace, high-level policies will be more effective, particularly in postconflict settings where they are usually previously absent. More precisely, I believe that peace treaties that contain high-level instruments for gender inclusion will be more successful at fostering gendered peace and will thus be less likely to relapse into conflict than those that contain more targeted policies.

Data and design

To test my theory, I used an updated version of the Women-PAX database maintained by the University of Edinburgh. The Gender PA-X is derived from the broader Peace Agreements database (PA-X) and is a repository of 351 peace agreements from 1990 to 2020. It provides detailed information on 225 substantive variables, including 53 provisions relating to women and gender (Bell et al., 2020). The database contains considerably more data on policies related to women and gender, making it uniquely useful for measuring what gender-focused components of peace treaties may lend themselves to fostering gendered peace.

The principal disadvantage of the Women-PAX database is that, although it does include treaty start date, it does not reflect if and when treaties end, making calculating the length of a treaty impossible using the database alone. To include the pertinent biographical information for the treaties, I used the Peace Agreement ID of observations to merge the dataset with the Uppsala Conflict Data Program (UCDP) data set.[5] I matched observations in the Women-PAX database with the same treaty in the UCDP database and imported end days of treaties in order to create the variable "days." The variable "days" reflects the number of days a treaty lives for—or lasts until it falls back into conflict.[6]

Finally, not all the observations in the Women-PAX database are found in the UCDP database. Observations for which the end date cannot be found in the UCDP database were dropped from the updated Women-PAX database for the sake of the analysis because an end date could not be verified. One hundred observations remained in the updated Women-PAX table, which allows for confidence of quantitative analysis as it exceeds an n of 40.

Dependent variables

As previously mentioned, the Women-PAX dataset catalogs 53 variables related to gender that can be components of peace treaties. Based on the literature review, I identified two groups of gender-related policies that I believed would foster gendered peace: high-level policies and targeted policies. Fostering gendered peace should manifest itself by elongating the life of a peace treaty. The high-level policies include women's social equality (Model 2), reforming the constitution to incorporate women (Model 7), and references to international law regarding the rights of women—specifically UNSCR 1325 (Model 4).

Targeted policies that would facilitate gendered peace and may elongate the lifespan of peace treaties based on existing literature include effective participation of women in governance (Model 1),[7] creating new institutions for women (Model 5), having female signatories to the peace treaty (Model 3), socioeconomic development for women (Model 8), and prohibiting or denouncing sexual violence (Model 6). The independent variable of the design is the length of the peace treaty, measured in days from treaty start date to end date. As not all treaties ended and some remain viable to this day, these treaties all took the same end date, which was the day the research was conducted in this investigation. In order to explore the relationship between treaty length and gendered peace variables, an end date was required to measure length. To identify whether these hypothesized instruments of gendered peace prove salient, I ran a linear regression for each high-level and targeted policy variable and gauged which policies and which group of policies were more correlated with longer peace treaties and could be important mechanisms with which to engender gendered peace.

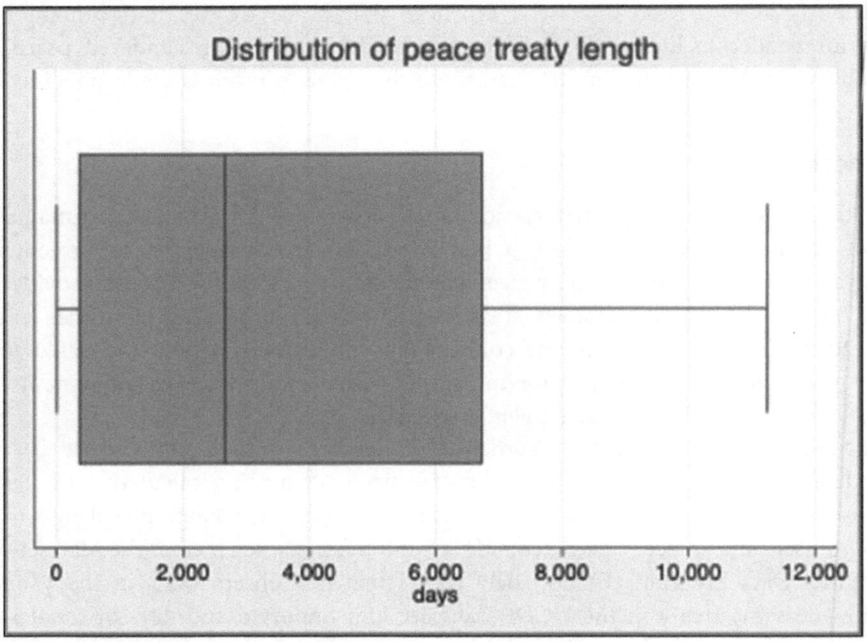

Graph 1. Distribution of peace treaty length in the sample (days).

Control variables

For the controls variables, I used different power-sharing variables that have been shown to have a significant impact on the durability of peace (DeRouen et al., 2009; Hartzell and Hoddie, 2003; Hartzell et al., 2001; Jarstad and Nilsson, 2008; Mattes and Savun, 2009; Mukherjee, 2006). These variables include territorial provisions for power-sharing (terr-prov), military provisions (mil-prov) for power-sharing, and political provisions for power-sharing (pol-prov). In the datasets, each of these variables acts as a binary umbrella indicator that captures whether any variation of that type of power-sharing is included within the peace treaty. For example, terr-prov flags mentions of any of the following territorial provisions in a peace agreement for a disputed region: regional autonomy, federal state solution, call for referendums for status of disputed regions, representation in local government for disputed regions, cultural freedoms for disputed regions, the recognition of a disputed regions, border demarcation, and permission of local governance of the disputed region.

Results

The length of peace treaties in the database range from 1 to 11,247 days. The mean number of days a peace treaty lasts is 4016.04 days, with a standard deviation of 3629.32 days, and the length of treaties in general skews to the right (Graph 1). Within this context, I found that certain gender-related policies are indeed correlated with notably longer-lasting peace treaties (Table 1).

Women's social equality, recognition of UNSCR 1325, and constitution making and reform to include women are all correlated with longer lasting peace treaties. Any mention of social equality; property rights; and health, financial, or worker's rights with reference to women results in a peace treaty lasting on average 1722 days more than one without such mention, and this finding is statistically significant at $p < .05$. Peace agreements that make any reference to international law with regard to UNSCR 1325 also last longer. A treaty referencing UNSCR 1325 will last 2459 more days than one without, and this finding is significant at $p < .05$. Finally, any mention of

Table 1. OLS regression models (DV: The number of days a peace treaty lasts).

Variables		Women's participation	Social equality	Female signatories	UNSCR 1325	New women's institutions	Preventing sexual violence	Constitutional reform	Development
Women's participation		−6.833							
		(1.088)							
Women's social equality			1.722**						
			(824.5)						
Female signatories				−2.285*					
				(1.224)					
Recognition of UNSCR 1325					2.459**				
					(1.133)				
New institutions						−2.705			
						(2.699)			
Preventing sexual violence							−1.385*		
							(825.8)		
Constitutional reform								1.385*	
								(797.2)	
Development									−3.352
									(3.749)
mil.prov		257.2	483.0	623.2	408.2	597.7	626.4	200.5	562.6
		(811.6)	(765.4)	(771.4)	(765.3)	(784.1)	(774.8)	(790.3)	(782.1)
terr.prov		44.62	−363.8	5.705	−430.4	122.9	−43.52	−171.3	71.67
		(756.1)	(753.1)	(737.3)	(757.7)	(758.8)	(740.0)	(744.7)	(753.4)
pol.prov		−482.5	−472.6	−336.2	−497.7	−49.08	−100.7	−69.50	−82.45
		(831.9)	(766.6)	(760.4)	(766.5)	(767.6)	(755.8)	(755.7)	(765.8)
justice.prov		1.118							
		(835.6)							
Constant		3.450***	3.653***	4.054***	3.944***	3.670***	4.082***	3.558***	3.715***
	(871.8)	(821.6)	(834.9)	(820.7)	(841.8)	(843.8)	(835.3)	(838.3)	(838.3)
Observations	**100**	100	100	100	100	100	100	100	100
R-squared	**0.023**	0.048	0.040	0.052	0.015	0.033	0.035	0.013	0.013

Notes. Standard errors in parentheses. $*p < .1$, $**p < .05$, $***p < .01$.

women in connection with constitution making and constitutional reform is also attributed with treaties lasting 1385 more days than those without this mention, and this finding is significant at a $p < .01$ level. These results suggest that the variables may be representative variables of gendered peace. They also suggest that overarching, high-level policies do have a positive correlation with the length of peace treaties.

When considering the models for targeted policies, the outcomes are not entirely as expected. In accordance with my hypothesis, none of the targeted policies is positively correlated with treaty length. Treaties with language on effective participation of women do not prove to have a significant relation with increased treaty length. Neither does a focus on the development of women, or the creation of new institutions to improve the status of women. Yet treaties with female signatories have a negative correlation with treaty length. Treaties with female signatories tend to last 2285 days *less* than those without, and this is significant at a $p < .1$ level. Prohibition or mention of sexual violence, rape, sexual harassment, and so on in a peace agreement also corresponds to a peace treaty being shortened by 1385 days, and this is also significant at $p < .1$ level.

The finding that peace treaties are generally shorter when they have female signatories or language prohibiting sexual violence is perplexing. If including women and policies that help women have been observed to reinforce peace, why would policies that so clearly represent the inclusion of women and protection of their physical security appear in opposition to the survival of peace treaties? It could be that because gender-mainstreaming and gender-balancing are new components of peace treaties they are included in recently ratified peace treaties, which would result in the length of these treaties being shorter, not because they failed, but because they were ratified more recently.

On the other hand, the fact that targeted policies are a combination of statistically insignificant or significant but negatively related to peace treaty length may suggest that these policies are not the best means with which to foster gendered peace. Although they may seem more effectual because they are more clearly defined and applied, targeted policies may be putting the cart before the horse. In order for peace treaties to leverage the capabilities of gendered peace, the state may first need to introduce the more overarching and high-level policies. Although difficult to implement and measure, high-level policies such as improving women's social equality or recognizing the need for the *foci* outlined in UNSCR 1325 play an important role in introducing gender-equity norms into society. These abstract policies become the foundations on which more targeted policies arise following the cascade of norms (Finnemore & Sikkink, 1998). Applying targeted policies without first introducing high-level policies may negatively affect the domestic legitimacy of that gender policy, because there is yet no domestic demand for it (Finnemore & Sikkink, 1998).

Enacting high-level gender inclusivity policies may be the way to go. States developing peace treaties may find it beneficial to focus on establishing general support for gender inclusivity and amending their legal and constitutional frameworks to include women before branching out to employ more targeted policies. Without these foundations, it is possible that sudden social changes may add stress to newly forged peace treaties in societies that are vulnerable to conflict relapse.

Conclusion

Moving beyond the anecdotal evidence for gendered peace theory, contemporary empirical research is increasingly finding evidence for the phenomenon. Still, we are left with the question of how to best harness the capabilities of gendered peace theory. Uncovering what gender-based variables best facilitate gendered peace is an important step toward this end. Gender-based variables that are attributed to longer-lasting peace can be instrumentalized as policy and included in future treaties to improve the status of women and bolster the survivability of peace.

This research highlights possible variables for producing gendered peace and disaggregates them into high-level and targeted policy. It finds that treaties that include high-level policies—such as a focus on the social equality of women, reforming constitutions to incorporate women, and the inclusion of international humanitarian laws pertaining to women—tend to last longer. By contrast, treaties that include more targeted gender policies—such as a focus on the socioeconomic development of women or reducing sexual violence—either have no effect on treaty length or are attributed to shorter treaties.

There are two plausible reasons for this counterintuitive outcome. It could be that incorporating targeted policies into treaties in which high-level policies have not already taken hold may interrupt the order of norm cascades. Rather than reinforcing peace, the introduction of alien values could act as a disruption to already fragile postconflict dynamics. Such a relationship could be evaluated using an interaction model that could gauge whether such policies need to be introduced in tandem or in a certain order. Second, it could be that because including gender-inclusivity policies in peace treaties is a newer practice, the treaties that incorporate more targeted policies happen to be "younger" treaties. It maybe that these treaties reflect shorter lifespans not because the treaty ended but because the treaty is fairly new. This could be tested by performing a robustness check to assess whether treaties in the dataset are live or have expired and how this interacts with the dependent variables.

Increasing the number of observations would also improve the internal and external validity of the investigation. Expanding PAX-Women to document any end dates for treaties in the database would help in this effort. The administrators of the database intentionally do not include this information because they believe there are many challenges to labeling a peace treaty as "ended." Yet not including this key detail impedes empirical research that might find support for gender inclusivity. Without this key information, scholars cannot assess if or how gender reinforces peace in a quantitative fashion. The lack of metrics makes policy prescription difficult and is possibly acting as an obstacle to gender inclusivity itself.

Although the PAX-Women database houses the most extensive data on women and peace treaties, it should expand to include more measurable variables regarding women and peace that would open the field to more quantitative investigations.

Notes

1. This is not to say that women mythologically or empirically are always more peaceful and proponents of peace over conflict. To the contrary, women have been shown to choose conflict over peace and be equally as violent as their male counterparts in a variety of studies (Bjarnegård & Melander, 2013; Cohen, 2013; Cunningham, 2003). However, peace processes tend to be more successful when women and gender equality are incorporated in the effort than when these two elements are absent.
2. That is to say, increasing the number of women included to provide gender equity in representation.
3. That is to say, incorporating policies that provide gender equity.
4. For example, UNSCR 1325.
5. The absence of this biographical information is intentional and one the creators of the database are hesitant to include because of epistemological challenges in declaring a peace treaty as "ended." Per the authors, there are a variety of ways for a treaty to end, including never really being implemented to begin with, simply being abandoned, or ending due to the resumption of conflict. For the sake of my study, I am not concerned with these nuanced details and am concerned with whether the treaty ceased, if at all. To overcome the problem of missing possible end dates, I use the Conflict ID of observations to merge the dataset with the UCDP data set.
6. If a treaty does not fall back into conflict, it takes the artificial end date of March 15, 2021.
7. This entails the inclusion of nonnumeric commitments to have women's representation, requirements to address gender participation or equality in political institutions, commitments to adequate representation, effective/equal participation, and so on.

Acknowledgments

I would like to recognize the NSF funded workshop on Human Rights Law that helped shape this paper, along with its organizers Dr. Magda Hinojosa and Dr. Heather Smith-Cannoy. I also greatly appreciate the reviewers, who pushed me to refine my theory and models. Lastly, I would like to extend a debt of gratitude to those that provided invaluable feedback including Dr. Thorin Wright, Kathy Schauer, Elena Shumskaya and Bruno Cooper.

References

Akyol, R. (2019). For Bosnian women, no justice—and no seats. *Foreign Policy*.

Barr, H. (2020). *A crucial moment for women's rights in Afghanistan*. Human Rights Watch.

Basini, H. S. A. (2013). Gender mainstreaming unraveled: The case of DDRR in Liberia. *International Interactions*, *39*(4), 535–557. doi:10.1080/03050629.2013.805129

Bell, C., Badanjak, S., Beaujouan, J. Forster, F., Epple, T., Jamar, A., McNicholl, K., Molloy, S., Nash, K., Pospisil, J., Wilson, R., & Wise, W. (2021). *PA-X codebook, version 5*. Political Settlements Research Programme, University of Edinburgh, Edinburgh. www.peaceagreements.org

Bjarnegård, E., & Melander, E. (2011). Disentangling gender, peace and democratization: The negative effects of militarized masculinity. *Journal of Gender Studies*, *20*(2), 139–154. doi:10.1080/09589236.2011.565194

Bjarnegård, E., & Melander, E. (2013). Revisiting representation: Communism, women in politics, and the decline of armed conflict in East Asia. *International Interactions*, *39*(4), 558–574. doi:10.1080/03050629.2013.805132

Björkdahl, A. (2012). A gender-just peace? Exploring the Post-Dayton peace process in Bosnia. *Peace & Change*, *37*(2), 286–317. doi:10.1111/j.1468-0130.2011.00746.x

Caprioli, M. (2000). Gendered conflict. *Journal of Peace Research*, *37*(1), 51–68. doi:10.1177/0022343300037001003

Caprioli, M. (2005). Primed for violence: The role of gender inequality in predicting internal conflict. *International Studies Quarterly*, *49*(2), 161–178. doi:10.1111/j.0020-8833.2005.00340.x

Caprioli, M., & Boyer, M. A. (2001). Gender, violence, and international crisis. *Journal of Conflict Resolution*, *45*(4), 503–518. doi:10.1177/0022002701045004005

Charlesworth, H. (2008). Are women peaceful? Reflections on the role of women in peace-building. *Feminist Legal Studies*, *16*(3), 347–361. doi:10.1007/s10691-008-9101-6

Cohen, D. K. (2013). Female combatants and the perpetration of violence: Wartime rape in the Sierra Leone civil war. *World Politics*, *65*(3), 383–415. doi:10.1017/S0043887113000105

Collier, P. (2007). *The bottom billion: Why the poorest countries are failing and what can be done about it*. Oxford University Press.

Cunningham, K. J. (2003). Cross-regional trends in female terrorism. *Studies in Conflict & Terrorism*, *26*(3), 171–195. doi:10.1080/10576100390211419

Dayal, A. K., & Christien, A. (2020). Women's participation in informal peace processes. *Global Governance: A Review of Multilateralism and International Organizations*, *26*(1), 69–98. doi:10.1163/19426720-02601002

de Jonge Oudraat, C. (2013). UNSCR 1325-conundrums and opportunities. *International Interactions*, *39*(4), 612–619. doi:10.1080/03050629.2013.805328

Derouen, K., Lea, J., and Wallensteen, P. (2009). The duration of Civil War peace agreements. *Conflict Management and Peace Science*, *26*(4), 367–87.

Early, F. H. (1995). New historical perspectives on gendered peace studies. *Women's Studies Quarterly*, *23*(3/4), 22–31. http://www.jstor.org/stable/40003497

Ellerby, K. (2013). (En)gendered security? The complexities of women's inclusion in peace processes. *International Interactions*, *39*(4), 435–460. doi:10.1080/03050629.2013.805130

Ellerby, K. (2016). A seat at the table is not enough: Understanding women's substantive representation in peace processes. *Peacebuilding*, *4*(2), 136–150. doi:10.1080/21647259.2016.1192240

Enloe, C. H. (1990). *Bananas, beaches & bases: Making feminist sense of international politics*. University of California Press.

Ferguson, J. (2019). Peace talks, the Taliban, and Afghan women's uncertain future. *The New Yorker*.

Finnemore, M., & Sikkink, K. (1998). International norm dynamics and political change. *International Organization*, *52*(4), 887–917. doi:10.1162/002081898550789

Funk, K. D., Hinojosa, M., & Piscopo, J. M. (2021). Women to the rescue: The gendered effects of public discontent on legislative nominations in Latin America. *Party Politics*, *27*(3), 465–477. doi:10.1177/1354068819856614

Gizelis, T. I. (2009). Gender empowerment and United Nations peacebuilding. *Journal of Peace Research*, *46*(4), 505–523. doi:10.1177/0022343309334576

Gizelis, T. I. (2011). A country of their own: Women and peacebuilding. *Conflict Management and Peace Science*, *28*(5), 522–542. doi:10.1177/0738894211418412

Gizelis, T. I., & Pierre, N. A. (2013). Gender equality and postconflict reconstruction: What do we need to know in order to make gender mainstreaming work? *International Interactions*, *39*(4), 601–611. doi:10.1080/03050629.2013.805324

Hartzell, C., & Hoddie, M. (2003). Institutionalizing peace: Power sharing and post-civil war conflict management. *American Journal of Political Science*, *47*(2), 318–332. https://doi.org/10.2307/3186141

Hartzell, C., Hoddie, M., & Rothchild, D. (2001). Stabilizing the peace after civil war: an investigation of some key variables. *International Organization*, *55*(1), 183–208. doi:10.1162/002081801551450

Hinojosa, M., & Kittilson, M. C. (2020). *Seeing women, strengthening democracy*. Oxford University Press. 10.1093/oso/9780197526941.001.0001

Hudson, V. M., Caprioli, M., Ballif-Spanvill, B., McDermott, R., & Emmett, C. F. (2009). The heart of the matter: The security of women and the security of states. *International Security*, *33*(3), 7–45. doi:10.1162/isec.2009.33.3.7

Huntington, S. P. (1993). The clash of civilizations? *Foreign Affairs*, *72*(3), 22. doi:10.2307/20045621

Jarstad, A. K., & Nilsson, D. (2008). From words to deeds: The implementation of power-sharing pacts in peace accords. *Conflict Management and Peace Science*, *25*(3), 206–223. https://doi.org/10.1080/07388940802218945

Karim, S., & Hill, D. (2018). *The study of gender and women in cross-national political science research: Rethinking concepts and measurement* [paper presentation]. Annual Convention of the International Studies Association, San Francisco, CA USA.

Krause, J., Krause, W., & Bränfors, P. (2018). Women's participation in peace negotiations and the durability of peace. *International Interactions*, *44*(6), 985–1016. doi:10.1080/03050629.2018.1492386

Mattes, M., & Savun, B. (2009). Fostering peace after civil war: Commitment problems and agreement design. *International Studies Quarterly*, *53*(3), 737–759. http://www.jstor.org/stable/27735119

Mckay, S. (2004). Women, human security, and peace-building: A feminist analysis. *A Search for New Approaches of Peace-Building*, *20*(1), 1–16. 10.11648/j.ijp.20140201.11

Melander, E. (2005). Political gender equality and state human rights abuse. *Journal of Peace Research*, *42*(2), 149–166. doi:10.1177/0022343305050688

Mukherjee, B. (2006). Why political power-sharing agreements lead to enduring peaceful resolution of some civil wars, but not others?. *International Studies Quarterly*, *50*(2), 479–504. http://www.jstor.org/stable/3693619

Nagel, R. U. (2019). The known knowns and known unknowns in data on women. Centre for Women, Peace and Security.

Nagel, R. U. (2021). Gendered preferences: How women's inclusion in society shapes negotiation occurrence in intrastate conflicts. *Journal of Peace Research*, *58*(3), 433–448.

Nordås, R., & Rustad, S. C. A. (2013). Sexual exploitation and abuse by peacekeepers: Understanding variation. *International Interactions*, *39*(4), 511–534. doi:10.1080/03050629.2013.805128

O'Reilly, M., Ó Súilleabháin, A., and Paffenholz, T. (2015). *Reimagining peacemaking: Women's roles in peace processes*. International Peace Institute.

Olsson, L., & Möller, F. (2013). Data on women's participation in UN, EU, and OSCE field missions: Trends, possibilities, and problems. *International Interactions*, *39*(4), 587–600. doi:10.1080/03050629.2013.805325

Paffenholz, T., Ross, N., Dixon, S., Schluchter, A.-L., & True, J. (2016). Making women count-not just counting women: Assessing women's inclusion and influence on peace negotiations. Inclusive Peace and Transition Initiative (Graduate Institute of International and Development Studies) and UN Women.

Peace Women (2002). *A special 1325 anniversary issue*. https://www.peacewomen.org/e-news/special-1325-anniversary-issue

Peterson, V. S., & Tickner, J. A. (1993). Gender in international relations: Feminist perspectives on achieving global security. *Political Science Quarterly*, *108*(2), 347. doi:10.2307/2152026

Porter, E. (2003). Women, political decision-making, and peace-building. *Global Change, Peace & Security*, *15*(3), 245–262. doi:10.1080/0951274032000124965

Schjølset, A. (2013). Data on women's participation in NATO forces and operations. *International Interactions*, *39*(4), 575–587. doi:10.1080/03050629.2013.805326

Sen, A. (1999). *Development as freedom*. Oxford University Press.

Shair-Rosenfield, S., & Wood, R. M. (2017). Governing well after war: How improving female representation prolongs post-conflict peace. *The Journal of Politics*, *79*(3), 995–1009. doi:10.1086/691056

Shulika, L. (2016). Women and Peace building: From historical to contemporary African perspectives. *Ubuntu: Journal of Conflict and Social Transformation*, *5*(1), 2016–2023. https://www.researchgate.net/publication/305744933_Women_and_Peace_building_From_Historical_to_Contemporary_African_Perspectives

Sultan, M. (2005). *From rhetoric to reality: Afghan women on the agenda for peace*. Hunt Alternatives Fund; Women Waging Peace Policy Commission.

Tickner, J. A. (1992). Engendered insecurities: Feminist perspectives on international relations. In *Gender in international relations feminist perspectives on achieving global security*. Columbia University Press.

Tickner, J. A. (2005). Gendering a discipline: Some feminist methodological contributions to international relations. *Signs: Journal of Women in Culture and Society*, *30*(4), 2173–2188. doi:10.1086/428416

UNSC (2012). *'Wherever there is conflict, women must be part of the solution,' Security Council told in day-long debate urging their inclusion in restoring fractured societies*. United Nations.

Wood, R., & Ramirez, M. D. (2018). Exploring the microfoundations of the gender equality peace hypothesis. *International Studies Review*, *20*(3), 345–367. doi:10.1093/isr/vix016

The evolution of the global movement to end child marriage

Andrea Vilán

ABSTRACT
Although international and domestic laws prohibit child marriage, millions of girls are married every year worldwide, a trend only aggravated by the COVID-19 pandemic. Since the turn of the century, the global advocacy movement to end child marriage has gained momentum by standardizing its framing, using testimonies and symbols to generate empathy and mobilize solidarity, and engaging with policymakers to end the practice. In this article, I draw on newspaper articles, advocacy reports, and interviews with activists in the United States and Latin America to identify the reasons behind its success. I also discuss several challenges activists are grappling with as the movement evolves, including intra-network dynamics regarding the centrality of sexuality and the forms child marriage adopts around the world.

Introduction

The United Nations (UN) has estimated that over half a billion women alive today were married as children (United Nations Children's Fund, 2021b). Child marriage—the formal or informal union of a child under the age of 18—is a harmful practice with lasting physical, emotional, and economic consequences.

Despite its prevalence and harmful effects, child marriage would not be on the international community's agenda without the global network of human rights activists working to end this practice. Since the turn of the century, a growing number of organizations worldwide have campaigned to end child marriage, advocating for domestic and international policy changes. I provide evidence suggesting that their efforts have had a real impact: Child marriage was included as a specific target of the UN's Sustainable Development Goal (SDG) of ending gender inequality (Shawki, 2015), thus firmly establishing the issue on the international agenda, and the rate of domestic legislative reforms has accelerated in recent years. What explains the success of the global movement to end child marriage? And what factors might hinder its future success?

To answer these questions, I draw on in-depth interviews, dozens of advocacy reports and newspaper articles, and the literature on transnational advocacy networks. I spoke to activists based in the United States who campaign to reform state laws and coordinate global advocacy efforts. I also interviewed activists and representatives of international organizations during my fieldwork in Latin America. These data allowed me to draw connections across a variety of institutional and economic contexts to reconstruct the evolution of the movement to end child marriage.

After providing a short overview of the prevalence of child marriage, in the third section I analyze the framing and tactics activists chose to raise awareness about child marriage, mobilize solidarity, and encourage policy reforms. I find that the movement to end child marriage gained momentum by choosing a human rights frame that allowed activists to build a broad coalition and employing many of the tactics suggested by previous literature on transnational advocacy, such as using shocking imagery and survivors' testimonies to appeal to the public and policymakers. I show that the movement has been able to secure policy changes that could lead to reductions in child marriage, including the elimination of legal loopholes allowing children to marry.

However, as the movement evolves to focus more on changing social norms, it faces new challenges. In the fourth section, I draw on the qualitative data to explore how inherent tensions in the framing that activists chose, regional differences, and societal resistance to women's and girls' empowerment could jeopardize the next phase of the movement's advocacy efforts. I conclude by discussing why studying the movement against child marriage is important for scholars and activists interested in raising human rights standards around the world.

Understanding child marriage

The United Nations defines child marriage as "any formal marriage or informal union between a child under the age of 18 and an adult or another child" (United Nations Children's Fund, 2021a). Even though in most regions of the world child marriage rates are declining, approximately 650 million women alive today were married before turning 18 (United Nations Children's Fund, 2021b). Although boys are also affected, the prevalence of child marriage among boys is one sixth that among girls (United Nations Children's Fund, 2021a), so it is a practice that disproportionately affects girls.

Child marriage occurs in every region of the world—even in high-income countries. Data show that nearly 300,000 children were married in the United States between 2000 and 2018; most were girls married to adult men about four years older (Unchained At Last, 2021). Koski and Heymann (2018) estimate that six of every 1,000 children living in the country between 2010 and 2014 were either formally married or had been married and then separated or divorced. Similarly, a recent study of Canada estimated that nearly 2,300 children between 15 and 17 years of age were in union in 2016 (Koski & Clark, 2021).

However, the prevalence of child marriage is higher in the Global South, particularly in Sub-Saharan Africa and South Asia. Table 1 shows the percentage by region of women 20–24 years old who were married before they turned 18. Nonetheless, even within high-prevalence regions there is encouraging evidence: Ethiopia was once among the top five countries for child marriage in Sub-Saharan Africa but has seen a one-third decline in prevalence since 2006, for example (United Nations Children's Fund, 2021b, p. 5).

Not every child faces the same risk. The averages reported in Table 1 conceal the disproportionate burden shouldered by children from the poorest and most marginalized communities, where we observe the compounding effect of gender, income, and racial exclusion. For example, girls who married before 18 years in Latin America are more likely to live in rural areas, in poor households, and have less access to education (United Nations Children's Fund, 2019). In the

Table 1. Percentage of women aged 20 to 24 who were married or in union as children, 2014–2020.

Region	Percentage (%)
Sub-Saharan Africa	34
South Asia	28
Latin America and the Caribbean	22
Middle East and North Africa	15
East Asia and the Pacific	7

Notes. Data refer to the most recent year available between 2014 and 2020 as of February 2021. Data for Europe and Central Asia, East Asia and Pacific, and North America are unavailable. **Source:** United Nations Children's Fund 2021c, 235.

Dominican Republic, for example, the combination of these factors produces a stunning 51 percent disparity: about 16 percent of those girls from the richest quintile, with secondary education, and living in urban settings are married, compared to 67 percent of those girls from the lowest income quintile, with no primary or secondary education, and living in rural areas (p. 9). The latest data also reveal that the gap in child marriage prevalence between the richest and poorest households has widened in most parts of the world (United Nations Children's Fund 2021b, p. 16).

The long-lasting effects marriage has on a child's well-being make these staggering statistics even more concerning. Women who marry as children are more likely to suffer from intimate partner violence (Kidman, 2017), for example. They are also more likely to become pregnant, which can negatively impact maternal and child health outcomes (e.g., Nour, 2006; Raj & Boehmer, 2013). In fact, pregnancy and childbirth complications are the leading causes of death for girls between 15 and 19 (World Health Organization, 2020). Moreover, child marriage often isolates girls from their families and communities and interrupts their education, thereby decreasing their labor force participation and taking a toll on a country's development and prosperity (Parsons et al., 2015; Wodon et al., 2017a).

In sum, child marriage is a global problem with lasting, detrimental consequences for the lives of girls. The next two sections analyze how activists have come together to put an end to this practice and what the future holds for this movement.

Drivers of progress

I conceptualize a human rights movement's success as "progress along a spectrum that runs from getting attention through mobilizing solidarity to the end point: securing policy change that diminishes or ends the violation, or transforms accountability for past or future violations of this type" (Brysk, 2013, p. 10). This definition encompasses aspects of the mobilization campaign as well as the actual outcomes of interest. Using this definition, in this section I explore whether the global movement to end child marriage has been successful and, if so, what factors explain its success so far.

To answer these questions, I use different types of data. I review quantitative evidence showing that legal protections against child marriage have been strengthening around the world. In the rest of the section, I use qualitative data to reconstruct the evolution of the movement to end child marriage and understand the strategic choices activists made to mobilize solidarity for the cause. Besides analyzing newspaper articles and reports from advocacy organizations, I draw from in-depth interviews conducted over the last five years with activists, researchers, and UN representatives based in Latin America and the United States.

I focus on Latin America because most advocacy efforts have focused on other regions of the world, such as South Asia, even though almost one in four Latin American women were married as girls (United Nations Children's Fund, 2018). Furthermore, in contrast to most regions of the world, child marriage rates in Latin America have stagnated: The prevalence of child marriage in Latin America and the Caribbean is as high as it was 25 years ago (United Nations Children's Fund, 2021b, p. 11). Although I spoke to activists and UN representatives in Latin America to complement advocacy efforts in other regions of the world, my goal is to draw connections across national frontiers to understand global efforts to end child marriage. For that reason, I interviewed activists in the United States and include cases that span the globe whenever possible. The Appendix provides further information on the interviews.

Setting the agenda

Throughout the twentieth century, international legal frameworks emerged to address the issue of child marriage. The 1948 Universal Declaration of Human Rights established that only intending spouses able to give "free and full consent" should be married. In the early 1960s, after UN members negotiated the Convention on Consent to Marriage, Minimum Age for Marriage, and Registration of Marriages, they adopted a resolution recommending that states establish a minimum age for marriage of 15 (United Nations General Assembly, 1965).

Subsequently, treaty-monitoring bodies recommended raising the minimum age for marriage to 18 years for girls and boys. The committee that supervises the implementation of the Convention on the Elimination of All Forms of Discrimination Against Women (CEDAW) has stated, "the minimum age for marriage should be 18 years for both man and woman" and that laws establishing different ages for girls and boys contravene the Convention and "should be abolished" (Committee on the Elimination of Discrimination against Women, 1994). The committee that supervises compliance with the Convention on the Rights of the Child has also called on states to "increase the minimum age for marriage with and without parental consent to 18 years, for both girls and boys" (Committee on the Rights of the Child, 2003). Most UN members have committed to comply with these standards by ratifying the CEDAW and CRC treaties.

While these legal standards show that child marriage was part of the multilateral agenda, it was not articulated as a global phenomenon until the turn of the century. To be sure, the UN pressured states to ban child marriage. For example, following Bolivia's first country report submission to the Committee on the Rights of the Child, the Committee urged the government to eliminate a legal loophole allowing girls to marry at a younger age (Committee on the Rights of the Child, 1993, Paragraph 9). But before the 2000s, child marriage was seen as a "niche" or specialty topic. An activist explained, "People viewed it as something that Muslims and Hindus were doing in South Asia" and that it was a comparatively rare phenomenon (Interview 10, 2021). Efevbera and Bhabha (2020) traced the origin of the term "child marriage" to discussions about marital relations in India.

Since the 2000s, the global movement to end child marriage has gained momentum by increasing coordination between organizations around the world. In 2011, a group of global leaders known as the Elders launched Girls Not Brides (GNB), a global partnership of more than 1,500 civil society organizations from more than 100 countries committed to ending child marriage. As more nongovernmental organizations have gotten involved with the child marriage issue, documentation demonstrating the practice's existence around the world has grown. One interviewee noted, "it's actually a very large phenomenon that is very widely culturally accepted practically everywhere … everybody's doing it because it's deeply gendered sexism, and that's why we see it all over the place" (Interview 10, 2021).

Not only have more organizations dedicated their advocacy efforts to ending child marriage, but funders have also allocated more grant money toward this end. For the last decade, the Ford Foundation, Kendeda Fund, NoVo Foundation, Gates Foundation, Nike Foundation, and others have funded efforts to end child marriage around the world. In 2018, donors and philanthropists established the Girls First Fund to support local organizations working to prevent child marriage. In partnership with VOW for Girls—an organization that accepts donations from couples' wedding registries, the wedding industry and brands that donate proceeds from sales—the Girls First Fund has already committed over $10 million to grantees in six countries.

Choosing the frame

The literature on transnational advocacy has emphasized the importance of framing rights claims to garner attention and mobilize solidarity. Scholars have argued that the content of the message delivered by the frame is important (Brysk, 2013, p. 78), and that the most persuasive content involves physical harm done to innocent individuals (Keck & Sikkink, 1998). When advocates refer to the impact of child marriage on intimate partner violence or the risk of complications during childbirth, they draw connections between the practice and the physical harm girls experience.

Additionally, Keck and Sikkink (1998, p. 27) argued that "issues involving legal equality of opportunity" help transnational advocacy networks organize most effectively. To garner attention in the early stages of the movement to end child marriage, activists have emphasized that girls are legally denied the protection of international standards against child marriage and are thus not equal under the law. Even though family law reform is not without its opponents, choosing to focus on legal equality has helped broaden the coalition to end child marriage, as it is easier for organizations to agree on the need to eliminate discriminatory laws than on what exactly is needed to eliminate child marriage in practice.

Scholars have argued that activists consider how the issue fits with other adjacent claims (e.g., Finnemore & Sikkink, 1998; Murdie et al., 2019). Child marriage is portrayed as a "cross-cutting" or "multisectoral" issue that relates to other goals of human rights advocates (Shawki, 2015, p. 60). In my interviews, many activists referred to child marriage as a specific form of gender-based violence. Similarly, the director of Plan International Honduras noted, "the fight against child marriage is a strategic way to promote the rights and empowerment of women in different areas, such as health, education, work and freedom from violence" (Plan International, 2017). Fitting the issue of child marriage within the broader human rights agenda has allowed activists to bring organizations that might previously not have been working on child marriage into the coalition, such as those working on children's education and health. It also means they can apply for funding earmarked for multiple issues (Interviews 8 and 11, 2021).

These framing choices reflect the strategies typically identified in the literature on transnational activism, but advocates' preference for the term "child marriage" was also important for the movement's success and deserves an explanation. Other phrases—such as "forced marriage," "girl brides," and "early marriage"—emerged as options in the past. By 2000, leading international organizations favored the term "early marriage" (Efevbera & Bhabha, 2020, p. 3). But activists engaged in a process of creative reframing in an effort to build a broad coalition (Murdie et al., 2019). Nour (2009) suggested that "early marriage," unlike "child marriage," excludes the connection to children and is vague "because an early marriage for one society may be considered late by another." The term "child brides," on the other hand, "glorifies the tradition by portraying an image of joy and celebration" (Nour, 2009, pp. 22–23).

A gender activist and researcher told me that the term "child marriage" is great for "advocacy reasons" because it glues two cultural constructs—childhood and marriage—in a way that is "shocking" and helps advocates raise awareness or persuade policymakers (Interview 10, 2021). Explaining to a reporter why her organization focuses on child marriage when its ultimate goal is to end forced marriage, an activist spoke of the advantages of the term "child marriage" over "forced marriage" by saying, "We do a lot on child marriage because (a) it's easy to define, quantify, and legislate, and (b) it's easy for people to understand why it's a problem" (Dahya, 2020).

Although advocacy organizations have coalesced around the term "child marriage" (Murdie et al., 2019), it is possible that as the movement evolves, so will its preferred terminology. Efevbera and Bhabha (2020), for example, proposed the term "girl child marriage" to highlight the gendered nature of the problem. Other reports have also recently used terms like "child, early, and forced marriage and unions" to account for the different forms child marriage can take (see, for example, Child, Early and Forced Marriage & Sexuality Programs Working Group, 2019).

Tactics to mobilize solidarity

Activists have mobilized support for the issue of child marriage by choosing tactics that are "especially powerful for conveying empathy, contention, and empowerment" (Brysk, 2013, p. 12).

The advocacy movement has relied on the courageous survivors who shared their testimonies to generate awareness and build empathy for the issue of child marriage. As Lusvardi (2021,

p. 13) noted, "the statistics of child marriage can deliver the shock factor," but leaders of advocacy organizations believe "the stories of survivors go further" in terms of impact.

Activists have built on the "shocking" terminology of child marriage by using symbolic images of girls dressed as brides and employing overt protest tactics to draw policymakers' attention to the issue. In the United States, Unchained at Last has pioneered "chain-in" events, at which groups of between 30 and 50 activists wear bridal gowns, veils, and chain their wrists and tape their mouths. The organization's founder described the impact of the chain-in protests:

> It's hard to ignore a group of chained brides! Apparently, legislators find it easy to discount the heartbreaking testimony of the survivors of child marriage who share their stories. But what you can't ignore is, on your way to the office, a group of chained brides standing there chanting, "Let's end child marriage!" (Dahya, 2020)

The media has also played a critical role in amplifying activists' messages. Chain-in events provide striking images in newspapers and on TV and social media, which help spread the message beyond the immediate legislators who witness the protest. But even in places like Pennsylvania, where the issue of child marriage did not receive sustained media attention, a few key accounts in elite outlets were enough to spur policy adoption (Lusvardi, 2021).

The movement to end child marriage has also relied on celebrity messengers like Oprah Winfrey and Desmond Tutu, who have raised visibility about the issue and demanded action to curb girls' inequality, including ending child marriage (Global Citizen, 2017). In this way, the campaign to end child marriage has relied on the support of charismatic speakers, another factor linked to advocacy success (Brysk, 2013).

Pressured by advocacy organizations such as Plan International (Murdie et al., 2019, p. 20), in December 2011 the UN General Assembly resolved that October 11, 2012, would be the first International Day of the Girl Child and would highlight the need to end to child marriage. In his message to mark this day, Secretary-General Ban Ki-moon urged the international community to "do our part to let girls be girls, not brides" (United Nations, 2012). Murdie et al. (2019) showed that the number of advocacy reports produced using the term "child marriage" increased substantially after this date.

In fact, the United Nations has been critical to coordinate global efforts to end child marriage. In 2013, the UN Human Rights Council adopted its first resolution on child marriage, urging states to bolster efforts to prevent and eliminate this practice. In 2015, ending child marriage was included as a target of the UN's SDG 5, which seeks to "Eliminate all harmful practices, such as child, early and forced marriage and female genital mutilation." The inclusion of child marriage resulted, at least in part, from the pressure from civil society advocates during the negotiations of the SDG agenda (Shawki, 2015). As a result, 193 countries have committed to ending child marriage by 2030. In my interviews, multiple activists identified the adoption of this target as a catalyst for domestic and international change. A US activist said that including child marriage as an SDG gave the movement "momentum" (Interview 10, 2021). Another activist from Brazil singled out the adoption of Target 5.3 as a significant moment in eliminating gender inequality (Interview 5, 2017).

During the last decade, different UN agencies—including UN Women, UNICEF, and the United Nations Population Fund (UNFPA)—have increased cooperation on the child marriage issue. A representative of the UN Women regional office in Latin America said that in the past, her organization had focused on topics like violence against women, whereas the UNFPA dealt with the child marriage issue. But since the 2010s, UN Women and other UN agencies began prioritizing child marriage after the insistence of civil society organizations led senior management to make a "political decision" to focus on the issue (Interview 7, 2018). In 2016, UNFPA and UNICEF launched the Global Programme to End Child Marriage, illustrating the increased agency coordination on the child marriage issue.

While the United Nations' leadership has been crucial to the success of the movement (Interview 4, 2016), the activists I interviewed also highlighted the importance of regional initiatives. The African Charter on the Rights and Welfare of the Child, for example, explicitly states, "child marriage and the betrothal of girls and boys shall be prohibited" (Article 21 [2]) and mandates states to incorporate this standard (African Union, 1990). Activists believe that regional initiatives give countries ownership and protect states' "sensitivities" to the imposition of a foreign agenda (Interview 10, 2021).

Securing policy change

The previous sections show how activists have used many of the tactics identified by previous literature to raise awareness about the harmful effects of child marriage and build solidarity to end the practice. Have their efforts translated into concrete policy changes to end child marriage?

Until recently, no cross-national, time-series data existed to answer this question. The reports states submit to the UN treaty bodies that monitor the implementation of human rights standards contain information on policy changes, but are not easily comparable across time and space. In the last five years, several efforts have been made to collect quantitative data on one key policy dimension: the adoption of laws that prohibit child marriage. Different datasets reveal that, although states have established a minimum age of marriage in compliance with international standards, they have also included loopholes allowing children to marry in special circumstances. These loopholes are prohibited by international law.

A systematic review of legislation available as of June 2013 found that 52 percent and 18 percent of countries allowed girls to marry legally when loopholes for parental consent and religious and customary law were included, respectively (Arthur et al., 2018). The loophole for parental consent is particularly common in the Americas, whereas the loophole for religious and customary law is most common in the Middle East and North Africa (Arthur et al., 2018, p. 9–10).

Vilán (2018) collected longitudinal data for Latin American countries to analyze how rival civil society activism influences the elimination of loopholes allowing girls to marry. More recently, the UN found that, since 1995, 23 percent of countries have closed the parental consent loophole and 15 percent have closed the judicial/religious loophole (United Nations Children's Fund, 2021b, p. 28).

To provide a closer look at the rate of change, consider the number of legal reforms introduced in Latin America and the Caribbean over the last 10 years (see Table 2). In most cases, the reforms eliminated existing loopholes, and several governments even adopted a minimum age of marriage of 18 without exceptions, including the Dominican Republic, El Salvador, Guatemala, and Honduras. An advocate referred to the pace of these regional changes as "insane" (Interview 10, 2021). Other regions have witnessed similar progress, especially Europe and Central Asia, the Middle East and North Africa, South Asia, and Sub-Saharan Africa (United Nations Children's Fund, 2021b, p. 28). For example, in 2019 Mozambique eliminated all loopholes allowing child marriage, and Indonesia raised the minimum marriage age for girls from 16 to 19.

Table 2. Latin American and Caribbean countries that changed laws regulating child marriage, 2011–2021.

Year	Countries
2011	Belize, Suriname
2014	Bolivia, Nicaragua, Venezuela
2015	Argentina, Ecuador, Guatemala, Panama, Paraguay
2017	Costa Rica, El Salvador, Guatemala, Honduras, Trinidad and Tobago
2019	Brazil, Mexico
2021	Dominican Republic

Source: Author's calculations based on data from Girls Not Brides.

A representative from the UN Women regional office in Latin America told me that eliminating loopholes is extremely important and that the UN was "trying to do everything possible" to make them go away (Interview 7, 2018). The activists I interviewed also emphasized how important the elimination of loopholes is to end child marriage. For example, the leader of an organization fighting for children's rights said,

> Brazil is the fourth country in the world in terms of child marriage, so it is a big problem for us. ... We work to change the laws to prohibit children from marrying too young. There is a bill in Congress right now. ... The author of the bill set the minimum age of marriage at 16 with parental consent, but we are trying to convince her that the law should establish a minimum age of marriage at 18, no exceptions, which is what we defend. (Interview 5, 2017)

In the United States, where the minimum age of marriage is regulated at the state level, similar progress has occurred over the last five years thanks to the work of activists. Currently, six states—Delaware, New Jersey, Pennsylvania, Minnesota, Rhode Island, and New York—have set the minimum age of marriage at 18 without exceptions (Tahirih Justice Center, 2021). Six other states provide exceptions only for emancipated minors, including Virginia, which in 2016 became the first state to limit marriage licenses to individuals aged 18, with a limited exception for emancipated minors 16 and older.

These legislative changes support the view that the movement to end child marriage has been successful at nudging policymakers to adopt reforms to end child marriage. Of course, reducing *de jure* discrimination against girls and women by eliminating loopholes for early marriage is not enough to curb this practice. There are other important dimensions of policy change—such as creating national action plans on child marriage and funding government offices that deal with this issue—for which it would be useful to have systematic, cross-national evidence.

Furthermore, even when maintaining the narrow focus on the law there is debate among stakeholders about how useful it is to end the practice. A global study found that about 7.5 million girls marry illegally each year, even after accounting for loopholes for parental and judicial consent (Wodon, Tavares, et al., 2017b, p. 5). Other scholars have suggested that inconsistent and limited enforcement of child marriage laws limit their impact (Svanemyr et al., 2013), as well as other reasons, such as overlapping legal systems, that diminish legal reforms' impact (Santelli et al., 2019).

Even so, laws are considered a first step to broader social change, even if on their own they cannot change social practices. Laws act as focal points that encourage governments to fulfill their obligations, signal appropriate behavior to society, provide a framework to improve service provision for girls, and give civil society organizations leverage to hold leaders accountable. And some scholars have found that laws can influence the outcomes policymakers and activists ultimately care about: States with strict laws prohibiting child marriage, for example, experienced the most dramatic reductions in rates of adolescent fertility (Kim et al., 2013).

Remaining challenges

The previous section tracked the extraordinary efforts made by the global movement to end child marriage and suggested that activists' efforts have led to policy change. But the prevalence of child marriage remains high, and no region is on track to meet the SDG target of eliminating child marriage by 2030 (United Nations Children's Fund, 2021b, p. 68). In this section, I focus on how social resistance, debates over sexuality, and regional differences complicate the work of activists, particularly as they move past advocating for legal equality into developing gender-transformative programs to end child marriage (Child, Early, and Forced Marriage & Sexuality Programs Working Group, 2019).

Societal resistance

Around the world, feminist movements face backlash from conservative counter-movements denouncing the so-called "gender ideology" (Kuhar & Paternotte, 2017; Zaremberg et al., 2021) and stressing the need to protect the traditional family, the right to life, and parental rights. A Jordanian lawmaker bemoaned, "Where there is a defense for women's rights, there is a backlash from conservative patriarchal bodies" (Bailey-King 2020, March 6), and a feminist activist said, "The more progress on women's rights we observe, the more resistance there is" (Interview 3, 2016).

A major source of societal resistance comes from religious leaders who defend traditional values and oppose efforts to achieve gender equality. Although their influence varies globally, in many states religious leaders are influential members of their communities; in Colombia, a researcher considered the churches the "fourth political power" (Interview 2, 2016). In Uruguay, a UN representative told me that when a new law on violence against women was adopted in December 2017, it was "opposed by the churches," which "mobilized against the law," claiming it "was against men" (Interview 6, 2018). Cardinal Sturla is on record stating, "Although everyone shares the same goal of curbing violence against women, the law adds issues that have to do with a gender ideology, which is a form of ideological colonization" (El País, 2017). Evangelical churches are also "major opponents in everything related to women's rights" (Interview 6, 2018). Indeed, scholars have noted the surprising alliances among different Christian churches, pro-family and pro-life NGOs, and anti-gender politicians (Vaggione, 2020).

Given the gendered nature of child marriage, campaigns to end the practice face similar societal resistance. In fact, advocates working on the ground to end child marriage said that even the word "gender" is so contested that they avoid the word *género* and talk instead about "girls and boys" (Girls Not Brides, 2019, p. 10). In Chile, one activist told me that opposition to child marriage reforms stemmed from the Catholic and Evangelical churches that "influence Congress and government a lot" (Interview 1, 2015). Another interviewee mentioned that the Evangelical church is "very powerful" in Latin America and often supports civil society organizations under names that seem "perfectly acceptable" but hide an "anti-rights agenda" (Interview 7, 2018). Of course, this opposition is not unique to Latin America: The Council of Islamic Ideology in Pakistan, for example, has blocked attempts to raise the age of marriage by calling the bills "blasphemous" and "un-Islamic" (Tharoor, 2016).

The literature suggests that religious leaders condone child marriage for several reasons. Some view marriage as a tool to control girls' sexuality and limit their premarital relations. If a pregnancy occurs, marriage is presented as a "solution." Religious leaders may also ignore that child marriage is illegal (Girls Not Brides, 2019, p. 6), interpret religious texts as condoning child marriage, or be unaware of its negative effects because the physical and social consequences of the practice are often hidden from public view (Le Roux & Palm, 2018, p. 6).

Furthermore, some religious leaders oppose reforms to the age of marriage because arranging and performing religious marriages is a key aspect of their identity and a source of influence in their communities (Le Roux & Palm, 2018, p. 14). In some states, the minimum age of marriage is regulated exclusively by religious laws, such as in Lebanon, where Shiite girls can marry at nine and Catholic girls at 14 (Committee on the Elimination of Discrimination against Women, 2006, p. 87). In other states, overlapping legal systems allow children of certain religions to marry at a younger age than is prescribed by civil law (Arthur et al., 2018, p. 9). For these reasons, some organizations have developed programs to work with religious and traditional leaders to change social norms in their communities (Groves et al., 2019).

In the United States, activists recognized that religious leaders play an important role in opposing efforts to raise the minimum age of marriage, but they emphasized other sources of social resistance as well. Fraidy Reiss, founder of Unchained at Last, was forced to marry a stranger in New York's ultra-Orthodox Jewish community. Yet during our interview, she mentioned how religious leaders publicly supported efforts to eradicate child marriage, including Catholic leaders in Maryland (Interview 12, 2021). In her opinion, although many religious communities in the United States oppose child marriage, politicians incorrectly believe the communities support it and act to protect their religious prerogatives. Governor Chris Christie, for example, vetoed a bill banning child marriage on the grounds it did not "comport with the … religious customs" of the people of New Jersey (Thoet, 2017). Another US advocate said that religious opposition was "a really obvious" source of opposition, but added that the blame should not be "laid completely at the feet of religious folks" (Interview 11, 2021).

US advocates also identified other sources of societal resistance. For instance, parental rights advocates believe that parents—not the government—should decide what is best for their child. John Schickel, a state senator from Kentucky, opposed a 2018 bill that removed parental consent loopholes, saying he "had some problems with the bill" because "Decisions involving a minor child should be made by a parent, not the court" (Gerth, 2018). Senator Julie Raque Adams, who sponsored the bill, declined to explicitly name who lobbied against the bill, saying that, "it involved people concerned about parents' rights" (Yetter, 2018), but Donna Pollard, a survivor and advocate, said the Kentucky Family Foundation opposed the bill. While the strength of these parental rights advocates varies by state, "it can be very hard to get to the bright line of 18 in states where 'parental rights groups' have a lot of sway" (Interview 11, 2021).

At times, the rationales of opponents to child marriage reforms can overlap. In communities in which pregnancy can ostracize a girl and limit her ability to go to school, child marriage is framed as a form of parental protection from social discrimination (Le Roux & Palm, 2018, p. 10) and from the effects of a negligent partner (Taylor et al., 2015, p. 13). In the United States, an activist mentioned that some resistance came from parents who believed that, "the government doesn't get to tell me what's right for my kid—I do. And if my kid is pregnant, then I think they should get married" (Interview 11, 2021).

Two other groups resisting reforms to the minimum age of marriage in the United States are libertarians and youth advocates. Libertarians see marriage as a fundamental right and an expression of individual liberty. Although they do not campaign to lower the age of marriage, efforts to raise the marriage age make them "uncomfortable" because they are perceived as restricting individual liberties (Interview 11, 2021). In California, a bid to raise the minimum age of marriage in 2017 was opposed by the American Civil Liberties Union, which argued that the proposal "unnecessarily and unduly intrudes on the fundamental right of marriage" (Tsui, 2017). This bill was also opposed by Planned Parenthood and the Children's Law Center of California on the grounds that it restricted children's autonomy and could restrict access to social services (Tsui, 2017).

The societal resistance faced by activists in the United States and abroad brings together a diverse set of actors who oppose raising the minimum age of marriage without exceptions. This resistance matters because it leaves the present successes of the global movement to end child marriage vulnerable to policy reversals. Activists and UN representatives are well aware that the social and political context that fosters reforms may change rapidly. A UN Women representative told me that, because "these anti-rights movements have infiltrated governments and other power structures," what she observed was that "[n]ormative progress that has taken decades falls in just a few months" (Interview 7, 2018). During our interview, she mentioned the swift dismantling of key institutions protecting women in Brazil, and that in Colombia, Peru, and Panama, "we are seeing not only the risk of reversal but clear reversals."

Addressing the role of sexuality

A further challenge that has emerged as a consequence of the strategies adopted by the global movement against child marriage is that, in an effort to build a broad coalition, activists have chosen a frame that organizations focused on women's rights and those focused on child protection could support. But advocacy organizations within the movement place different emphasis on sexuality and gender norms. Some experts believe that "[w]e will be unable to put an end to the practice of child marriage if we fail to see and address the central role of sexuality in limiting girls' prospects" (Greene et al., 2018, p. 35).

In particular, some activists draw a connection between pregnancy and child marriage; an activist said the stereotypical case in which child marriage occurs in the United States is a pregnant teenager (Interview 12, 2021). Similarly, Promundo's groundbreaking report on child marriage in Brazil identified two primary factors associated with child marriage: first, the "desire, often by a family member, to deal with an unwanted pregnancy in order to protect the girl's and family's reputation," and, second, the desire "to control girls' sexuality and limit perceived 'risky' behaviors associated with girls being single, such as casual sex and going out" (Taylor et al., 2015, p. 13).

An expert on El Salvador said, "the majority of unions are the solutions to unplanned pregnancies or unwanted pregnancies in the majority of cases to avoid that the family be criticized and the adolescent stigmatized" (quoted in Sorhaindo, 2013, p. 17).

In many countries, the connection between pregnancy and child marriage is even explicit in the law, as legal loopholes allow pregnant girls to marry at a younger age (Arthur et al., 2018, p. 12). And civil society organizations that oppose legal reforms also connect pregnancy to marriage. In 2017, the New Jersey Right to Life organization urged Governor Christie to veto a bill prohibiting child marriage expressing concern "with the 16- and 17-year-old who becomes pregnant and wants to marry the father of her child." Marie Tasy, the group's executive director, worried that the girl "may feel that she has no choice than to have an abortion" (Tsui, 2017).

The connection between marriage and pregnancy is also observed in cases of rape. When 11-year-old Sherry Johnson became pregnant after a member of her church raped her, "her family and church officials decided the simplest way to avoid a messy criminal case was to organize a wedding" (Kristof, 2017). An expert in Honduras said, "If a girl is raped then, they arrange it. … For the family this saves their honor, right, of the family and of the girl. Therefore if they marry that [the rape] doesn't carry the stigma" (quoted in Sorhaindo, 2013, p. 17).

Furthermore, child marriage often allows adults to escape prosecution for statutory rape. In the United States, marriage is a defense against criminal prosecution of statutory rape of 12- to 15-year-olds at the federal level (U.S.C. Section 2243(c)(2)), and at least 40 states and the District of Columbia allow marriage as an exception to prosecutions for statutory rape (Tahirih Justice Center, 2020). Around the world, activists are fighting to eliminate so-called "marry-the-rapist" laws, including in Latin America and the Middle East (Sengupta, 2017).

Although the connection between child marriage and sexuality is key to some activists, other organizations, especially those with a child protection background, deemphasize the connection between sexuality and child marriage and focus their message on other dimensions that are perhaps less contentious, such as the need for girls to remain in school. One US-based child protection expert side bemoaned that policymakers connect child marriage to access to reproductive healthcare. In her opinion, this connection can obstruct the movement's progress:

> We see from conservative offices quite a bit of concern around reproductive health. "So, you know, you're advocating for girls to stay in school and not get pregnant. When you are talking about ways that they don't get pregnant, is it abortion?" That's the line of questioning, even with something as simple as girls' education. … It seems that [eliminating child marriage] should be totally bipartisan, but somehow those anti-abortion advocates get into the narrative. And that's been a huge barrier for us in Congress … it is hard for us to reckon with some of that feedback too because we feel like this bill has nothing to do with reproductive health. It doesn't even say health! So I don't understand where that's coming from, but it's an obstacle for sure. (Interview 8, 2021)

Deemphasizing the role of sexuality and gender is a strategic framing choice of activists. According to Greene et al. (2018, p. 31), "One of the reasons the term 'child marriage' has gained so much currency is that by referring to children involved in this practice, one avoids talking about adolescents and their complicated sexuality." To some experts, by not referring to the practice as "girl child marriage," the term also conceals the gendered nature of the practice (Efevbera & Bhabha, 2020). As a result, most programs to end child marriage do not center their efforts on the issue of sexuality (Child, Early, and Forced Marriage & Sexuality Programs Working Group, 2019; Greene et al., 2018).

Although the literature on transnational activism has mostly focused on activists' cooperation, some scholars have explored how advocacy groups contest one another's causes or their specific framings (e.g., Bob, 2005; Hertel, 2006), as well as other intra- and inter-network dynamics that influence the work of activists. Carpenter (2007, p. 116) argued that when issues bridge overlapping advocacy networks, activists "pass the buck" to others in adjacent areas. As a result, some human rights issues do not emerge as transnational causes. She explored this dynamic for the issue of "children born of war," which, as in the child marriage case, engages activists working on child protection and gender-based violence, specifically in situations of conflict.

Although the diversity between the organizations working to end child marriage has not prevented the issue from becoming visible in the global agenda, the unresolved tension regarding sexuality could weaken the unity of the movement which, in turn, can impact global efforts to end this practice. First, it might increase the likelihood that loopholes are maintained. An advocate explained the tension between organizations securing minors' access to reproductive healthcare and those pushing to raise the marriage age in the United States:

> At some point, a client of mine is going to need an abortion in Georgia. And if people in Georgia are telling me, "Well, your child marriage bill is a potential threat to this progress we made to allow those under 18 to get a judicial bypass for abortion access, so they don't need parental consent," we had to—and we did—come to the table … and say, "How can we run this campaign and craft this bill in a way that doesn't do damage to your movement, while we can continue to pursue ours?" (Interview 11, 2021)

In this case, the activist described efforts to change the messaging strategy away from a frame that infantilized minors and emphasized their limited cognitive ability to make decisions. This cooperation was possible because advocates prioritized compromise; the activist took the view that "we're all in a broader movement together, and I am not comfortable with my particular campaign doing damage to another" (Interview 11, 2021).

However, this example suggests that progress on eliminating legal loopholes might require compromises that fall short of the blanket prohibition against child marriage found in international law. The Tahirih Justice Center, one of the key advocacy groups campaigning to end child marriage in the United States, warned that "the fast pace of these reforms also has a downside, inclining towards lowest-common-denominator approaches that can garner broad consensus" (Tahirih Justice Center, 2021).

Second, even if laws conform to international standards perfectly, these underlying tensions might emerge in subsequent phases of the implementation process, such as the improvement of birth and marriage registration efforts or the enforcement of legal standards. They may also influence the design of programs to end child marriage. Greene et al. (2018) discussed how policymakers' and development practitioners' discomfort with children's sexuality has led them to sidestep the issue entirely when dealing with child marriage. They have suggested best practices to end child marriage—such as building communication across generations and genders—that might be otherwise ignored (Greene et al., 2018, p. 31). Another report cautioned, "Unless control of sexuality and harmful gender norms that subordinate the position of women and girls in society are addressed head on, [child, early, and forced marriage and unions] will persist" (Child, Early, and Forced Marriage (CEFM) & Sexuality Programs Working Group, 2019, p. 5).

Regional differences

Although child marriage is a widespread practice, there are important differences in the form it takes around the world. These differences present a challenge to activists, who must mobilize solidarity across borders while navigating the idiosyncrasies of local contexts. In particular, activists disagree about the extent to which child marriage is always forced, or may sometimes reflect children's agency. Moreover, in some cases, children form informal unions instead of formally marrying.

To some activists, children are unable to consent to marriage, so all child marriage is, by definition, a form of forced marriage. But these "perspectives have not yet been universally adopted" (Efevbera & Bhabha, 2020, p. 8); in fact, activists disagree about how much emphasis to put on the agency of girls who choose to marry. One researcher talked about child marriage as a "spectrum," where at one extreme, girls are forced into arranged marriages with a large age differential, and on the other extreme, girls choose to enter into informal unions (Interview 9, 2021). One organization reported that "even among experts a common reason cited for early unions was 'free will' among adolescents," so "it was sometimes even described as a manifestation of the empowered youth" (Sorhaindo, 2013, p. 16). Taylor et al. (2015) similarly emphasized the consensual nature of unions in Brazil, while recognizing that limited economic opportunities and high regulation of girls' sexuality leaves them with few alternatives to marriage.

Even at the United Nations girls' agency is a contentious topic. In 2014, the CEDAW and CRC committees issued a joint statement explaining why states could have judicial authorization loopholes to the minimum age of marriage for children aged 16 or older. The rationale was that this loophole would respect a child's "evolving capacities and autonomy in making decisions that affect her or his life" (CEDAW/C/GC/31-CRC/C/GC/18,18 2014). At the same time, a UN representative told me that the emphasis on agency merely reflected how girls themselves had internalized discriminatory gender roles and norms (Interview 7, 2018).

Another difference relates to whether unions are formal or informal. In Latin America, many of the marriages are, in fact, informal unions. Consequently, many reports from local advocates and UN agencies in Spanish discuss "early unions"—as opposed to child marriage—because of the informal nature of the marriage, even if the United Nations' own definition includes formal and informal marriages. A representative of the UN Women regional office justified the decision to use the term "early union" by saying, "if not, they tell us that it is not important. So we chose that in this region" (Interview 7, 2018).

Similarly, an advocacy organization described how it "sent an online survey to a long list of national and international experts," telling them that they were selected because they worked on issues "related to child marriage," but it received "very minimal response" (quoted in Sorhaindo, 2013, p. 13). When they reapproached experts for interviews by changing the terminology to "early unions," they received more responses.

The activists from the global movement to end child marriage must juggle universal claims with regional differences that can complicate their advocacy efforts. One US-based advocate said that different languages might offer varied "linguistic clarity," which is "why it has been hard to get the conversation [about child marriage] going in other parts of the world, like Latin America and the Caribbean" (Interview 10, 2021).

The problem with varying the language to accommodate regional differences is that norms strengthen when the terminology is standardized. In fact, the movement to end child marriage strengthened over the last decade, in part, as a result of this standardization (Murdie et al., 2019). Reversing this trend could challenge the universality of the norm and complicate advocates' efforts to mobilize policymakers against this practice.

Conclusion

Over the last two decades, the global movement to end child marriage has gained momentum by standardizing its framing, using survivors' stories and shocking symbolism to generate empathy and mobilize solidarity, and coordinating strategies with domestic and international partners.

These efforts have led to tangible successes, as shown by the number of countries that introduced legal reforms to the minimum age of marriage.

The activists with whom I spoke, however, were hardly complacent. They spoke of the enormous challenges they still face to raise (and sustain) attention on the issue, of the societal resistance they encounter, and about how their own thinking has evolved over the years. Besides explaining challenges to the movement emerging from society, in this article I have explored the internal dynamics of the coalition to end child marriage regarding, first, the centrality of sexuality and, second, the variation in the forms child marriage adopts.

Activists have worked hard to build a broad coalition that includes a convergence of organizations with different perspectives, backgrounds, and views on how to end this practice. Organizations working on child protection, violence against women, and gender equality have used their time and resources to end child marriage. Although these organizations ultimately share the same goal, their focuses create inherent tensions that manifest themselves whenever global norms are put into practice, such as adopting a new law or program to curb child marriage. These tensions were not as salient when activists tried to raise awareness about child marriage and focused on legal changes. But as activists have focused on the more challenging goal of changing social norms, they have expressed different views on the importance of addressing the issue of sexuality and the regional differences in the practice of child marriage.

Accommodating diverse views while sustaining a unified campaign can be difficult. While we do not know enough about how activists resolve intra-network disagreements after norms emerge, the literature on transnational activism suggests that resolving these challenges cooperatively can help sustain awareness about this practice and prevent policy reversals. Following closely if and how activists in the movement to end child marriage resolve these tensions will illustrate how others can overcome the challenges that come with successfully building a broad advocacy coalition.

By exploring the evolution and internal dynamics of the global movement to end child marriage, this article underscores that activists are central to the improvement of human rights. Their mobilization is necessary to put human rights on the agenda and to nudge governments toward compliance with international standards. At a time when activists around the world are under threat (Chaudhry & Heiss, 2022), guaranteeing their ability to operate freely is paramount. In the child marriage case, supporting activists' work will be especially important now that the COVID-19 pandemic has put an estimated 10 extra million girls at risk of child marriage in the next decade (United Nations Children's Fund, 2021a).

Acknowledgments

I thank the activists who took the time to discuss their important work and share their expertise with me. Without their help, this research would not have been possible. I gratefully acknowledge the feedback I received from Suparna Chaudhry, Esther Spindler, an anonymous reviewer, and participants at the 2021 conference convened by the Global Human Rights Hub at the Arizona State University and sponsored by the National Science Foundation. All translations from Spanish to English, as well as any errors, are my own.

Funding

This work was supported by the Latin American Institute and the International Institute of the University of California, Los Angeles, and by the National Science Foundation award #2029490.

ORCID

Andrea Vilán http://orcid.org/0000-0003-0968-0893

References

African Union. (1990). *African charter on the rights and welfare of the child.* Retrieved December 20, 2021, from https://au.int/en/treaties/african-charter-rights-and-welfare-child

Arthur, M., Earle, A., Raub, A., Vincent, I., Atabay, E., Latz, I., Kranz, G., Nandi, A., & Heymann, J. (2018). Child marriage laws around the world: Minimum marriage age, legal exceptions, and gender disparities. *Journal of Women, Politics & Policy, 39*(1), 51–74. doi:10.1080/1554477X.2017.1375786

Bailey-King, E. (2020, March 6). *Three extraordinary women who are rewriting the rules for girls.* Girls Not Brides. Retrieved December 20, 2021, from https://www.girlsnotbrides.org/articles/meet-the-extraordinary-women-who-are-rewriting-the-rules-for-girls/

Bob, C. (2005). *The marketing of rebellion: Insurgents, media, and international activism.* Cambridge University Press.

Brysk, A. (2013). *Speaking rights to power: Constructing political will.* Oxford University Press.

Carpenter, R. C. (2007). Setting the advocacy agenda: Theorizing issue emergence and nonemergence in transnational advocacy networks. *International Studies Quarterly, 51*(1), 99–120. doi:10.1111/j.1468-2478.2007.00441.x

Chaudhry, S., & Heiss, A. (2022). Closing space and the restructuring of global activism. In C. L. Pallas & E. A. Bloodgood (Eds.), *Beyond the boomerang: From transnational advocacy networks to transcalar advocacy in international politics.* (pp. 23–35). The University of Alabama Press.

Child, Early and Forced Marriage and Sexuality Programs Working Group. (2019. June). Tackling the taboo: Sexuality and gender-transformative programmes to end child, early, and forced marriage and unions. https://www.girlsnotbrides.org/documents/905/Tackling-the-Taboo_-Full_English.pdf

Committee on the Elimination of Discrimination against Women. (1994). *General recommendation no. 21: Equality in marriage and family relations.* Retrieved December 20, 2021, from https://tbinternet.ohchr.org/Treaties/CEDAW/Shared%20Documents/1_Global/A_49_38(SUPP)_4733_E.pdf

Committee on the Elimination of Discrimination against Women. (2006). *Lebanon third periodic state party report.* CEDAW/C/LBN/3. Retrieved December 20, 2021, from https://tbinternet.ohchr.org/_layouts/15/treatybodyexternal/Download.aspx?symbolno=CEDAW%2fC%2fLBN%2f3&Lang=en

Committee on the Elimination of Discrimination against Women. (2014). Joint General Recommendation No. 31 of the Committee on the Elimination of Discrimination against Women/General Comment No. 18 of the Committee on the Rights of the Child on Harmful Practices. CEDAW/C/GC/31-CRC/C/GC/18. Retrieved December 20, 2021, from https://tbinternet.ohchr.org/_layouts/15/treatybodyexternal/TBSearch.aspx?SymbolNo=CEDAW/C/GC/31/CRC/C/GC/18

Committee on the Rights of the Child. (1993). *Concluding observations of the Committee on the Rights of the Child: Bolivia.* CRC/C/15/Add.1. https://tbinternet.ohchr.org/_layouts/15/treatybodyexternal/Download.aspx?symbolno=CRC%2fGC%2f2003%2f4&Lang=en

Committee on the Rights of the Child. (2003). *General comment no. 4.* CRC/GC/2003/4. https://tbinternet.ohchr.org/_layouts/15/treatybodyexternal/Download.aspx?symbolno=CRC%2fGC%2f2003%2f4&Lang=en

Dahya, A. (2020, May 26). *An interview with child marriage activist Fraidy Reiss.* Retrieved December 20, 2021, from https://womensmediacenter.com/fbomb/an-interview-with-child-marriage-activist-fraidy-reiss

Efevbera, Y., & Bhabha, J. (2020). Defining and deconstructing girl child marriage and applications to global public health. *BMC Public Health, 20*(1), 1–11. doi:10.1186/s12889-020-09545-0

El País (2017, December 21). *Sturla sobre la ley contra la violencia de género: 'estoy en contra'.* Retrieved December 20, 2021, from https://www.elpais.com.uy/informacion/sturla-ley-violencia-genero.html

Finnemore, M., & Sikkink, K. (1998). International norm dynamics and political change. *International Organization, 52*(4), 887–917. doi:10.1162/002081898550789

Gerth, J. (2018, March 2). If Kentucky parents are too stupid to stop child marriage, judges must step in. *The Courier Journal.* Retrieved December 20, 2021, from https://www.courier-journal.com/story/news/local/joseph-gerth/2018/03/02/child-marriage-kentucky-parents-rights -judges-republican-party/388424002/

Girls Not Brides. (2019). *Working with religious leaders to address child marriage.* Retrieved December 20, 2021, from https://www.girlsnotbrides.org/resource-centre/working-with-religious-leaders-to-address-child-marriage/

Global Citizen. (2017, December 18). *10 celebrities who spoke up against child marriage in 2017.* Retrieved December 20, 2021, from https://www.globalcitizen.org/en/content/celebrities-speaking-out-child-marriage-2017/

Greene, M. E., Perlson, S. M., Hart, J., & Mullinax, M. (2018). *The centrality of sexuality for understanding child, early and forced marriage.* GreeneWorks and American Jewish World Service.

Groves, W., Lance, N., & Stephens, M. (2019). *New vows: Empowering communities to end child marriage.* World Vision.

Hertel, S. (2006). *Unexpected power: Conflict and change among transnational activists.* Cornell University Press.

Keck, M. E., & Sikkink, K. (1998). *Activists beyond borders: Advocacy networks in international politics.* Cornell University Press.

Kidman, R. (2017). Child marriage and intimate partner violence: A comparative study of 34 countries. *International Journal of Epidemiology, 46*(2), 662–675.

Kim, M., Longhofer, W., Boyle, E. H., & Nyseth, H. (2013). When do laws matter? National minimum-age-of-marriage laws, child rights, and adolescent fertility, 1989-2007. *Law & Society Review, 47*(3), 589–619. doi:10.1111/lasr.12033

Koski, A., & Clark, S. (2021). Child marriage in Canada. *Population and Development Review, 47*(1), 57–78. doi:10.1111/padr.12369

Koski, A., & Heymann, J. (2018). Child marriage in the United States: How common is the practice, and which children are at greater risk? *Perspectives on Sexual and Reproductive Health, 50*(2), 59–65. doi:10.1363/psrh.12055

Kristof, N. (2017, 26 May). 11 years old, a mom, and pushed to marry her rapist in Florida. *The New York Times.* Retrieved December 20, 2021, from https://www.nytimes.com/2017/05/26/opinion/sunday/it-was-forced-on-me-child-marriage-in-the-us.html?mcubz=2& r=0

Kuhar, R., & Paternotte, D. (Eds.). (2017). *Anti-gender campaigns in Europe: Mobilizing against equality.* Rowman & Littlefield Publishers.

Le Roux, E., & Palm, S. (2018). *What lies beneath? Tackling the roots of religious resistance to ending child marriage.* Girls Not Brides.

Lusvardi, A. (2021). *An end to the child bride: State legislative action on low-salience issues.* Prepared for the 117th American Political Science Association's Annual Meeting & Exhibition, Sept. 30-Oct. 3, Seattle Washington.

Murdie, A., Park, B., Hart, J., & Mullinax, M. (2019). Building momentum: Changes in advocacy discourse around early child marriage, 2011–2017. In A. Brysk & M. Stohl (Eds.), *Contesting human rights.* Edward Elgar Publishing.

Nour, N. M. (2006). Health consequences of child marriage in Africa. *Emerging Infectious Diseases, 12*(11), 1644–1649. doi:10.3201/eid1211.060510

Nour, N. M. (2009). Child marriage: A silent health and human rights issue. *Reviews in Obstetrics & Gynecology, 2*(1), 51–56.

Parsons, J., Edmeades, J., Kes, A., Petroni, S., Sexton, M., & Wodon, Q. (2015). Economic impacts of child marriage: A review of the literature. *The Review of Faith & International Affairs, 13*(3), 12–22. doi:10.1080/15570274.2015.1075757

Raj, A., & Boehmer, U. (2013). Girl child marriage and its association with national rates of HIV, maternal health, and infant mortality across 97 countries. *Violence against Women, 19*(4), 536–551. doi:10.1177/1077801213487747

Santelli, J. S., Spindler, E., Moore, E., & McGovern, T. (2019). Criminalising sexuality or preventing child marriage: Legal interventions and girls' empowerment. *The Lancet Child & Adolescent Health, 3*(4), 206–208. doi:10.1016/S2352-4642(18)30370-5

Sengupta, S. (2017, July 22). One by one, marry-your-rapist laws are falling in the Middle East. *The New York Times.* Retrieved December 20, 2021, from https://www.nytimes.com/2017/07/22/world/middleeast/marry-your-rapist-laws-middle-east.html?smid=url-share.

Shawki, N. (2015). Norm-based advocacy and social change: An analysis of advocacy efforts to end child marriage. *Social Alternatives, 34*(4), 57–62.

Sorhainco, A. M. (2013). *Exploratory research to assess the problem of child marriage in five Latin American countries: El Salvador, Guatemala, Honduras, Nicaragua and southern Mexico.* Population Council Report.

Svanemyr, J., Scolaro, E., Blondeel, K., Chandra-Mouli, V., & Temmerman, M. (2013, October). *The contribution of laws to change the practice of child marriage in Africa.* Department of Reproductive Health and Research, World Health Organization.

Tahirih Justice Center. (2020, August). *The alarming disconnect between age-based sex offenses and minimum marriage age.* Retrieved December 20, 2021, from https://www.tahirih.org/wp-content/uploads/2020/08/FINAL-Aug-2020-Policy-Brief-Disconnect-btwn-Stat-Rape-and-Marriage-Age.pdf

Tahirih Justice Center (2021, August 26). *Making progress, but still falling short: The movement to end child marriage in America.* Forced Marriage Initiative. Retrieved December 20, 2021, from https://www.tahirih.org/pubs/making-progress-but-still-falling-short-a-report-on-the-movement-to-end-child-marriage-in-america/

Taylor, A.Y., Lauro, G., Segundo, M., Greene, M.E. (2015, July). "She goes with me in my boat." Child and Adolescent Marriage in Brazil. Results from Mixed-Methods Research. Rio de Janeiro and Washington DC: Instituto Promundo & Promundo-US.

Tharoor, I. (2016). *Pakistan prevented from banning child marriages because it is 'unIslamic'.* Retrieved December 20, 2021, from https://www.independent.co.uk/news/world/asia/pakistan-prevented-from-banning-child-marriages-because-it-is-unislamic-a6817066.html.

Thoet, A. (2017). *Activists in NJ push to ban child marriage before Christie leaves office.* PBS NewsHour. Retrieved December 20, 2021, from https://www.pbs.org/newshour/nation/activists-in-n-j-push-to-ban-child-marriage-before-christie-leaves-office.

Tsui, A. (2017, July 6). *In fights over child marriage laws, states resist calls for a total ban.* PBS Frontline. Retrieved December 20, 2021, from https://www.pbs.org/wgbh/frontline/article/in-fight-over-child-marriage-laws-states-resist-calls-for-a-total-ban/.

Unchained At Last. (2021, April). *United States' child marriage problem: Study findings.* Retrieved December 20, 2021, from https://www.unchainedatlast.org/united-states-child-marriage-problem-study-findings-april-2021/.

United Nations. (2012, October 11). *On world's first international day of the girl child, UN calls for end to child marriage.* Retrieved December 20, 2021, from https://news.un.org/en/story/2012/10/423262-worlds-first-international-day-girl-child-un-calls-end-child-marriage.

United Nations Children's Fund. (2018). *Latin America and the Caribbean: A decade lost in ending child marriage.* UNICEF. Retrieved December 20, 2021, from https://www.unicef.org/press-releases/latin-america-and-caribbean-decade-lost-ending-child-marriage.

United Nations Children's Fund. (2019, August). *A profile of child marriage and early unions in Latin America and the Caribbean.* UNICEF. Retrieved December 20, 2021, from https://www.unicef.org/lac/en/reports/profile-child-marriage-and-early-unions.

United Nations Children's Fund. (2021a, June). *Child marriage: Child marriage threatens the lives, well-being, and futures of girls around the world.* UNICEF. Retrieved December 20, 2021, from https://www.unicef.org/protection/child-marriage.

United Nations Children's Fund. (2021b, October). *Towards ending child marriage: Global trends and profiles of progress.* UNICEF. https://data.unicef.org/resources/towards-ending-child-marriage/

United Nations Children's Fund. (2021c, October). *The State of the world's children. On my mind: Promoting, protecting and caring for children's mental health.* UNICEF. Retrieved December 20, 2021, from https://www.unicef.org/reports/state-worlds-children-2021.

United Nations General Assembly. (1965). *Recommendation on consent to marriage, minimum age for marriage and registration of marriages.* Retrieved December 20, 2021, from https://www.ohchr.org/EN/ProfessionalInterest/Pages/RecommendationOnConsentToMarriage.aspx.

Vaggione, J. M. (2020). The conservative uses of law: The catholic mobilization against gender ideology. *Social Compass, 67*(2), 252–266. doi:10.1177/0037768620907561

Vilán, A. (2018). *The domestic incorporation of human rights treaties.* Doctoral Dissertation, University of California, Los Angeles. https://escholarship.org/uc/item/7728765v

Plan International. (2017). *Congreso hondureño eleva a 18 años la edad mínima para contraer matrimonio.* Retrieved December 20, 2021 from https://plan-international.es/noticias/2017-07-14-honduras-eleva-18-anos-la-edad-minima-para-contraer-matrimonio.

Wodon, Q., Male, C., Nayihouba, A., Onagoruwa, A., Savadogo, A., Yedan, A., & Petroni, S. (2017a). *Economic impacts of child marriage: Global synthesis report. 116829.* World Bank Group. Retrieved December 20, 2021, from https://documents.worldbank.org/curated/en/530891498511398503/Economic-impacts-of-child-marriage-global-synthesis-report.

Wodon, Q., Tavares, P., Fiala, O., Le Nestour, A., & Wise, L. (2017b, October). *Ending child marriage: Child marriage laws and their limitations.* World Bank.

World Health Organization. (2020, January 31). *Adolescent pregnancy.* Retrieved December 20, 2021, from https://www.who.int/news-room/fact-sheets/detail/adolescent-pregnancy

Yetter, D. (2018, March 1). Kentucky's 'child bride' bill stalls as groups fight to let 13-year-olds wed. *The Courier Journal.* Retrieved December 20, 2021, from https://www.courier-journal.com/story/news/politics/2018/03/01/child-marriage-kentucky-brides-parents-rights/385489002/

Zaremberg, G., Tabbush, C., & Friedman, E. J. (2021). Feminism(s) and anti-gender backlash: lessons from Latin America. *International Feminist Journal of Politics, 23*(4), 527–534. doi:10.1080/14616742.2021.1956093

Appendix

Interviews

To understand the evolution of the global movement to end child marriage, I conducted interviews with activists, researchers, and UN representatives based in the United States and in Latin America. Interviews were conducted in person or virtually. For virtual interviews, I note what was, to the best of my knowledge, the location of the interviewee during the interview. On average, interviews lasted between an hour and ninety minutes.

To map out the global advocacy landscape and identify interview respondents, I used newspaper articles and reports from civil society organizations. I conducted interviews in English and Spanish and assume responsibility for all translations from Spanish to English used in this article. I followed informed consent procedures for all interview respondents (University of California, Los Angeles IRB #16-001720 and Princeton University IRB #12135). Most respondents preferred that I refer to their comments by their position instead of their names.

These are the interviews referenced in this article:

1. Gender activist, Santiago de Chile, Chile. Virtual interview: January 18, 2015.
2. Associate Researcher, Bogotá, Colombia. November 8, 2016.
3. Gender consultant, Montevideo, Uruguay. November 22, 2016.
4. UNICEF Representative, Montevideo, Uruguay. November 24, 2016.
5. Children's rights activist, São Paulo, Brasil. Virtual interview: January 24, 2017.
6. UN Women Representative, Montevideo, Uruguay. Virtual interview: March 26, 2018.
7. UN Women Latin American Regional Office Representative, Clayton, Panamá. Virtual interview: May 18, 2018.
8. Children's rights activist, Washington, DC, United States. Virtual interview: March 10, 2021.
9. Gender activist, Washington, DC, United States. Virtual interview: March 16, 2021.
10. Gender activist, Washington, DC, United States. Virtual interview: March 23, 2021.
11. Gender activist, Washington, DC, United States. Virtual interview: March 26, 2021.
12. Fraidy Reiss, CEO and founder of Unchained at Last, Westfield, New Jersey, United States. Virtual interview: March 30, 2021.

Index

Note: Figures are indicated by *italics*. Tables are indicated by **bold**. Endnotes are indicated by the page number followed by 'n' and the endnote number e.g., 20n1 refers to endnote 1 on page 20.